Yellow Star, Red Star

by

Agnes Kaposi

with contributions

by

László Csősz

ISBN: 978-1-9161066-8-0

ABOUT THE AUTHORS

Dr Agnes Kaposi is a Chartered Engineer, Churchill Fellow, and Fellow of the Royal Academy of Engineering.

Dr László Csősz is historian, Senior Archivist of the National Archives in Hungary, Research Fellow of the Wiener Holocaust Library, London.

Published by

i2i Publishing. Manchester.

www.i2ipublishing.co.uk

To Ella, Molly, Jay, Tabitha and Dylan

ACKNOWLEDGEMENTS

It would take a whole book to express my gratitude to all those of my family, friends and scholarly acquaintances who contributed to my work on this book. Even interested strangers helped, posing questions that offered guidance and sharpened focus. I thank them all, but can mention here only a few.

It was the curiosity of my granddaughter Tabitha when still a child that prompted me to embark on writing a book such as this. My husband's dedication and enthusiasm aided me until the end of his life. His role was taken over by my daughter Anna, always perceptive, thorough and sensitive. Marina Smith and Aneesa Riffat at Beth Shalom offered encouragement, as did audiences I addressed there and elsewhere. Gabor Lacko, my comrade in the camps, helped with dates and facts, and my friends and readers Lilian Gordon, Phyllis Vangelder, Kusoom Vadgama and Louise Taylor scrutinized the text at various stages of its preparation. Strict criticism from my cousin Ágnes Gál and her husband Péter reinforced my conviction that support of a historian was essential, but the idea to run a historian's commentary alongside the narrative came from Francois Guesnet of POLIN, University College of London. Closing the circle, the title of the book was inspired by Tabitha's father, my son-in-law Boyd Steemson. It was Ben Barkow, former Director of the Wiener Holocaust Library, who introduced to me my co-author, the historian László Csősz. In turn, it was Dr Csősz who enlisted the incomparable expertise of the museologist Katalin Jalsovszky. I am grateful to them all.

Finally, yet importantly, I must record my appreciation of my publisher Lionel Ross of i2i for his kindness, patience and attention to detail.

CONTENTS

A FIRST GLANCE

I should have had a good start in life. I had a loving family, my parents were young, good-looking, talented. Only two things were against me: the place and time. Hungary is a small country at the very heart of Central Europe. Its people are gifted, musical, its folk art is rich, its literature exquisite but its location puts it in the way of the storms of history. This is the country I was born into in 1932, a Jewish child of socialist parents.

It was a fateful period right after the Great Depression, with the extreme right on the rise throughout Europe. Gömbös Gyula, race protectionist and pro-fascist, became Prime Minister of Hungary. A year later, in 1933, Adolf Hitler came to power in Germany. Predictably, Hungary entered World War II on Hitler's side. Two-thirds of my family was lost in the turmoil of the war. A Stalinist dictatorship followed.

Against all odds, I survived murderous Nazism and vicious Communism; tyrannical regimes both, with different ideology and methods, but fundamental similarities. After the 1989 fall of Communism there was a serious effort in Hungary to establish a liberal democracy, but the attempt faltered, as it had many times before. Today the country has a fiercely populist government. Antisemitism, always present, was silenced under the Communists, but once again it is out in the open, and on the rise.[1]

For over half a century, I avoided talking about my personal history. I did not wish to burden my children with their family's troubled origins, and when friends and colleagues asked, I thought they were being polite rather than genuinely interested. Then one day my ten-year-old granddaughter Tabitha surprised me with a show of sincere interest. It was she who inspired me to write about my two survivals. Recounting my story, I realised that I owe my life to improbable coincidences, or unbelievable luck, or a series of miracles. My memories were vivid, visual; past events appeared to me almost like film clips. I could recall places and people, even colours flashed before my eyes, and sometimes they still come to me in my dreams. But my recollections were buried in my distant childhood and youth. Could I trust them? I was the author of many technical books and scientific papers, but I had no experience as a storyteller.

I looked to journalists for advice on writing non-fiction, and found that they offered techniques, whereas my problems were with the content itself. A clue came from Molly, another of my grandchildren. When a small girl, she told her cousins that they could believe Grandma Kaposi's every word, because she had no imagination. Here was my lead: I had to tell my story straight, without engaging the imagination, but taking nothing away, and adding nothing.[2]

Searching for the truth, scientists and engineers are guided by the *scientific method*, testing and continuously refining their knowledge of a complicated world. I found that honest historians proceed along similar lines; questioning and revising 'known facts'. The need to do so is especially important at a time when denial of the truth is not just the preserve of a few angry zealots, but has almost become a part of some governments' policy.[3]

So, my task was to follow scientists and historians: test my memories against eyewitness accounts, letters, photographs and documents, books, historical monographs, articles and broadcasts. It took me ten busy years to record this story, telling the truth to the best of

1   See *HISTORIAN'S VOICE* in Chapter 10: Hungary since 1956.

2   Mark Kramer–Wendy Call, *Telling True Stories. A Nonfiction Writer's Guide*. New York: Plume, 2007.

3   Martha Howell–Walter Prevenier, *From Reliable Sources. An Introduction to Historical Methods*. Ithaca, NY: Cornell University Press, 2001; Aviezer Tucker, ed. *A Companion to the Philosophy of History and Historiography*. Oxford: Wiley-Blackwell, 2010. Martha Howell–Walter Prevenier, *From Reliable Sources. An Introduction to Historical Methods*. Ithaca, NY: Cornell University Press, 2001; Aviezer Tucker, ed. *A Companion to the Philosophy of History and Historiography*. Oxford: Wiley-Blackwell, 2010; Karl Raimund Popper, *The Myth of the Framework: In Defence of Science and Rationality*. London–New York, Routledge, 2007; Mario Bunge, *Scientific Research*. Berlin: Springer Verlag, 1967.

my ability at the moment of writing. I sought and found the support of a historian, László Csősz. His 'historian's voice' runs alongside my story, adding background, depth, detail and authenticity.

This a personal account, told in a historical context, offering a glimpse of life and attitudes in those distant places and at those long-ago times. I recount tragic events, but this story is not all gloom and doom, and has a happy ending. My husband and I escaped from our native land and found acceptance in liberal tolerant Britain. We fled from our country of origin, but did not come as refugees. We worked from the moment of our arrival, contributing to the industrial development and higher education of our generous adoptive country.

We also founded a family. The last chapter shows our family tree and a recent photograph.

ABOUT NAMES

My story refers to Hungarian names of people and places. Unlike English, Hungarian is a phonetic language: if you know its alphabet, the accents over vowels guide the pronunciation. On the other hand, Hungarian people's names are unusual. They go the other way around from names elsewhere: surname first, forenames after. For people born in Hungary, the Hungarian version is used in this story. However, the commentaries (*HISTORIAN'S VOICE*) and the footnotes follow the regular order of Hungarian names.

Most Hungarian Jews had German surnames, like Grün, Goldberger and the like. 'Klein' was a particularly frequent surname among Jews, like 'Smith' is in England and 'Jones' in Wales. I was born under that name, and so was my husband, although we were not related. German surnames set Jews apart from the rest of the Hungarian population, so many Jews adopted Hungarian-sounding surnames.[4] Both my husband's and my own family changed our surname Klein when we were children: his to Kaposi, mine to Kristóf. This proved to be a futile enterprise: Jews were just as conspicuous under their new names, and the anti-Jewish laws tracked down Jewish ancestry, whatever the surname.

In case of forenames, it seems that Hungarians were dominated by fashion. You could often guess people's ages by their forenames. Three people of my family are called Margit; there are two Kláras and two Mariskas – all popular names for the generation before mine. 'Ágnes' is the Hungarian-style spelling of my name. It spread like an epidemic after I was born. No fewer than five women of my extended family suffer under that name. Men's names are similarly treated; for example, we have three important family members called András, and several people in this story have the forename Gábor.

Hungarians often use abbreviated names or pet names for people they love, and even for people whom they tease, or for whom they don't care. I shall introduce people by their formal name first, but will mostly adopt general usage thereafter.

The words 'néni' and 'bácsi' translate into 'aunt' and 'uncle', but this is not quite right. Hungarians use 'néni' and 'bácsi' to address older and respected people. As an example, we addressed our primary teachers by their first name, followed by 'néni'.

---

4   See *HISTORIAN'S VOICE: Jewish surnames in Hungary*

My story refers to historical figures, and also to members of my family, friends, colleagues and foes. I remember most people's names, but sometimes I adopt pseudonyms.

And just a word about place names. *Utca* means street, *út* is road, and *tér* is a city square.

HISTORIAN'S VOICE

Jewish surnames in Hungary

In 1783, Austro-Hungarian Emperor Joseph II issued the 'Edict of Tolerance', a ruling which recognised Judaism throughout the Austro-Hungarian Empire, and granted Jews freedom to pursue various types of crafts and trade from which they were previously excluded. However, the edict imposed several requirements upon the Jews, including compulsory secular education, usage of the state language (German, instead of Hebrew and Yiddish), state taxation and conscription. Until this time, Jews in Hungary did not use fixed surnames. In 1787 another Patent came into force, requiring Jews to register births, marriages and deaths, and adopt German surnames for ease of administration. From the 1860s, the politics of homogenisation of the multiethnic kingdom and the integration efforts of Jews led some of Hungary's Jews to 'Magyarise' their surnames: replace their German surnames by Hungarian-sounding ones. Later, waves of antisemitism added an extra impetus to this movement. Such Magyarisation was particularly frequent among the urban middle and upper classes, and among followers of the Neolog (reform) movement of Judaism.[5]

---

5   For the Latin and German originals of the edicts (and Hungarian translations), see Géza Komoróczy, ed., *"Nekem itt zsidónak kell lenni". Források és dokumentumok (965-2012).* Pozsony: Kalligram, 2013. 379-395., 399-405. Online versions: http://www.hebraisztika.hu/szovgyujt/KG_chrest_074.pdf; http://www.hebraisztika.hu/szovgyujt/KG_chrest_077.pdf (accessed 19 October, 2019)

1   ORIGINS

My family came from Debrecen, which is the second largest city of Hungary today. It is a dusty market town near the Romanian border, with a largely Protestant population. In my childhood, Debrecen's Jews loved their city, expecting empathy from its people who were themselves a minority in a predominantly Catholic country. How wrong those Jews were proven to be![6]

Most of Hungary's Jews were 'integrated', 'emancipated', 'secular'. My parents might have been typical, considering themselves loyal Jews, without being actively religious. They viewed with equal disdain marriages with Christians and with traditional orthodox Jews. There had not been active religious practice in my family for generations. My father and uncles were cultured and knowledgeable men, but their learning did not extend to Jewish philosophy or history. They were not members of any synagogue and did not attend religious services. Nobody followed the Jewish dietary rules of kashrut; no one observed the Shabbat, the Jewish holy day of rest. Religious education was compulsory country-wide, so we attended religion classes and could read Hebrew script – I only with difficulty – but almost nobody understood a word of what they read. Before World War II, my husband's family had a kosher home, not because of religious conviction, but as respect towards the grandparents who had been observant.

We must have been lower middle class. My family rented rather than owned their homes. Older people left school early to practice a craft, or run small shops: drapery, grocery, haberdashery. My mother's generation, born around World War I, was the first of which some advanced to vocational higher education, but by the time they graduated, anti-Jewish laws gave them little chance to pursue their professions.

Hungarian Jewish society was deeply stratified and diverse economically, culturally, and regarding religious practice. My elementary school was situated in the prime area of the capital; some of my schoolmates were children of wealthy Jews, but their world was closed to me. On the other end of the economic scale were Jews who were even poorer than we were.[7]

---

6   See *HISTORIAN'S VOICE: Debrecen*
7   See *HISTORIAN'S VOICE: Hungary's Jews: Culture and Religion*

The Jewish society of my native city was particularly complicated. Many of my grandmother's neighbours were orthodox men with beards and women with wigs. Their community was small, but it was further stratified according to financial circumstances. We also heard about – but never met – the Yiddish-speaking ultra-religious Hasidic Jews from Munkács and Szatmár in the northeast of Hungary. These remote people were unkindly called Fins, an abbreviation of the Yiddish '*Fin Munkács*' – from Munkács. They were considered utterly beyond the pale.[8]

MY FATHER

It was my father Imre who shaped my ideas and set me on my path of life. He was a remarkable man: a gifted mathematician, socialist, and humanist. He was learned in many spheres, particularly physics, astronomy and the classics. He was a fluent speaker of ancient Greek and an inexhaustible source of the tales of mythology from the world over. How did he acquire his thirst for knowledge? What was the secret of his strength of character?

Born in 1901, Imre was the youngest of a family of many children – he himself was unsure how many. Few of his siblings reached adulthood, others dying later of tuberculosis or diphtheria. I only knew his sister Margit, and Klári, the daughter of his oldest brother. Both feature in my story.

My grandfather Klein Sámuel was a master cobbler. I just found a picture from around 1910, of the front of his workshop, with some of his assistants.

Klein Sámuel's workshop, Debrecen, around 1910.
Kaposi family collection

---

8   See *HISTORIAN'S VOICE: Jews in Debrecen*

He was a small, round, jovial-looking man with ruddy cheeks and bushy white moustaches. He looked jolly, but he was mean, unkind, his jokes more vicious than funny.

Imre's beautiful golden-haired mother was aptly named Aranka (Golda). After a miserable marriage and many pregnancies, she died of cancer at 35. By Jewish custom, I was named after her, so I have two names: Agnes and Aranka.

Soon after Aranka's death, Sámuel married the widow Szeréna, who brought a son to the marriage: Sándor, a clever boy, a year my father's senior. The boys got on well, no thanks to Szeréna, a wicked stepmother fit for a fairytale. We had a photograph, now lost, of the two boys aged about 10: Sándor in a velvet suit and frilly silk shirt, Imre in rags and barefoot (a master shoemaker's son!). Sámuel and Szeréna had a son, Laci, together. Laci was 11 years my father's junior.

Here is a picture of the family, in 1927. At that time almost nobody owned a camera, and in my family even snapshots were rare. A studio photograph like this would have been a luxury. My grandfather looks smug, radiating pride at being able to afford it. Margit is missing from the picture – by then she had escaped into an early marriage and left Hungary, fleeing from country to country across Europe, never to return.

Imre rarely talked of his childhood, but I knew my grandfather and his home, which lacked any trace of comfort, any sign of Jewish culture or culture of any kind, and I was familiar with the story told by that boyhood photograph with stepbrother Sándor.

The author's father's family, Debrecen, 1927. Sitting: Klein Szeréna and Sámuel.
Standing: Klein Sándor, Laci, Klári, and the author's father Imre.

Kaposi family collection

When Imre finished primary school at the age of ten, his father expected him to join the apprentice cobblers at his workshop, to earn his keep and pay for his board and lodgings. Imre had other ideas. The story of his education reads like another fairytale. He located the gate of the nearest senior school, which happened to be a fee-paying *gimnázium* (grammar school), run by Piarist priests. He rang the bell and said to the janitor monk that he wanted to come here to study. Surprised at the initiative of the raggedy youngster, the janitor took him to the headmaster who was amused and, by asking some questions, established that Imre was a natural mathematician of rare gifts; Jewish, but knowing nothing about Judaism. Impressed by the child's determination and ability, the headmaster said yes, Imre could join the school. Imre said Thank You, but only if he could earn money while at school, to pay his father for his bed and keep. The headmaster agreed even to that, promising to find him pupils to coach in mathematics. Throughout his schooling, my father acted as mathematics tutor to his classmates, and even to pupils older than himself.

This famous establishment was run by Piarists, a small Catholic teaching order, strict but generously liberal. My father was not the only Jew, and his class also included a few girls.

The author's father's (Klein Imre's) tableau, 1918-19 graduates of Debrecen's Piarist High School.
Kaposi family collection

The school was founded in 1621 and was disbanded by the Communists in 1948. Standards were high. Science and mathematics were thoroughly covered, but the curriculum was dominated by the classics. Ancient languages were in everyday use, history being taught in Latin, and geometry in Greek. Biblical Hebrew was also on the timetable, but 'lightweight' subjects, such as art, music or modern languages, were excluded. Imre soon outstripped the mathematics curriculum, and the Reverend Fathers devised lessons especially for him. I came to appreciate the depth and quality of this personalised instruction during my university years, when I found that my father knew most of the higher mathematics of the engineering curriculum.[9]

Until I came on the scene, Imre was the only member of his family to graduate from grammar school. It is a tradition for Hungarian secondary schools to display photographs of their graduating students, together with their teachers, on a large tableau in the window of a prominent shop in the main street. My father's picture is in pride of place at the top, next to the Headmaster.

The author's father Klein Imre

Kaposi family collection

The Piarist Fathers were proud of their brilliant Jewish protégé, and were ready to sponsor him through university. However, by that time Imre was involved in politics, and in 1919 he became active in the revolutionary movement which established a Marxist/Communist government in Hungary. Imre's youthful participation in the Commune compromised him, marked him for life, and ended his association with the Piarists. During my childhood I came across several distinguished people, among them an MP, an eminent paediatrician, a chemistry professor, and a judge who had all been Imre's pupils at school. Imre himself would never go to university.[10]

In 1919 Imre only just survived the Spanish 'flu, an epidemic which claimed millions of lives all around the world. He had encephalitis as a complication, which deprived him of the sight in one eye. Encephalitis was also thought to be responsible for the Parkinson's disease from which he later suffered.

---

9   Piarists are a Roman Catholic teaching order, founded in 17th century Italy. They established several famous schools in Hungary, including some of the most prestigious grammar schools that still exist today. Despite the antireligious stance of the communist regime, two Piarist schools were still allowed to exist in Hungary under the decades of communism.

10   See *HISTORIAN'S VOICE: Red Terror, White Terror*

Soon after graduation from school, the family curse caught up with my father: he contracted tuberculosis. Before antibiotics, the best treatment was thought to be a long stay in a sanatorium in the high mountains. There was no question of Sámuel paying for such treatment for his son, so 19-year-old Imre found a cure for himself. With his copperplate handwriting and spectacular numeracy, he obtained an accountant's job with a large lumber-and-glass company in *Feketeerdő* in the Carpathians, a high Transylvanian mountain area which is now in Romania. He learnt about glass manufacture and trees, their species, growing habits, the processes of logging and transporting logs down mountains, and uses of timber in the furniture and building trades. He enjoyed the frosty air, the snow-capped mountains and the beauty of waterfalls, and even acquired a companion, a tiny dog which he carried around in wintertime in the inner pocket of his greatcoat. He was valued by his employers, and when he was well enough to leave the mountains, they presented him with two personalised ornamental paperweights made at the glassworks: one bearing his signature, the other his initials.

Paperweights made for Klein Imre by his employers in the Carpathian glassworks, around 1920.

Photo: László Csősz, 2019

Imre was a well-built, good-looking man, but he was a misfit, born at the wrong time to the wrong family: progressive among traditionalists, idealist among opportunists, generous among the mean, tolerant among the prejudiced. He was the champion of the weak and of lost causes, a Jew in a Protestant city of a Catholic country, a socialist persecuted with equal venom by fascists and Stalinists. He respected all people, rich or poor, men or women, old or young, Jews, gentiles or atheists. In an age when children were to be 'seen but not heard', he outraged adults by encouraging children, especially his own child, to ask questions, always willing to answer, often taking the child's side against adults, acknowledging the child to be in the right if justice demanded.

MY MOTHER

Her given name was Magda, and her maiden name was Csengeri, a beautiful old Hungarian name, very different from the German names of most Hungarian Jews. Also, unusually for Jews, most Csengeris were blond and blue- or green-eyed, and the wealthy branch of the family (not our branch of course) had extensive land estates. It was rare for Jews to be landowners; yet, a Csengeri estate in Margitta, east of Debrecen, was already mentioned in statistical bulletins in 1897.

Grandfather Dezső had five sisters. I remember them all. The oldest, Giza, was everyone's favourite. We all called her Giza mama. She had sparse hair and no teeth, and yet she was beautiful: sweet, gentle, clever and funny. She taught me to cook delicious dishes from cheap ingredients, and to knit, crochet and embroider. Most of all, she taught me beautiful Hungarian folksongs. Hungarian fascists shot her into the river in Budapest in February 1945.

My mother's mother was widowed at 35, a businesswoman who brought up three daughters on her own. Her name was Ilona. I called her Nanóka, as did all who followed me into the family: her grandchildren, their spouses, and my daughters. She was the sun of my childhood, the source of wisdom, skills and loving care. She imposed an iron discipline on herself and on all around her. Her family adored her, her employees feared and admired her, customers trusted her, business associates respected her, and everyone learned from her. She had boundless energy, stood just under 4ft 8in tall with size 3 feet, and her cushioned little hands had a surprisingly strong grip.

Author's grandmother Csengeri Dezsőné née Rosinger Ilona (Nanóka)
and grandfather Csengeri Dezső.
Kaposi family collection

Ilona was the second youngest of 13 children, of whom I knew only three. Their father had been an agronomist, superintendent of a huge country estate, so she grew up in a remote rural area. She and her siblings never went to school – they had governesses at home. This may account for my grandmother being semi-literate. She never read a book. I have many of her letters: lively chronicles, full of spelling errors, totally lacking punctuation. Ilona never learnt accounting or management, but she ran a successful business, and looked after the administration herself. Her mental arithmetic was faster and more accurate than that of anybody else, except of course my father. In my grandfather's time the business stretched an impressive distance each way on the corner of Dégenfeld tér, one of the main squares of Debrecen, catering for the entire clothing requirements of the peasant class: boots, shoes and underwear; clothing material for work, church and weddings; hats and caps for men, bonnets and ribbons for women. There were textiles by the yard for the household: table linen, bedlinen and kitchen linen. Later the business had to contract somewhat, but the shop always flourished, and Ilona had two and sometimes three employees. Always exquisitely turned out, she only wore dark clothes. She had many suitors, but never remarried. My favourite picture of her catches her smile and her ramrod-straight back.

Nanóka's first home, I remember, was typical of the provincial lower middle class: a single-storey building, divided into several dwellings. There was a tiny entrance hall, a dining room, and a bedroom. The kitchen was in the basement, accessed by an outside staircase. There was no bathroom. The toilet was across the yard in a shed, shared by several families. It had a wooden seat with a lid, also of wood, both well-scrubbed. To use it, summer or winter, one had to cross the yard, carrying one's own paper and a jug of water.

The rooms had heavy oak furniture, with much silver and ornamental china on display. There were no easy chairs; one sat on heavy straight-backed dining chairs. The bottom of the pedestal dining table was covered with ornately beaten copper, polished to a high shine, like the door handles and the kitchen utensils. In summer the thick wool carpets were shielded by cotton 'carpet protectors'. Windows had delicate lace curtains and heavy inner curtains. The wide tapestry pelmets and side-hangings had tropical scenes, embroidered by Nanóka, as were the framed tapestry pictures. The bed was covered by a double bedspread, lilac silk below, white crochet above, and had embroidered scatter cushions. The entrance hall had rag carpet mats, woven by Nanóka of used stockings. The spacious kitchen had a water tap but no sink, gas or electricity. It was a friendly place, with brightly painted walls and furniture. There were samplers, ornamental embroidery and monogrammed tea towels, all made by Nanóka herself. The wood fire in the range was comforting, and the paraffin lamp gave a warm glow.

Even modest households like ours had a resident maid. Nanóka engaged simple country girls, and trained them to her exacting standards. She drove them hard, but treated them generously, so they were loyal, and stayed for many years. I loved Mari, a cheerful young hunchback, and I missed her when she left suddenly – I think she must have got pregnant. Her successor was Flora, a dour woman, with an illegitimate child somewhere.

Nobody had vacuum cleaners at the time. Nanóka's home was cleaned daily by the servant girl, all of us helping, all following Nanóka's set procedures. The girl also cooked the meals, and prepared home-made pasta of various shapes, dried on white cloths on the kitchen table and stored in muslin sacks in the larder. There was a special board and hand tool for making shell-shaped pasta. Jams, compotes, tomato purée and pickles, not available in shops, were prepared by Nanóka herself when fruits and vegetables were in season. Jars and bottles of preserves were ranked in the larder on tiers of shelves decorated with embroidered runners, some of which I still have.

Nanóka baked cakes and pastries on Sunday mornings. Strudel-making was a ritual, and great fun. Nanóka placed a ball of special dough in the precise middle of a white-cloth-covered round table. She stretched the dough gently to just beyond the table edge, carefully avoiding tears (I could teach you the method). The pastry had to cover the whole table evenly, the weight of its all-round overhang providing the final gentle pull. At last, when the pastry was paper thin, Nanóka ran around the table to tear off the excess. Strudels were made with several fillings: walnut, poppyseed, sweet cheese with sultanas, semi-sweet peppered cabbage (everyone's favourite), apple, and morello cherry, when in season. Nanóka also baked variously shaped braided brioches, kalács (challah), chocolate-filled 'dirty' kalács, pies, and beautifully decorated petit fours, drizzled with chocolate through a spoon with a hole in the middle. As a special treat, a helpful little girl could lick the spoon at the end of the proceedings. Another special treat was supper on a rainy evening: sweet lemon tea, and bread toasted on long two-pronged forks over the embers of the kitchen range, the toast rubbed with a clove of garlic, spread with goose fat, and sprinkled with salt and paprika. Grownups' lemon tea was sometimes laced with rum, and I longed for the day when I too would qualify.

For each meal, the table was covered with a crisply starched, figured linen tablecloth with large matching serviettes, all embroidered and monogrammed, more of Nanóka's handiwork. For decoration, an embroidery called *tablet* was placed in the middle. Here is a beautiful example, made by Nanóka in the traditional folk style of *kalotaszegi vagdalásos*. Most of the tablecloths are lost, but several tablets and a couple of sets of serviettes remain, now used as guest towels. I donated a small tablecloth with matching serviettes to the National Holocaust Centre and Museum.

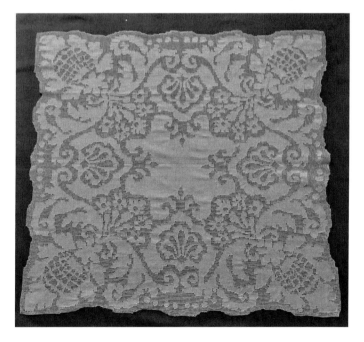

Traditional Transylvanian "kalotaszegi vagdalásos" embroidery, Nanóka's handiwork.
Photo: László Csősz, 2019

Everyone had their own silver serviette ring. Crockery, cutlery, glasses, serviettes, salt and pepper, water jug, bread basket, serving spoons and condiment sets all had their appointed places on the table. For each meal, a particular person was entrusted with setting the table: my mother, one of her sisters, or I. Each dish was brought in by the servant girl, and set before Nanóka, who served everyone in turn. We waited until she served herself at last, and gave us a smile, a quick nod indicating that we could start eating. Once we sat down, nobody was allowed to leave the table until the meal was over. Should any item be missing, such as a glass or the salt cellar, we had to do without; Nanóka never chastised the culprit – the one who set the table – but her eyes told all.

Even after my marriage, washing machines were still unheard of. In Nanóka's house washing and ironing was done by tall, beautiful Mariska, a washerwoman who went from house to house, spending a day a fortnight in the washhouse in her clients' courtyards. Her daughter Little Mariska was one of my summertime playmates. The washhouse was shared among all tenants. It had a big wooden tub, a cauldron over a stove for heating the water, a mangle, and three ironing boards: one for larger items, another for dresses and shirts, and a special one for sleeves. Mariska was always pale, with a constant headache caused, I am sure, by fumes of the charcoal iron. Her job was precisely specified by Nanóka. Everything had to be ironed, even socks and dusters. Fiddly bits of blouses and dresses had to be ironed first, seams came next, smooth parts last. I taught the procedure to my granddaughter Molly, the only one interested. Embroidery was first pressed on the good side, then on the reverse side, making ornamental stitches prominent. Personal linen and table linen were folded to sizes specified on rectangles of paper. Lilac-coloured tissue paper lined each item of Nanóka's lingerie. The colour for her oldest daughter was gold, pink was for the middle girl, blue for the youngest. Each had their own wardrobe section with a silk curtain inside, the colour matching the tissue paper. This colour code accompanied Ilona's daughters into married life, and yellow remained my mother's favourite colour.

Nanóka was a country girl at heart, although in her adult life she lived in cities. She knew the plants of the field and the trees of the forest, and later this helped us survive the wartime hardships of the camps.

Dezső and Ilona had three daughters at two-year intervals: Magda, Terka, and Klára, whom we all called *Pici* (Tiny). Here is a solemn and faintly funny picture of them.

The girls differed in looks, abilities and character, but were united in loyalty to each other, and to their mother. Although she had little education herself, Ilona's natural intelligence guided her to choose learning opportunities to suit each daughter, and from her very limited income she set aside money for their language and music lessons. My mother Magda, the oldest, was attractive but not conventionally pretty. She handed down her fair complexion to two of my grandchildren. She never wore makeup, and to the end of her life, at 96, she had porcelain skin and no wrinkles. When she was a girl, her hair was a shiny, wavy gold-blonde, and the local hairdresser pestered Ilona to allow her daughter to model hairstyles for local competitions. Ilona was scandalised at the very idea.

The Csengeri girls, from the left: Klára (Pici, 2), Terka (4)
and the author's mother Magda (6), Debrecen, 1918.
Kaposi family collection

Magda found learning easy and was naturally numerate. Instead of leaving school at 14, she attended commercial school and gained a diploma. While still a student, she travelled to Budapest regularly, acting as buyer for her mother's business, choosing merchandise, negotiating prices and deliveries, and becoming knowledgeable about textiles and competent at business. This girlhood experience stood the family in good stead in our difficult later life.

A gifted musician, Magda was the first in the family to start piano lessons at the age of six, a practice which has continued for all later generations. She attended the local music school (Debreceni Zenede). Standards were high; the Zenede launched many noted musicians, the pianist Vásáry Tamás among them. Magda was a star pupil, expected to become a professional pianist. Marriage at 19 stopped these ambitions, but music stayed her dominant interest through life.

The author's mother Magda
in Glyndebourne, England,
around 2002.

Kaposi family collection

A family like theirs would not have owned a radio, and of course television was yet to be invented. Magda bought sheet music, piano transcriptions of operas and symphonies, and played them to herself, becoming familiar with the musical literature.

My aunts Terka and Pici will come into my story later; meanwhile here is a picture I found among my mother's papers after her death. It was taken in August 1932, a jolly outing to the Great Forest of Debrecen, when a huge storm broke out. My mother was pregnant with me and was so frightened that she thought she was losing her baby. They managed to get home safely and here I am to prove it, but she was petrified of storms for the rest of her life. I recognise several of those happy young people on the photo. The war meted out a cruel fate to them all, killing most of the men and many of the women.

The author's mother Magda, her sisters, cousins and friends in the Debrecen Great Forest, 1932.
Kaposi family collection

HISTORIAN'S VOICE

Debrecen

Debrecen is the economic and cultural centre of Eastern Hungary, a bulwark of Protestantism in a largely Catholic country. The city is symbolised by two landmarks, the Calvinist (Reformed) Great Church and the Calvinist College, dating back to the 16th century.

In 1941, Debrecen had 125,933 inhabitants: two-thirds Calvinists (82,580), about one-fifth Catholics (25,491), and 9142 said to belong to the 'Israelite' denomination. Another 305 souls were Jews by origin who had converted to Christianity. In all, some 7.5% of the city population was Jewish. The overwhelming majority was ethnic Hungarian, almost exclusively Hungarian-speaking.

Hungary's Jews – Culture and Religion

In the 19th century, various Jewish religious-liturgical branches appeared in Hungary. Proponents of modernisation, known as the Haskalah *or the 'Jewish Enlightenment', introduced various reforms, including the loosening of dress and dietary codes, changing the mother tongue from traditional Yiddish to the language of the indigenous population, transforming the structure of the synagogue, and implementing innovations in service. Differences went far beyond liturgical variation; for example, reform communities were characterised by lower birth rates, more frequent divorces, and the spread of women's education. Traditionalists, however, insisted on conserving the strict, rabbinical religious heritage.[11]*

In 1869, the differences between Hungarian Jewish communities were institutionalised. Three liturgical-organisational branches were created: pro-modernist Neolog, *anti-reform* Orthodox, *and* Status Quo, *with religious practices closer to the Orthodox. Uniquely in European Jewish history, the state gave official recognition to this 'schism'. In addition to these three-way opposing movements,* Hassidism *– a religious renewal folk movement – also appeared in Hungary. This became especially popular among poor, closed communities of eastern immigrants who were strongly holding on to their traditions.[12]*

Before World War I, traditionalist communities were in the majority, representing some 60% of Hungary's Jews. There was a geographical divide: Orthodox Judaism had almost exclusive influence in the eastern and northeastern regions, while the Neolog bloc mostly covered western-southwestern and central areas, and was dominant in Budapest. However, after World War I, with Hungary losing most of its Orthodox-dominated territories, Neolog became the largest community branch.

---

11   Kinga Frojimovics, *Szétszakadt történelem. Zsidó vallási irányzatok Magyarországon, 1868-1950*. Budapest: Balassi, 2008.

12   The expression *'status quo ante'* (Latin: "the way things were before") refers to the fact that the communities belonging here did not recognize the events of the 1868-69 Israelite Congress. They instead insisted on the situation prior to the meeting. For details about the schism, see Jacob Katz, *A House Divided. Orthodoxy and Schism in Nineteenth-Century Central European Jewry*. Waltham, MA: Brandeis University Press, 1998.

Jews in Debrecen

The position of Debrecen was unique: it was on the dividing line between the traditional and modernist worlds, the only locality in Hungary where all four branches of Judaism were present. It was home to the largest Status Quo community in Hungary. For about two decades, a Neolog community also existed, but eventually joined the Status Quo community, engulfing the majority of Debrecen Jews, including the bulk of the elite and the middle class. At the same time, some Hasidim joined the Orthodox community.

The Jewish neighbourhood started to spread from the city's main square towards the south-west, between the then Nagy Hatvan and the Széchényi streets. Symbolising their social status, economic power and integration, at the very end of the 19th century the Status Quo community built a magnificent two-towered synagogue on the main street. The synagogue survived the Holocaust, but was damaged in a fire, and was ultimately demolished after the war. Another Status Quo synagogue had existed in the traditional Jewish district, in close proximity to the main synagogue of the Orthodox community. Unlike most of the synagogue buildings in Hungary, both are still serving the community, the latter recently renovated by the Hungarian state.[13]

Red Terror, White Terror

The Commune, also known as the Republic of Councils (Tanácsköztársaság) or the Hungarian Soviet Republic, was a short-lived Communist rump state that reigned in the central parts of Hungary between 21st March and 1st August, 1919. Following the Soviet example, the Communist government attempted at radical transformation of the economic and social order, including nationalisation of larger industrial, commercial and financial enterprises, collectivisation of agriculture, and reform of culture and education. These actions stirred stout resistance against the government, especially in the provinces. To suppress 'internal enemies', the Communists organised armed detachments who often committed violent excesses and arbitrary executions of hundreds, known as the 'Red Terror'. Jews often played a leading role in anti-Communist resistance and some were murdered; however, the majority of the Commune leadership was also of Jewish origin. Hence, antisemitic counter-revolutionary propaganda referred to the Republic of Councils as a 'Jewish' takeover, which has remained a dominant interpretation in Hungarian historical consciousness until the present day.

The subsequent retaliatory campaign of Vice Admiral Horthy's right-wing National Army, also known as 'White Terror', targeted left-wing sympathisers, and also Jews, who rarely had any responsibility in the politics of the Commune. Hundreds of people were executed or killed in 'spontaneous' pogroms throughout the country. Thousands were imprisoned, harassed, or forced to emigrate. By 1921, Horthy halted violence for pragmatic considerations, and a period of political

---

13   For more details, see the *Yivo Encyclopedia of Jews in Eastern Europe* (New Haven, Yale University Press, 2008) Vol. 1. p. 399. http://www.yivoencyclopedia.org/article.aspx/Debrecen (accessed 19 October, 2019)

and social consolidation followed. However, antisemitic sentiments and implicitly anti-Jewish practices lingered on. The economic crisis of the early 1930s hit Hungary hard, brought about another right-wing political turn, and increasingly radicalised the political climate.

Violent swings of Hungary's politics continuing through the war and beyond, are well demonstrated in case of Kun Béla, Jewish leader of the 1919 Commune. During the White Terror he was vilified and then soon forgotten, but after the war the Communist regime elevated him to the status of national hero. To commemorate the 100th anniversary of his birth, in 1986 a memorial was erected in Vérmező (Field of Blood), one of Budapest's historical squares. Work of Hungary's great sculptor Varga Imre, it is a dramatic masterpiece, hailed by the **Daily Telegraph** *as 'one of the world's most incredible sculptures'. Its central figure is Kun Béla himself, surrounded by historical characters, Red Army soldiers and captured enemy officers. Kun Béla's second coming ended abruptly at the 1989 change of regime, when the statue was removed from its prominent position, and is now stashed away in Memento Park in a distant suburban corner of Budapest.*

Imre Varga: Béla Kun Memorial (1986), Memento Park, Budapest
Courtesy of Frankemann, <u>*creativecommons.org*</u>

2   EARLY DAYS

1932 – 1938

In October 1932, when I was born, my 31-year-old father had a job which suited him perfectly. He was co-founder and Managing Director of a range of financial, legal and educational advisory services and businesses run by socialist sympathisers for the benefit of Debrecen's working people. He was well known and highly respected in the city. This was the only job in his life worthy of his talents.

It fell to my father to register my birth. Agnes was the name chosen for a girl and Aranka was to be my second name, but at the Registry Office my father was too excited, and made one of his rare mistakes: he interchanged the two names. My school certificates show that I was branded as Aranka throughout primary school, although I hated the old-fashioned name.[14]

In the first six weeks of my life, my 20-year-old mother and I were strangers to each other, and our relationship never quite recovered. Immediately after childbirth, Magda was diagnosed with

The author at the age of 1, Debrecen, 1933.
Kaposi family collection

---

14   'Ágnes' is the Hungarian spelling, but the accent is omitted when referring to the author herself.

thrombosis of the leg. The condition was potentially lethal, requiring six weeks of bed rest. As far as I was concerned, she was out of the picture. Under the watchful eye of Nanóka, my 18-year-old aunt Terka nursed both my mother and me. Unusually for those times, and unheard-of for a man of my father's elevated position, he pushed my pram all around town, to the delight and amusement of a fair section of the public. This was the start of the close relationship between my father and me.

Terka never tired of saying what a beautiful baby I used to be. For years, my photograph was displayed in the window of the town's most fashionable photographer, and the Austrian food company Julius Meinl used my pictures for decades, advertising baby rusks.

Rumour had it that I was a clever and happy toddler. Aged two, I knew my Walt Disney books by heart, pointing to the right words, making people think that I could read. Music was part of my life from the start. Whenever my aunt Pici was playing, I used to sit under her piano on a *sámli*, a very low stool. When I was tall enough to reach the keys, I picked out the odd tune. Chopin's Raindrop Prelude was my party piece. Everyone thought that the family had a prodigy ...

And then, when I was two, the roof fell in. The reasons lay in international and Hungarian politics. When Hitler seized power in Germany and Gömbös became Prime Minister in Hungary, my father's organisation was disbanded; he lost his job and, as a socialist activist, he was branded a dangerous rebel. Being well known in Debrecen, he had no chance ever again of finding employment there. Hoping for better fortunes or at least anonymity in the capital, my parents moved to Budapest, leaving me behind with Nanóka. His socialist past cast a long shadow; my father remained unemployed during most of my childhood. My young mother suddenly became the breadwinner.

Although I was lovingly cared for in Debrecen by Nanóka, Terka and Pici, parting from my parents must have been a trauma. I acquired a bad stammer, and did not shake it off until well into my school years. Neither was I beautiful anymore. My hair became frizzy. Shampoo and conditioner had not yet been invented, and hair washing was a torment. My left eye was lazy and the right none too good, so at age three I was given glasses. The lazy eye soon became dysfunctional. It could have been corrected by exercise, but my parents were not there to pick up on the possibility. I have lived my whole life with just one none-too-good working eye.

Arriving in the capital, my parents had no money, no home, no means of livelihood. They found shelter with my mother's lovely aunt Giza mama and her daughter Rózsi, who had made the move from Debrecen some years before.

Rózsi was as protective of my mother as only an older sister might have been. She was manager of a branch of *Központi Tejcsarnok* (Central Dairy), a chain of food shops. She adopted Magda as assistant, taught her how to run the business, and helped her to obtain a post as manager of another branch. The company was a well organised business, with over 150 outlets throughout the capital. Staff training was comprehensive, with skills continuously updated. Supervision was thorough, and there was a monthly competition for the prize of 'Best Branch'. From 1936 until 1943, when increasing numbers of Jews lost their jobs, Magda and Rózsi alternated gaining the prize. They were the last Jews to be dismissed from Central Dairy.

My mother got her first job when I was four. I was reunited with my parents. Magda's shop was in Aréna út (now Dózsa György út), a busy thoroughfare linking Budapest's famous *Hősök Tere* (Hero's Square) to a poor district near the Eastern Railway Station. The shop was in a run-down building, with a greengrocer and a tobacconist on either side, and a pub two doors away. A Hungarian pub was a very different institution from one in Britain today. Standing room only, a clientele of drunks and vagrants, sawdust on the floor to soak up mud and worse, drunken swearing, and ever-pending violence. Just around the corner was Garay tér, a large noisy square full of layabouts, housing the meat, fish and vegetable market.

Magda's shop was small, and behind it was an even smaller windowless room where we lived. There was a water tap but no sink, the kitchen range was in one corner, and a table with three chairs in another. There was just enough room for my parents' bed and my cot. The toilet was across the yard in the basement, shared with the families of staff of other businesses and customers of the pub.

My father could not get a job. He helped my mother in the shop: took orders for milk, cream or whatever, packed deliverables into large rectangular baskets, and carried the foodstuff to customers' homes early in the morning, before breakfast. He also did the business accounts. Sometimes he tried, so hard and yet so unsuccessfully, to serve behind the counter, but he was slow and clumsy. Used to the speed and skill of my mother, customers objected to being attended by him. He found other ways of making a few pennies. I remember two of his pathetic enterprises: shelling walnuts and making filter-tip cigarettes.

Walnut shelling was seasonal. In October/November, Imre brought over from the greengrocer sacks of freshly harvested walnuts. If the shells were still soft, the walnuts were spread out under the bed to dry. Imre would crack and peel off the shells, taking care not to break the nut inside, he would prise the two halves apart, and would try to remove the dividing membrane without damaging the half-nuts. The greengrocer paid less for broken halves.

Cigarette work was all the year around, but it was difficult. A carefully judged quantity of tobacco was sprinkled into a hinged brass tube. Inserting the closed tube into the flimsy paper shell of the filter-tipped cigarette, a brass plunger was applied, delicately pushing the tobacco into the shell, releasing the tube. If the tube had too much tobacco, the shell would burst; if it had too little, the cigarette would be floppy, a reject. Worst of all, sometimes a grain of tobacco was trapped in the tube when snapping it shut, the grain acting as a blade and slicing open the shell. On many an occasion the money the tobacconist paid for the completed cigarettes was less than the money Imre paid for the tobacco and the paper shells.

We had no money for toys. There were no children in our block. Sometimes the publican next door let me play with the billiard balls. Városliget, the biggest park of Budapest, was nearby, on the other side of the road, full of children and exciting things to do, but I was too small to go on my own, and who was to take me? My mother worked from dawn to evening, and was constantly exhausted, always preoccupied; she hardly ever talked to me. My father was my companion, letting me help him with his little jobs. School was years away, but he taught me the numbers and how to add them, and later showed me how to add whole columns of numbers for my mother's books. Next, he taught me to read. He invented for me word games, number games and memory games. On Sunday the shop was closed, so sometimes, rarely, we all went by tram across town to visit relatives, but most Sundays my mother just slept, trying to recover from the work of the week before, gathering strength for the week to come.

The summer of 1937 brought some events which changed our lives.

My aunt Terka married the handsome young lawyer Feri who found a junior lawyer's job in Újpest, a nearby town which later became a suburb of Greater Budapest.

By then, few law offices were willing to engage Jews. I never met the principal, Nádasi, but hated him, because he treated Feri meanly. Feri's monthly pay of 40 Pengő was a pittance, less than a third of the average earnings of the time. Feri also had an occasional job, a big secret: he sat law examinations and wrote law theses in place of weak students, some of them highborn playboys. But where would the young couple live?[15]

The second happy event was also problematical. Pici was one of the few Jews accepted to Budapest's famous Liszt Ferenc Music Academy, becoming a pupil of the renowned pianist Faragó György. But where would she live? Our little room behind the shop was too small for my parents and me, let alone another three adults.

Great news: a turn of events to solve all problems! After years of unsuccessful trials, at last my father found a job! My mother's cousin, József, a slow learner at school, was now a well-regarded accountant at Lichtmann Cipőgyár, a firm of shoe manufacturers. At his recommendation, my brilliant classicist/mathematician father obtained a junior clerk's post at the same factory. Better than cracking nuts or filling cigarette shells. His pay was under 200 Pengő a month. Combining my mother's earnings with my father's and Feri's, we could rent a flat for us all!

The Managing Director of Lichtmann Cipőgyár was a splendid white-haired gentleman. I was not yet six when my father had one of his frequent bicycle accidents, and I had to collect his wages. The MD was surprised at my independence, and invited me to his office, where the chairs smelt of leather. He gave me a glass of lemonade and asked when I was going to school. I said September after next. When is my birthday? he asked. I said

---

15   Aleksander Ekstein gives the total annual earnings in the country in 1940 as 6.360 million Pengő, and an active working population as 4.2 million. The average income was 1514 Pengő per annum, 126 Pengő per month. See: National Income and Capital Formation in Hungary, 1900-1950. In *Review of Income and Wealth*, 1955, Vol. 5 (1) 152-223.

in October. Two magnificent birthday presents followed. The first was a scooter which I loved and rode on the pavement in front of my mother's shop. Just before I started school, he sent me another grand present which caused me much misery. It was a beautiful beige hand-made soft leather briefcase. Other children had stiff brown schoolbags strapped to their backs, while for four years I was saddled with this great floppy grownup's briefcase, to be carried by its handle. Yet another thing setting me apart, when I longed to be like everyone else.

My parents found a spacious flat to house us all! It was on dirty Garay tér, but who cared? – it had two nice rooms, each with two tall windows; one room even had a small balcony, and the only time I saw it, the sun streamed in. There was a kitchen and a bathroom with our own toilet. One room was for Terka and Feri, another for my parents and me, and Pici was to sleep in the kitchen, on a folding bed. It seemed that life was changing for the better!

And then again, the roof fell in.

This was supposed to be another happy event. Recognising my mother's good work, Central Dairy promoted her from the run-down Aréna út branch in one of the worst districts of the city to Honvéd utca, the very best. The whole family was rejoicing; only I was sad – the sunny Garay tér flat had to be forgotten.

Houses of Parliament, Kossuth square, Budapest, 1937. Photo: Ernő Vadas.
Hungarian National Museum Historical Photo Department

33

The wartime drama of my primary school years unfolded within a radius of half a mile from Budapest's Parliament. The iconic building is well known: the tourist industry uses its riverside picture to advertise city breaks and cruises. This photograph is the view from the garden square where I had an almost fatal accident as a child – a story soon to be told.

This was the district of state administration: Ministries all round, the Law Courts a corner away. My mother's shop was in an imposing turn-of-the-century Art Nouveau edifice, one of four huge, intercommunicating seven-floor buildings of elegant flats, housing Members of Parliament, university professors, judges, senior civil servants, famous artists, rich businessmen – the cream of Hungarian society. There were just a few shops in the block, my mother's dairy and a men's hairdresser among them.

The shop was like the one at Aréna út, but smarter and bigger. There were tables and chairs for customers to have a snack. A display cabinet had enticing small cakes, including Linzer and Ischler, my favourites to this day. A vestibule separated the shop from the back room, housing huge refrigerators and milk crates from which unpasteurised milk was measured into customers' own bottles. This milk had to be boiled before drinking. More expensive pasteurised milk arrived in sealed bottles of 1 litre, half litre and 0.2 litre sizes. There were bottles of cocoa and barrels of cream, soured cream and yoghurt, to be measured into customers' containers. There were cheeses, to be cut by wire, and great slabs of butter to be shaped with special tools. There was a great variety of merchandise: not just dairy, but eggs, hams and salamis, jams, preserves and honey, cakes, gateaux and fruit. To be fresh for breakfast, lunch, afternoon tea and evening, four times a day, bakers delivered plain, crossed and poppyseed rolls, salty, plain and semi-sweet crescents, round and platted brioches, and

The shop managed by the author's mother between 1938 and 1942, in Honvéd street, Budapest, which is a bank today.

'pacsni', a crispy savoury confection. There was brown, semi-brown, rye and white bread, the last also in cumin variety. Loaves were all the same shape and weight: 2kg.

Bread delivery was fun. One baker's boy stood at the back of the lorry, another at the door of the shop, and a third at the bread shelves inside, all wearing crisp white aprons, hats and gloves. The one at the van grabbed two fragrant, freshly baked, sometimes even hot loaves, turned them back-to-back, and threw them to the boy at the door, who forwarded them in an elegant volley to the one at the shelves, who put them into place. Serving bread, my mother cut the loaf with a huge razor-sharp bread knife which I still have, and she was proud to get the weight exactly right to the requirement of each customer. All dairy goods came from Central Dairy depots, but the rest was brought in. My mother selected suppliers to be approved by Central Dairy, negotiated prices, paid bills, and controlled delivery and quality. The training centre of Central Dairy taught the manager the correct method of storing, handling and serving food; the manager was then responsible for training staff. Hairstyle was specified, head covered, hands gloved. Food handling was regulated. For example, fruit had to be picked piece-by-piece from the crate, because even a small impact could bruise apples or peaches. Plain-clothes inspectors circulated, checking that the shop was spotless and procedures were observed. Small errors were punished by salary deduction, but larger digressions could bring about summary dismissal. The company issued a monthly bulletin with new instructions and ranking of branches.

Schoolgirl! The author, Budapest, 1939, photo by the author's uncle Laci.

Kaposi family collection

The shop opened for business at 7 am, but work started two hours earlier. Deliveries were received, customers' orders assembled, delivery baskets filled, delivery boys dispatched. Panics were frequent: a delivery was late, quality was unacceptable, a delivery boy was sick or fell on the stairs, breaking a bottle of milk or his arm. Snow slowed down everything, and customers' housemaids came complaining about late delivery.

My mother's eyes were everywhere. She was strict with the staff as she had learned from Nanóka, but was also popular, always quick and courteous; however, she never smiled: not in the shop, not at home. She appeared tireless, but absolutely *had* to take a 30-minute lunchtime break, putting her hands on the table and her head on her hands.

Terka was nominally a partner in the shop. She did her best, but was not well suited to the task. My mother and Terka tried to alternate doing the preparatory work from 5 to 7am, but Terka sometimes overslept; she was too thorough and slow, was not authoritative, and staff took advantage. Busy at the Academy, Pici was at hand sometimes; what she lacked in skill, she made up in charm.

35

As in the old place, there was a windowless room behind the shop, opening into the courtyard. This room was bigger, but even darker: not much light could penetrate into the small courtyard of a seven-floor building. There was a water tap, a kitchen range where our meals were cooked, a table with chairs, and a deckchair, in case anyone was unwell. I had a corner, with a tiny wicker table and armchair, of which I still have a picture. Toilet arrangements were familiar: across the courtyard, downstairs to the basement, shared with other shops. Although we now had a flat, we lived all day in that gloomy room behind the shop.

A new home had to be found. We had a resident maid, Bözsi, so we were seven: two couples without much income, two people with no income at all (music student Pici and me), and Bözsi, a financial liability. Central Dairy demanded a quick move, the flat had to be in the expensive district of the new shop and had to be near a school: I was approaching school age. Perfect location was the only good feature of our flat. It was ugly, cramped, airless, and dark. My father said it did not matter, we only used it for sleeping. Our new address was Vilmos Császár út 58 (now Bajcsy-Zsilinszky út). One of the city's major thoroughfares, the road runs parallel with the Danube from the Belváros (Inner City) to the Western Railway Station where it changes its name to Váci út, continuing northwards for miles, to Újpest and far beyond. Our building was fairly typical of the time: two storeys around a courtyard with a stand for beating carpets (there were no vacuum cleaners). Facing the street were two shops, one of them Fischers, a renowned antiquarian bookshop where, in his boyhood, my husband bought his miniature orchestral scores of the Beethoven symphonies. I did not meet him until much later, but I still have those scores.

Mr Hajdu, the stern skeletal concierge, lived on the ground floor with his shrewish fat wife and his daughter, ten years my senior. Mrs Hajdu locked the gate at 10pm precisely. 'Gate money' (kapupénz) was payable by anyone chancing their arm to go in or out after 10pm.

In all the years we lived there, I was the only one of the family ever to visit another flat – once. Next door lived the stocky mustachioed tailor Mr Somogyi with his beautiful wife and their daughter Elvira, my age. I had great hopes for Elvira, the only other child in the building, but my hopes were dashed at once. Mr Somogyi worked at home, making men's suits and coats in his small kitchen. I heard that he beat his wife.

Propaganda stamp of the Arrow Cross Party, 1938. Caption: "We are winning!"
Hungarian National Museum, Small Prints Collection

Even in his own kitchen, Mr Somogyi wore the armband of the Fascist Arrow Cross. I soon learnt that this meant that Elvira was not allowed to play with me. In any case where could we play? Mrs Hajdu did not tolerate children in the courtyard or on the corridors.

Smart flats overlooked the street, but our second-floor flat was at the back. The front door opened into the tiny entrance hall. The little stone-floored kitchen on the right was heated (somewhat, sometimes) by a fire in the range. It had a folding bed for maid Bözsi. By the unpleasant parlance of the day she was termed *mindenes*, for which the nearest translation would be 'all-purpose'. My socialist parents never referred to her this way.

The door on the left led to the room I shared with my parents. When Nanóka came to visit at Christmas, she slept on my sofa, and I slept on folded blankets on the floor. Our room had a small narrow window opening to a *lichthof*, a tiny back yard between our house and other buildings around. Inhabitants were not supposed to throw rubbish out of the window, but they did, and the lichthof usually smelled. Another reason for the smell was that the windows of the bathroom/toilet of other flats opened to the lichthof. Our bathroom/toilet had no window at all, it only had ventilation through the door to our room. Our flat was immaculate, and yet there were hundreds of shiny black cockroaches in the bathroom. They came out in the dark, scuttling away when the lamp was lit. I feared them, and often waited for a grownup to go to the loo first, so I could follow when the light was still on and the bugs were hiding.

Other than the door to the windowless bathroom, another door from our room led to Terka and Feri's room, a bit larger than ours, with windows to the corridor. Terka and Feri had to go through our room to access theirs.

We had no telephone in the flat or in the shop; in fact, my first home with a telephone was in England, in 1965.

My mother was the main breadwinner, the senior sister. It was she who decided that Terka and Feri should have the bigger, lighter room. Why not my parents and me? Only once did my father question her decision. Her answer is lost in the fog of the past. When thinking to write this book, I asked Pici, who said that my mother's arrangement showed what a good sister she was. That flat remained a constant reminder that my mother's affection for her sisters almost exhausted her repertoire of love, and she hadn't much left for me.

Whatever its limitations, the flat was a great improvement on the room behind the shop at Aréna út. The kitchen had a tap, and the bathroom had a bath (no shower), a flush toilet, and a stove with a water tank. A wood fire heated water once a week for a bath and a hair wash, everyone using as little water as possible, mindful of the cost of fuel and the needs of the next along the line. To wash clothes, all-purpose Bözsi perched a wooden tub over the bath, and dried small items on a *fregoli*: a frame fitted with parallel wires, suspended from the ceiling. Mrs Hajdu permitting, bedlinen could be dried in the unheated loft, but winter-time drying would have been impossible. Bedclothes were changed frequently, but used bedclothes were stored in a huge chest in the bathroom, washing postponed until the spring.

The room I shared with my parents was cramped. Very cramped. If the cupboard door was open, one could not get to the bathroom. If a chair was pulled out, one could not get around the table. Books were under the bed: we had neither money nor space for a bookcase. On my mother's bedside table there was a radio. My father loved radio dramas and sports commentaries. My mother liked any good music, but was particularly partial to the voice. This is how I became familiar with lieder and operas, and learned the names, and sometimes even recognised the voices, of great singers of the day: Galli Curci, Totti dal Monte, Tito Schipa, Fleta, Caruso, Chaliapin.

The flat had two large ceramic-tiled stoves: one in Terka's room, one in ours. On winter mornings Bözsi lit wood fires in both. An hour later the last person leaving the flat shut down the stoves. The tiles stored the heat, so the air remained temperate in daytime, while we were in the shop. By the time we returned in the evening the tiles were cold, but that did not matter: one could sleep in the cold.

From time to time the courtyard had visitors: gypsy traders buying up old clothes and shoes, an old man calling to sharpen knives and scissors on his rotating pumice stone, mounted on a small cart. They were usually chased away by Mrs Hajdu before anyone could answer their call. Sometimes buskers came, singing in tuneless voices, plucking an ancient guitar, banging a tin drum. On the rare occasion when we were there to hear them, a grownup would wrap a few coins for me to throw down, before they were chased away by Mrs Hajdu.

The Hajdus made an important contribution to our lives. After the war we learned that Mr Hajdu had been a prominent underground Communist. As such, he had secrets to guard, and this would have explained his reticence. When we left our home in 1944 on the arrival of the Germans, my parents lodged some valued possessions with trusted Christian acquaintances for safekeeping. Not a single item did we see again. My parents never thought of asking the Hajdus for any favour, and yet they saved some of the contents of our flat. This is how I still have bits of my mother's table china, her exquisite coffee service, and some of our household linen.

Mr Hajdu came to an undeservedly horrible end. In 1945 the bridges of the Danube had been destroyed by the withdrawing German army, and after the war some makeshift bridges were rigged up. To clear bomb damage, Mr Hajdu brought, from Buda, some nitroglycerine in a container. He slipped on the bridge, the nitroglycerine exploded, and he was burnt to death.

Antisemitic leaflet, early 1940s.
Caption: "Ghetto for Them!"

Hungarian National Museum, Small Prints Collection

PLAYMATES

Throughout my Budapest childhood I was lonely, an outsider. Elvira, the fascist tailor's daughter, was out of bounds, so I had no playmate at our home. My mother's shop was not in a child-friendly area, but there were two potential playmates. Neither worked out.

Mr Czornek, a skinny elderly man, had a gentlemen's hairdresser's salon in the same block as my mother's shop. His wife, younger but almost a hunchback, was always at her sewing machine, a piece-worker. Their daughter Irénke was pale and skinny, a year younger than me. They lived in one room behind the shop, like we had done at Aréna út. Their room had crosses and candles everywhere, and was full of frightening pictures: a man nailed to a cross, another with his chest open and his heart dripping with blood, a tearful woman in blue robes precariously holding a grown man in her lap. The Czorneks were not unkind but neither were they welcoming, and Irénke was not much fun.

Opposite my mother's shop was a plot of land behind a tall fence, somehow forgotten when the Ministries and the splendid seven-floor blocks were built. The fence was covered in posters, like this one.

Behind the fence squatted the small bungalow of the Hegyi family. Aranka was a bit older than me, tall, with long straight hair. She was not allowed to play with me.

I did have one friend in Budapest, but he lived on the other side of town, so we rarely met. Here is the story.

Gabi was 18 months my senior, the handsome son of Rosinger Sándor, my mother's cousin. The Rosingers were religious Protestants. (Why did I never quiz my father about this?) My father and I met Gabi and Sándor some Sunday mornings after their church service. I suspect that Sándor too was a secret socialist; he and my father enjoyed each other's company. The Rosingers' flat was small and neat, crowded full of fascinating things: mechanical toys, a model railway, sports equipment, a tandem for the parents, a bike for the boy. On the wall hung father Sándor's medals from World War I: older than my father, he had had a distinguished wartime career in the Austro-Hungarian Army. Gabi taught me to ride his bike in the Városliget. Once, when I was five, the Rosingers took me on a week's holiday by Lake Velence, the only holiday of my childhood not spent in Nanóka's home in Debrecen. We stayed in a low-ceilinged peasant house with green shutters. We all shared a room which had carved, hand-painted furniture and lots of red-and-white embroidery. For breakfast, we had home-baked bread and poured home-made yoghurt from a huge porcelain jug. We hired a boat, Sándor and Gabi rowing. Another time we hired a sailing boat, and here is the picture.

In 1941 Sándor was called up into the army. One day, in 1944, Gabi was coming home from school when a kindly neighbour pulled him into her flat, saying that his mother had been taken away by the fascists because their family were Jews. Gabi must not go home, the neighbour said, otherwise he too would be taken away and might be killed.

Sándor and his wife were never seen again. When the war was over, Gabi went to Palestine. He was 14, tall and strong. He pretended to be 16, joined the Zionist paramilitary organisation *Irgun,* and volunteered for the most dangerous missions, until he managed to get himself killed in 1946.

Life in Budapest was gloomy, but I had happy summer holidays in Debrecen. Nanóka's home was my favourite place in the world. How it was spoilt for me later!

Lucky me: I stayed with Nanóka from early June until the end of August. The grownups could only come for two weeks, in pairs, one couple taking me to Debrecen at the start of my holiday, the other travelling back with me just before September. Nobody had telephones, so urgent correspondence between those in Debrecen and Budapest was by telegram, the cost being proportional to the number of words. My uncle Pista invented signing the telegram by chaining together the names of four senders, so a signature might have been *IMAGPICISTA* (Imre, Magda, Pici, Pista). I use these name combinations nowadays as passwords.

When I was four, Nanóka moved from Kígyó utca right across Debrecen to a predominantly Jewish area which later became designated as Debrecen's *ghetto*.

Rosinger Sándor, the author and Rosinger Gabi, Agárd, Hungary, around 1937.

Kaposi family collection

Debrecen, 42 Hatvan utca, the building where Nanóka lived, between around 1935 and 1944.
Photo: József Papp, 2019

Hatvan utca was a wide, long thoroughfare leading out westwards from the town centre. Near the centre houses were large and elegant, gradually deteriorating to crowded tenement blocks by the far end. Nanóka's home at number 42 was still respectable; a low, single-floor building on a corner.

Nanóka's home consisted of two rooms, a kitchen, and a tiny entrance hall. There was no bathroom. We washed in the kitchen, and the toilet was in the courtyard in a shed, shared among all inhabitants. Next door lived my mother's cousin Margit with her husband Lipót and their daughter Vera, my summertime shadow. Unbeknown to him, Lipót played an important role in my spiritual development.

Lipót was an insignificant-looking little man who had a small textile business near the orthodox synagogue. He prayed noisily every morning, swaying backwards and forwards, blanketed in a white silk prayer shawl, with a ceremonial little black box called *tefillin* strapped to his forehead, like the young boy in the picture. I was not yet school-age when I heard the grownups say that Lipót was not to be trusted in business, because he was a liar and a cheat. I waited impatiently for a chance to ask my father: wasn't religion meant to make people good? Yes, he said. So how was it, I asked, that Uncle Lipót was religious, but a liar and a cheat? My father said he could see my dilemma. I said if someone could be religious and bad, could someone not be religious and good? Of course, said my father. So, I said, did he mind if I was not religious, as long as I tried always to be good? My father said that would be fine by him. This is how Lipót finished off, for life, any leanings I might have had towards religion.

Young Jew Praying, 1940. Drypoint print by Hermann Struck

Courtesy of Hermann Struck Museum, Haifa

During my summers at Nanóka's I had several playmates, but even here, I was an outsider. My playmates were religious Jewish girls of Debrecen, whereas I had no religion, and came from Budapest.

At the end of Nanóka's courtyard lived the orthodox Lőwy family. The youngest was little blonde Lizi, two years my junior. I was an only child, and regretted this all my life. Lizi was the object of my envy because she had 12 older brothers. Between them, the boys covered most trades: house painter, carpenter, plumber, upholsterer, electrician, locksmith, etc. They were large, friendly, darkly handsome, and wore raggedy clothes and skullcaps. They treated Lizi and me like toys, giving us rides on their backs and on their tradesman's bikes, swinging us into the air, and bringing us toys: empty paint tins, scraps of wood, metal, materials left over from their jobs.

My favourite playmates were the Feldman girls Éva and Ági (not their real names) who lived on the opposite side of Hatvan utca. Theirs was an orthodox family of rich wine merchants, men with beards and side locks, and women with covered hair. Grandfather Feldman had several sons, and governed his family like a benevolent dictator, setting and policing the rules by which they lived. He and his eldest son occupied two big flats on either side of the deep wide gateway, their windows overlooking the street. The yard was flanked by the homes of younger brothers, each opening from a long covered porch. My playmates' father was the youngest, so their flat was the smallest and most distant from the gate. Usually a heavy cart was parked in the gateway, with a pair of shire horses, burly men rolling down barrels of wine into the cellars. There were young horses grazing in the courtyard. Across the back was a working yard, with stables and workshops for mending carts and barrels. For a city child like me, the place was a fairyland. Grandfather Feldman knew that my family had no religion, hence he was not keen on the girls playing with me, but he did not forbid our friendship outright. Éva was my age, blonde, always in blue. Ági was younger, brunette, her clothes matching her sister's, but in red. Like me, they usually wore *dirndl*: an Austrian-style cotton dress with full skirt, puffed short sleeves and a

starched white embroidered apron. On my yearly arrival from Budapest, the girls were waiting for me in front of Nanóka's flat. We played together every day, but of course they were never allowed to eat in Nanóka's house. We made our own toys and devised our own games. In high summer Nanóka's maid would put out in the yard the large wooden washing tub, two-thirds filled with water. By midday the water was warm enough to paddle in. We skipped on ropes, spared from the wine cellars. We made paper dolls and paper clothes for them. Nanóka had a tiny patch of garden which we planted with pansies and petunias with seeds given us by the gardener brother of little Lizi. We wrote short plays and performed 'shows', for which the big boys of the Lőwy family constructed a makeshift stage. We collected wildflowers from under the hooves of the Feldmans' baby horses, and sold bunches of them, gypsy-fashion, as good-luck tokens from a little table in front of the gate. On rainy days we played card games, noughts-and-crosses, and word and number puzzles taught to us by my father. For my friends' sake, I observed the rules of the Jewish Sabbath: dressed smartly, wore uncomfortable patent leather shoes, made do without pencils or scissors, avoided noisy games, read books, told stories, sang songs.

Author's second cousin Klein Vera and the author, on Nanóka's doorstep, Debrecen, 1940, photo by the author's uncle Laci.

Kaposi family collection

42

Lipót and Margit's daughter Vera, my second cousin, was six months my junior. The family made her my responsibility. Nobody liked her, and she must have hated me: I was taller, stronger, more popular, and the grownups held me up to her as an example. Matters got even worse when we started school. I did well, she badly, and she was constantly reminded of this by her stupid father. There is an ugly Hungarian word *bezzeg*, divisive and untranslatable, used to precede comparisons: 'Vera, once again you failed Maths/ Hungarian/whatever; bezzeg Agnes got top marks.' Vera often spoiled our games, ruined our little constructions, told on us when we did something naughty. Here is my uncle Laci's picture of Vera and me. We are eight. The picture catches a rare moment of Vera smiling. As a young woman, Vera remained true to her childish self, ruining the life of my sweet step-cousin Olga, luring away her fiancé, the love of Olga's life. Vera survived the camps and died in early middle age.

In 1943, the summer before the concentration camp period, Nanóka was persuaded to enrol me into a 'Summer Club', organised by the unmarried sister of Weisz Pál, the local Neolog Rabbi. There were 14 of us in the Club. Since Grandfather Feldman did not approve of the Neolog branch of Judaism, his granddaughters were not allowed to join, but inevitably Vera was there. Miss Weisz was a bookish spinster, a linguist or historian. She was cheerless and had no interest in children, but – as many other Jewish graduates – she had no job, and needed the income. She conscientiously mugged up on activities, and took us to the Great Forest of Debrecen to play games. Our favourite was 'number wars', everyone wearing a large four-digit number fastened to their forehead. If anyone shouted out your number, you were 'dead', and the winner was the last man standing. Disaster struck when Miss Weisz arranged a nature exploration trip to a barren island in the middle of a nearby lake. Boatmen rowed us across in small boats in the morning, and collected us at dusk. It was a hot summer's day, and there was no shade. Miss Weisz packed lunches for us, but forgot hats and drinking water. I was lucky, I only had sunstroke and fever, but most also had sunburn. All night, the doctor, an elderly man in a brown jacket, was doing the rounds of the 14 casualties of the expedition. He was thrilled to meet me, and told me about attending my mother and her sisters in their childhood. The club was promptly disbanded, and for the rest of the summer I happily returned to Nanóka's yard and my friends the Feldman girls.

AN UNUSUAL FRIEND

Although I had no playmates in Budapest, I had friends: adults who enriched my childhood. I lost most of them, but they will play major roles in my story. They were all young, with one exception.

My elderly friend Mrs Sommer was one of my mother's customers, a widow who lived with her chambermaid and cook in one of the elegant flats on the fifth floor of the block of my mother's shop. She noticed me in the shop, bought from my mother a small bottle of cocoa and a Linzer, and sat me down at one of the small tables. I was scared at first, but she was kind, told me that she loved children, and missed her own grandchildren who lived far away. She first asked my parents and then me if I would visit her for tea: she wanted to introduce me to her friends. I was five. My parents were as surprised as I was, but found no reason to refuse, and told me that Mrs Sommer was Jewish, and her son was dead. We were six at the tea party, not counting the two servant girls in black frocks, white aprons and frilly headdresses. I knew one of them, as she used to come to the shop. Mrs Sommer's friends were just as old and elegant as she was, wearing plenty of jewellery, with their hair stiffly coiffed. The table was set with ornate china, crystal glasses and heavy silver cutlery. That was the first time I came across a multicoloured, sculpted ice-cream confection called *parfait*, so beautiful that I was almost sorry when Mrs Sommer cut it up and served it to us. The ladies talked to me as my father did, not in children's language but treating me like one of them. They encouraged me to ask questions and listened to anything I said. Thereafter, once a month on a Wednesday afternoon, I went to tea with Mrs Sommer. She said we were friends.

I enjoyed Mrs Sommer's tea parties, but they worried me. More and more posters, graffiti and pictures appeared in newspapers, on walls, on leaflets. Here is a poster which I found particularly disturbing.

Antisemitic poster, 1938. Caption: "Brother! Do you want to change this?
Fight with us in the Arrow Cross camp!"
National Széchényi Library, Poster Collection

I thought the poor skinny people were like the family of Mr Czornek the barber, and the fat lady on the right with lots of jewellery was like Mrs Sommer and her friends. To me, the daughter of socialists, the message sounded right: it was unfair that some people should be rich and fat, while others were poor and starving. I knew about poverty and unemployment, and I knew my father to be fair and just, so I asked if he was joining the Arrow Cross to fight injustice. He said the subject was complicated, and we should discuss it at length on our Sunday mornings. He was patient, and I had plenty of time, having no playmates in Budapest.

When the time for our talks came, my father started by saying that the poster was dishonest: contrasting rich and poor was not its real message. He would never join a party such as the Arrow Cross because it stood for envy and hatred of people who were *different* from most others.

He showed on the map that our country was surrounded by several others. Most people in our country spoke Hungarian as we did, he said, but elsewhere people spoke *different* languages. He found me some foreign radio stations. He said we did not understand the speech of these *other* people, but they had songs, dances and art of their own just like we did and deserved our respect. Now came new words. He said some people lived in our country who spoke languages other than Hungarian, and some even looked and wore clothes different from ours. These were the *minority,* which meant that they were the *few* among the *majority,* the *many*. The many should be fair, and should respect the few, he said.

The next topic was harder. He said some people were *religious.* They believed in God, a wise and powerful being one cannot see, hear or touch. The world had many different religions, he said. The majority in our country were *Christians*, like the family of Mr Czornek the barber, who believed in God, and also believed that God had a son called Jesus who was like God himself. But there were several religious minorities in our country, he said, such as the *Jews*, like Uncle Lipót and his family, who believed in God, but not in Jesus. The religious majority should be fair and respect religious minorities.

Now we reached the hardest topic of all. He said people in our family were Jews, like Uncle Lipót, although we were not religious. I had trouble with this, and my father said so had he, but he explained about ancient religions and calendars, told me of the Ten Commandments which made sense, and showed me Hebrew script. He said many people disliked Jews, and some were cruel to them, some even wanted to kill them. The poster showing an ugly mean-looking big-nosed man wanted people to think that all Jews were like this, and invited Christians to hate and kill Jews. I said I did not understand: the man on the picture did not look like you my father, nor like my uncles Feri, Pista, or Laci. None of you have beards or wear skullcaps, I said, none of you are ugly with big noses, and none of you are mean. So why should Christian people hate you and other Jews? After a long pause he said that he could not answer me because he did not understand this either.

A WARTIME FAMILY

At last, I come around to talking about the young adults in my life, members of our family. Most were professional married people, but childless, because that was not a good time for bringing children into the world. These grownups were my teachers and playmates, and for some, I was the child they never had. On that family tree, names crossed out show those lost in the Holocaust. Six million Jews were killed in the Holocaust. More than half a million of these were Hungarian Jews. Only big Poland and vast Soviet Union lost more Jews than tiny Hungary. These numbers are so shocking as to be meaningless. What is meaningful is the fate of individuals. I knew and loved every person in that family tree, but by the time I was nine, some of them were already dead, and many more died before I reached the age of 12. The loss of those 19 members of the family is not just a statistic: it represents my lost childhood.

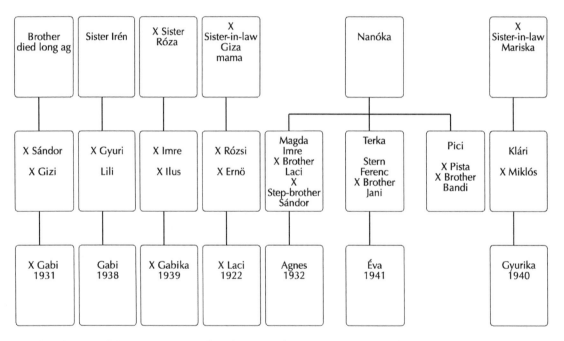

The family tree of the author's grandmother Nanóka in 1941. Victims of the Holocaust marked with 'X'

THE WOMEN

TERKA

My aunt Terka was beautiful, with light brown hair, creamy skin and large brown eyes. She loved books and had a delicious sense of humour and an original turn of phrase.

Unlike her sisters, Terka was not very interested in school, music or languages, and had no talent for business, but she was witty, had an excellent memory, and knew a lot of poetry. She was artistic – at art college she specialised in embroidery. I will always regret that her exquisite handiwork was lost in the war. Studying books of art, she knew great collections of masterpieces. When in England for the first time in 1960, she eagerly visited the National Gallery, and was upset when some of her favourites could not be found. I suggested that those pictures might be in some other gallery, but she was adamant. We located a curator who admitted that those pictures were indeed in the National, but not on display: they had several times as many pictures as wall space available. Seeing how upset this knowledgeable foreign visitor was, the curator took us to the basement, and showed the pictures to a happy, vindicated Terka.

Terka played a unique role in my childhood. She cared for me when I was born, and since in my early years my mother was the main breadwinner of the extended family, Terka continued to be the mother figure. She loved me and I was devoted to her, and yet we had daily conflicts, often resulting in me being punished and spanked. I stood in corners, sat on naughty chairs, wrote out lines ten, fifty, hundred times, forfeited treats – nothing worked. I was not a malicious child; the trouble may have been that in those days a child's asking questions amounted to impertinence, whereas my father did not bring me up to do unquestioningly as I was told. At her wits' end, Terka sometimes appealed to my mother. That fetched me more punishment and more heavy spanking. Only two things disrupted our feuds: my illnesses, and my summer holidays. I enjoyed every minute of summer with Nanóka, but I missed my father and Terka more than other members of the family. When Terka and I were reunited at the end of summer, peace reigned for a few days, but then the rows restarted, punishments came, all was as before. Year after year, and sometimes twice in a winter, I had tonsillitis. Antibiotics had not yet become available, and the illness could be quite severe. Fever was controlled by *priznic,* a small bedsheet dipped into cold water and wrapped around the torso.

When I got better, my appetite returned only slowly. Terka nursed me with infinite kindness. Only she could put on the priznic without causing distress; she knew when to bring a drink and when to tempt me with food, when to give me a cuddle and when to tuck me up, when to read me a story and when to leave me to rest. When I was 10, my tonsils had to be removed. I was almost sorry to miss being nursed by Terka.

In the camps, Terka could barely tolerate the harsh conditions. I regarded myself as one of her protectors. After we left Hungary for England, I visited her often, and spent many hours at her home chatting, or being silently companionable, holding hands. She died a few years ago. I shall always miss her.

PICI

The youngest Csengeri girl, Pici, was irresistible: charming, pretty, a dulcet-voiced singer and graceful dancer. She was cherished by her sisters, popular with friends, admired by young men, loved by all. By the time her third daughter was entering senior school, Nanóka realised the advantages of grammar school education, and sent her youngest to Debrecen's famous Dóczi Protestant girls' grammar school. Conscientious to a fault, Pici did particularly well in languages. Even in her 90s, she knew her Latin, had excellent German, good French, and a fair command of English.

Pici was musical, not as instinctively talented as Magda, but more studious. She passed all examinations of the Piano Faculty of Budapest's Liszt Ferenc Academy, but Hungary's Jewish laws prevented her from graduating. She never had the chance to be a professional musician, but remained a competent pianist to the end of her days.[16]

The author's aunt Csengeri Klára
(Pici,) aged 20, in Debrecen.
Kaposi family collection

Like everyone else, I was captivated by Pici's artless charm and natural grace. It was she who started me on the piano soon after she got married. Daily, I took the No. 10 tram to their home on my own, looking forward to lessons, practicing diligently.

The loss of her brilliant young husband in *Military Labour Service*[17] changed Pici completely. My children could not recognise, in the anxious, tense woman she became, the sweet, carefree, joyous Pici of my childhood. Years after losing her husband, she found a new partner, a charismatic doctor twice her age who had lost his first family in Auschwitz. Their only son is my cousin, the great pianist Sir András Schiff.

In the camps Pici was fearless and inventive, the pillar of the family. She remained one of the central figures of my life until she died in 2010.

---

16   See *HISTORIAN'S VOICE: Hungary's Jewish Laws and their Consequences*
17   See *HISTORIAN'S VOICE: Military Labour Service in Hungary*

KLÁRI

My cousin Klári was my mother's age, my closest relative: my first cousin (our fathers were brothers), and also my mother's first cousin (her mother was the sister of my mother's father). As a child, she had been outrageously naughty, so the strict father of the Csengeri girls did not allow his daughters to play with her. In adult life my father – her uncle – disapproved of her, Terka secretly envied her, and everyone thought her fun. She was flirtatious, vivacious, very attractive. She was a wonderful dancer and could entertain a roomful of people singing operettas and popular songs, accompanying herself on the piano. She had no idea about children and treated me as an adult. Later in life she showed many other sides of her character: a loyal member of the camp-time family, a thoroughly inadequate mother, a competent businesswoman, and, in old age, a *rachmones*: a Yiddish word, meaning a pitiful creature, a lost soul.

RÓZSI

When shops were closed for Christmas or other festivals, we spent our time with Rózsi and Giza mama.

Rózsi had bad posture, thin hair and blotchy skin. Toothless Giza mama's chin almost touched her nose. Never mind all that: they were both lovely.

Rózsi's teenage son was rarely at home, and her husband Ernő was almost never there. He was a commercial traveller, a shady character. As a child I was not told the details, but I suspect that imprisonment rather than business trips accounted for his absences. Rózsi was the breadwinner of their family, with support from Giza mama.

Giza mama's sewing machine never stopped: she slaved away as a pieceworker, making men's shirts, earning a pittance.

Their home was near ours. Their crumbling building has long since given way to an underground station. Their front door opened from the corridor directly into the kitchen, which housed the water tap, the kitchen range, and Giza mama's sewing machine. There was no bathroom; they washed in the kitchen, in an enamel basin. The toilet opened from the kitchen, as did a small room with no window, borrowing a little light through an internal glass panel. A second little room opened from the first and had a small window to a foul smelling *lichthof*. They shared this tiny flat with my parents when they first arrived in Budapest.

It was obvious even to me how poor they were. Instead of parquet floor and carpets, like we had, they had wooden floorboards and rags which always crumpled underfoot. No light fittings, just

Frank Ernőné Rózsi, her husband, and her mother Giza Mama. Budapest, around 1940.

Kaposi family collection

49

bare bulbs hanging from the ceiling. Bentwood chairs with broken raffia seats. Chipped china, a motley assembly of well-worn cutlery. None of this mattered. At their house you were always welcome, comfortable and happy. These were not jolly times, and my parents were not playful people, but they smiled more at Rózsi's than anywhere else. Rózsi could always quote a poem to illustrate an idea, and Giza mama had a song for every occasion. We played word games and poker, with beans for stakes. We boiled eyes of corn – usually fodder for geese – and ate them with salt, pepper and melted butter, a delicacy. One evening my father challenged us to a new game: he said a word and we had to find a poem, song or opera aria with the word in it. Even my mother joined in. I used to sing to my children the folksongs Giza mama taught me, and sometimes I still sing them to myself.

It was Rózsi who suggested to my mother that they should get a season ticket to the opera. Bizarre idea: neither could afford it, but both were devoted to music. Pici's fiancé Pista arranged the first purchase. Queues in front of the Opera House started the day before, and Pista slept on the pavement to secure two cheap but excellent first-row seats in the topmost tier. My mother and Rózsi had first refusal for these seats each year thereafter. Even I could go sometimes: the ushers got used to me and let me sit on the stairs.

The only trace left of Rózsi's family is a linen kitchen towel with her initials embroidered in red by Giza mama's cross-stitch. It had been part of Rózsi's trousseau. Who knows how it came to be in my possession? It had never been used, and I have just donated it to the Beth Shalom Holocaust Museum.

In 1945, Rózsi and Giza mama were taken from their home to be shot into the Danube. Their men died in Military Labour Service. They left behind nothing but that tea towel and my fond memories.

THE MEN

Most men of the family were about my mother's age. Some were my proper uncles, others strictly speaking not, but they deserve the status of honorary uncles. They all suffered under Hungary's Jewish laws, and with the single exception of Terka's husband Feri, they were all killed in Military Labour Service. I will never stop grieving for them. Am I repeating myself? I don't mind.

LACI
My father's half-brother Laci was a stylish, elegant man with the dark good looks of his mother Szeréna. He was an accomplished amateur photographer, the only member of my family who owned a camera, and there was a rumour that he sometimes visited nightclubs (!). He had

Klein László (Uncle Laci),
Debrecen, around 1940.
Kaposi family collection

50

a successful small business in Debrecen, designing and making uppers of hand-crafted shoes. He always carried a small sketchbook for jotting down ideas for new shoe designs, and never gave up the hopeless task of trying to teach me to draw. I loved to visit his workshop, where half-a-dozen tanners dyed and tooled skins, women turned Laci's designs into paper patterns, machinists made fancy motifs on leather, and cutters laid out the patterns, showing me which part of the skin had to be used for what part of the shoe.

Laci venerated my father, and visited us in Budapest at least twice a year, bringing a clutch of shoes for me, measuring my feet for the next delivery. He was devoted to the Csengeri girls; he admired Terka, unsuccessfully courted Pici, and was secretly in love with my mother. He was well liked by the ladies and had many girlfriends, but never married.

He never returned from Ukraine.

FERI

My uncle Feri was Terka's husband. His father had been an engine driver who died young, leaving a widow and three boys. Feri was the most handsome and most talented, well-known in the Jewish community: as a boy, he was the star singer of Debrecen's synagogue choir.

The Jewish Boys' Grammar School of Debrecen opened in 1925 with great expectations, proud achievement of the Jewish community. The first Headmaster was the charismatic Dr Kardos Albert, a famous scholar. Standards were extraordinarily high: few if any Jews could hold university posts, so eminent academics became schoolteachers. Feri was the first member of his family to continue into higher education and became a lawyer. I was briefly a pupil at that excellent school, as I will soon relate. The school fell victim to the Nazis and closed in 1944. A few years later the Communists also closed my father's wonderful Piarist school.

During my childhood, Feri was not involved in politics. He made up for it after the war. His carved bookcase contained all Stalin's writings. It is a testimony to Feri's memory that he could quote from these freely, but I doubt if he believed in their message.

Stern Ferenc (Uncle Feri) and his wife Aunt Terka, Budapest, around 1940

Kaposi family collection

JANI

I had no contact with Feri's elder brother, but his younger brother Jani was one of my honorary uncles. He was taller than Feri, less handsome, but more elegant. A sweet-natured man, he was a shop assistant in an upper-class men's outfitters' in Debrecen's main street. His job suited him well; he would have been a good model for the expensive clothing he sold but could not afford. He told me of the yearly changes and nuances of men's fashion and let me play with the fiendish mechanism which carried customers' cash in a copper cylinder from the shop floor to the glass cubicle of the cashier.

He was taken to Ukraine, never to return. His beautiful young widow will feature in my story: she played a memorable role in our camp life.

PISTA

Apart from my father, the most important man in my childhood was Pici's first husband Pista. My grandchildren would have called him 'cool'. He was only describable in superlatives: charismatic, larger-than-life, multi-talented. He was the only sporty member of the family: a mountaineer, swimmer, and cyclist. He understood good music and was a philosopher and a wit who coined epigrams and word puzzles in three languages. He was a calligrapher, a gifted draughtsman and painter. I have only one very poor photograph of him, and a faint crumpled drawing he made of me.

The only picture of Deutsch István (uncle Pista), Pici's husband

Kaposi family collection

Pista studied Civil Engineering in Paris and sent to the schoolgirl Pici beautifully scripted letters with his drawings of the city's buildings and monuments. He was passionately political, a secret member of the Communist Party. Because he was a Jew, he could not work in his profession openly, but did urgent clandestine jobs for an important design office, working day and night for a pittance to meet impossible deadlines. He designed part of the famous building complex of Budapest's Madách tér. Another of his projects would appeal to those with a sense of irony: this young left-wing Jew designed the structure of the monument for the right-wing antisemitic Prime Minister Gömbös Gyula. The monument was blown up by left-wing Jewish partisans in 1944.

We had no piano. When I arrived at their home for piano practice, Pista was often at work on his large multi-coloured drawings.

52

I thought the drawings were beautiful. He explained that each colour designated a type of utility in a building: a different colour for electricity, water, heating and sewage. He told me, a child of seven or eight, that the task of engineers was to link beauty and utility. Sometimes he gave me little sums to do and entered the results into his drawings in coloured ink, and showed my contributions to Pici and his parents, in whose home they all lived.

Typically, it was Pista who discovered that snowfalls were good news for unemployed Jews: he queued up at the municipal depot before sunrise, collected a shovel and a wheelbarrow, and cleaned roads before traffic started. Later, when my father and Feri lost their jobs, they joined Pista in those queues, Jewish professionals working as occasional street cleaners.

My great pal Pista died in the horror of Doroshich.[18]

BANDI

One of my precious honorary uncles was Pista's brother Bandi, a doctor. They were identical twins, and in childhood few could tell them apart. In adult life their resemblance was still striking, but amusing. Where Pista was muscular with a full head of hair, Bandi was podgy and balding, with gentler features and manner.

Bandi's explanations of the pictures of his medical books reassured me when I had any childhood ailment. He told me of the workings of the body, including the digestive system.

The next little story gives an example of his role in my childhood. The summer before starting school, I was taken to Debrecen's University Hospital with suspected appendicitis. After a few days of observation and 24 hours of 'nil by mouth', they took me to a big room with a lot of lights and many people. A doctor told me that they would examine the workings of my alimentary canal: *anyagcsere vizsgálat*. Remembering what Bandi taught me, I said how come? – I had eaten nothing for a day, so my alimentary canal was empty, it was not working at all. The doctors laughed, and said I was right, they were not testing my alimentary canal, but would put me to sleep to cut away the bit of useless gut that was causing the pain in my tummy. I wondered why they lied to me in the first place.

Bandi too was lost in Ukraine.

MIKLÓS

Cousin Klári's husband Miklós was my favourite honorary uncle. Unlike the others, he was far from handsome: skinny, balding, with glasses, narrow shoulders and prominent ears, but he was witty, brilliant, an already prominent young banker. While he was still allowed to work, he took me to his bank, and showed me the enormous hardbound ledgers in which clerks at high tables were writing great columns of numbers with black and red

---

18   See *HISTORIAN'S VOICE: Doroshich*

ink. He told me how accountants calculated the figures in two ways, and although the sums were huge, the results had to be correct to the nearest *fillér* (penny). I had a few fillérs in my pocket and offered him the money to make up any discrepancy. He patiently explained that any tiny difference had to be tracked down, because it could hide a big error.

It was Miklós who tried to teach me to swim. He splashed about in the children's pool, pretending to need rescuing. I teased him: 'Can't swim!' (*Nem tud úszni!*), and the little phrase remained my name for him for the rest of his short life.

He was lost, like the others, but his little son Gyurika will appear, an important member of our camp-time family; a survivor, but a victim of the Nazis.

SÁNDOR

My father's stepbrother was older than the others. He was an enigma. As a boy, he had been a promising sculptor and painter, with an analytic mind and a photographic memory. By the time I knew him, it was already clear that he was a failure. My father and I paid monthly visits to him, his crippled wife Elza,

Cousin Klári and her husband Frankel Miklós ('Can'tSwim'). Debrecen, 1938
Kaposi family collection

his beautiful daughter Olga, and his outrageously talented mathematician son Gyuri. These visits were distressing, but fascinating. He and my father engaged in erudite discussions on politics, science and the arts, Sándor matching the logic and learning of my father. I asked my father why Sándor and his family were not just poor like we were, but lived in squalor, sleeping on filthy rags in an unheated shed behind their pitiful greengrocer's shop. Reluctantly, my father explained that Sándor was a notorious drunk and gambler who had been disloyal to his wife, and Elza had given up fighting for herself and their children. My father said he would always love Sándor, but I should consider him a cautionary example.

Sándor too was lost in Ukraine.

As I am writing, more and more young men of my childhood emerge from my memory: distant members of the family, my parents' friends and schoolmates, all killed. Their tragic loss is the hardest part of my story to relate. I have no hate. I would not seek revenge. What I feel is pain, and a deep sense of pity for these young people who had such promise.

HISTORIAN'S VOICE

Hungary's Jewish Laws and their Consequences

There were altogether 22 anti-Jewish laws in Hungary, of which the major ones are listed here, the earliest dating from 1920.[19]

Act	Description	Function
Act XXV of 1920	Numerus Clausus (Closed Number)	Racial quota, restricts the number of Jews admitted to Higher Education
Act XV of 1938	First Jewish Law	Restricts to 20% the proportion of Jews in certain professions and white-collar positions in industrial and commercial companies
Act IV of 1939	Second Jewish Law	Restricts to 6% Jewish participation in professions, and measures restricting economic activities and civil rights of Jews
Act XV of 1941	Third Jewish Law, Race Protection Law	Bans marriage between Jews and Christians, and forbids sexual relations between Jewish men and non-Jewish women
Act XXV of 1942	Fourth Jewish Law	Nationalisation of Jewish landholdings

It is estimated that over 90,000 people lost their jobs because of the first two 'Jewish laws' in Hungary. Counting family members, about 220,000 people were affected. Jewish groups hit hardest included the lower middle class (craftsmen, petty tradesmen, shopkeepers, retailers, state employees, white-collar employees and young Jews living in the countryside), and young professionals entering the job market. There were major efforts to circumvent the restrictions. Had the laws been enforced strictly, and had they been applied immediately, the economy would have been crippled. For this reason, the authorities often turned a blind eye to attempts to bypass the laws, especially in branches of key importance, such as the military industry. There were also efforts in the opposite direction: out of antisemitic zeal, public administrators and the military would strive even to exceed regulations, and in some places this led to severe economic problems and skill shortages.[20]

To circumvent Jewish laws, an illegal 'Strohmann' system was created. A Strohmann would be a non-Jew, typically a friend or a friendly stranger who, usually in exchange for a sizeable sum, would represent the Jewish owner of a shop, factory or other enterprise, or would have the business

---

19   For details about the anti-Jewish laws in Hungary, see Zoltán Vági, László Csősz, and Gábor Kádár, *The Holocaust in Hungary. Evolution of a Genocide.* Lanham, MD–Washington, D.C., AltaMira Press–USHMM, 2013. Chapter 1.

20   Viktor Karády, Zsidótörvények és életfeltételek a szociális jelzők tükrében (1938-1943). In *Zsidóság, asszimiláció, polgárosodás.* Budapest: Cserépfalvi, 1997. 279-281.

signed over to his/her name. As a result, these years brought about effortless economic advances for many non-Jews. At the same time, quite a few Christians were hurt by the Jewish laws, for example employees and clients of shut-down Jewish enterprises. [21]

Military Labour Service in Hungary, 1939-45

Various forms of voluntary and compulsory labour service existed all around the world in the 20th century. Besides easing socio-economic crises, labour service could be used for the physical and ideological training of youth, and as a form of social engineering. However, in the context of World War II and the Holocaust, the term 'labour service' came primarily to mean an enforced and discriminatory institution. Throughout this book, 'munkaszolgálat', means the military (auxiliary) labour service imposed on Hungary's Jews and other minorities.

At the outbreak of World War II, with the exception of Finland, Axis countries excluded Jews from their armies. Instead, they exploited the workforce of Jewish men, employing them in war-related tasks, such as various forms of slave labour. Some Axis allies, including Romania and Bulgaria, also introduced unarmed military service for Jews, as an 'alternative' to regular military service. In practice, it meant that the conscripts were subjected to disciplinary training, and performed forced labour under military command. The system was also extended to various groups which these regimes deemed 'unreliable', including the political opposition, or members of ethnic and religious minorities. Jews were the integral part of the image of the enemy everywhere in the Axis bloc, so the majority of labour servicemen were Jews.

Hungary was the only country that systematically sent labour service units to the front line, as part of the regular army. Tens of thousands of labour servicemen were serving on the Eastern Front from the spring of 1942, dying in battles and in Soviet captivity. Many also fell victim to the cruelty of Hungarian labour service guards and officers. Over 10% of the estimated half a million victims of the Hungarian Holocaust died as labour servicemen. Paradoxically, after the German invasion of Hungary, labour service offered an avenue for rescue. Despite the collaboration of the Hungarian state apparatus in the mass deportation of Jews from the provinces in the spring and summer of 1944, the Hungarian Ministry of Defence protected the labour servicemen from deportation to Auschwitz, mostly for pragmatic reasons: they did not want to hand over valuable manpower to the Nazis. Despite their extremely high casualty rates, the majority of Jewish men drafted for military labour service survived the war. More than two-thirds of the labour servicemen serving in the Eastern front in the deadliest period from summer 1942 to spring 1943 perished, whereas the bulk of those who spared this maelstrom survived.[22]

---

21   Strohmann in German, straw man or layman in English, stróman in Hungarian.

22   For further details, see: Randolph L. Braham, *The Hungarian Labor Service System, 1939-1945*. Boulder, CO: East European Quarterly, 1977.

Doroshich

During World War II, thousands of Hungarian Jewish labour servicemen had typhoid fever, a disease carried by lice, due to the generally abysmal hygienic conditions. In the early spring of 1943, a makeshift field hospital was set up for some of the sick in the local kolkhoz in Doroshich, a Ukranian village named Kupyshche today, situated near Korosten, Zhytomyr District. Patients were crammed together in barns and stables in terrible sanitary conditions. Food was scarce, the hospital lacked adequate professional staff and medicines, and Hungarian guards often maltreated, blackmailed and robbed the inmates. Survivor Zoltán Zelk described the inferno like this: "Patients waiting for 'reception' to the hospital were lying in ankle-deep mud for days. Eight to ten patients died each day before they could even get into the tobacco dryer, where half-naked patients lay on each other's dirt among dead bodies. Some were lying completely naked on stinking, filthy straw."[23]

In the early morning of 30th April 1943, one of the barns containing some 700 labour servicemen caught fire. Most patients perished in the flames. Those who attempted to flee were machine-gunned down outside the building by the Hungarian guards, who later reported that they shot the burning victims in order to prevent the extension of the fire to other buildings of the kolkhoz. Survivors and eyewitnesses suspected that the guards deliberately set the building on fire. Attempting to put the blame on the victims for the tragedy, official investigation by Hungarian authorities concluded that the fire was caused by a cigarette. There is no evidence to prove the cause of the tragedy, but it is clear that inhumane conditions and brutal treatment were decisive factors, and the guards were at least partly responsible for the deaths. Even so, only one member of the unit which staffed the field hospital was put on trial and executed after the War.

According to the estimate of survivor historian Béla Katona, 478 people burnt to death in the barn, and another 56 were shot by the soldiers, bringing the total number of victims to 534.[24]

---

23   Zoltán Zelk, Dorosicsi tűz. In *Szabadság,* 11 February, 1945.
24   Béla Katona, *Várad a viharban.* Nagyvárad: Teala, 1946. 75.

3   INTERMEZZO

20ᵗʰ CENTURY HUNGARY AND ITS JEWS

When I was a child, my father told me that the roots of the sad events of our lives reached back to the early 20th Century history of our country. Remembering his words, when drafting this book I consulted many sources, of which I list but a few.[25]

Here is my own summary, with support from the expert.[26]

HUNGARY'S WORLD WAR I

In 1914, at the outbreak of World War I, the dualist monarchy of Austria-Hungary was one of the great powers of Europe. As part of the Austro-Hungarian Empire, Hungary had everything: a fertile agricultural plain surrounded by the crescent of the snowy peaks of the High Tatras, vast ancient forests and mineral-rich mountains of picturesque Transylvania, and as crowning glory, a port on the Adriatic.

The author's father-in-law Kaposi Ernő, Újpest, 1942
Kaposi family collection

25   For example: Randolph L Braham, *The Politics of Genocide. The Holocaust in Hungary*. Vol. I-II. 3ʳᵈ rev. ed. New York: Columbia University Press, 2016; Szita Szabolcs: *Utak a pokolból*. Sopron: Metalon, 1991; Martin Gilbert: *The Holocaust*. Fontana Press, 1987; Vági–Csősz–Kádár, *Evolution of a Genocide*; Braham: *The Hungarian Labour Service System*; Tamás Stark, *Hungarian Jews During the Holocaust and After the Second World War, 1939–1949*. New York: Columbia University Press, 2000; Nagybaczoni Nagy Vilmos: *Végzetes esztendők*. 2d rev. ed. Budapest: Gondolat, 1986.
26   *HISTORIAN'S VOICE: The History of Hungary in a nutshell*

World War I ended in 1918, with complete collapse of the Austro-Hungarian Empire. More than half a million Hungarian soldiers died in that war, many of them Jewish patriots. My husband's father, a handsome young officer at the time, was among the survivors. He was severely wounded, heavily decorated, and was officially declared a national hero. In 1941, when this picture was taken, he was still wearing proudly his uniform of the Imperial and Royal Army of Austria-Hungary. I have just donated his medals to London's Wiener Library.

The Treaty of Versailles imposed penalties on the vanquished, such as payment of restitution, curtailment of military capability, and reduction of territories. Conditions for Hungary were set out in the Trianon Treaty. To recognise the independence of ethnic groups, Greater Romania was established, and two new nation states were created: Czechoslovakia and Yugoslavia, the country of Southern Slavs. Hungary lost almost three-quarters of its former territory, close to two-thirds of its population, and much of its economic base.

To this day, nationalist Hungarians refer to the Trianon Treaty as the 'dismemberment of Hungary', the 'rape' of their beautiful country, a humiliating injustice that must be corrected to restore national pride. Maps contrasting 'whole' and 'broken' Hungary were used in nationalist propaganda when I was a child and are still used as such today. Was the Trianon Treaty the outrageous injustice proclaimed by Hungary's nationalist right?

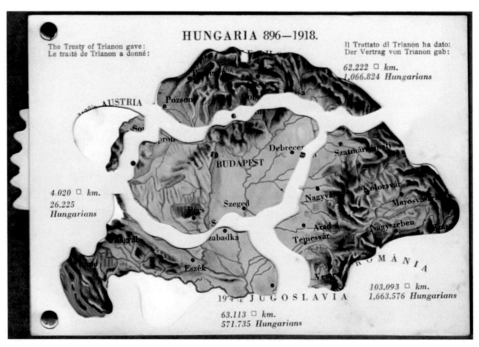

Hungarian revisionist poster, 1920s.
Courtesy of Daniel Crouch Rare Books (crouchrarebooks.com)

The Treaty was based on a census, giving a chance for self-determination to Hungary's minorities. Although it left over three million Hungarian speakers outside post-Trianon borders, the demographic map shows that, in all lost regions, Hungarians were in the minority.

Trianon meted out harsh punishments to the losers of the war, but its border adjustments might have been justifiable. Even as a child, I was aware of Hungary's minorities being belittled and despised. This attitude was reflected by the classical device of *epitheton ornans*. One rarely heard Romanians and Slovaks mentioned without a pejorative adjective. *Bocskoros oláh* was the typical crude Romanian who had neither shoes nor boots, but wore a *bocskor*, a piece of cloth strapped to the foot. The typical Slovak could be a *drótos tót*, a down-and-out tinker. These resonated with *büdös zsidó*, a Jew with the inevitable adjective 'stinking'. The Hungarian patriot of the day saw himself as above all others. They proclaim: *lovas nemzet vagyunk*, we are a proud equestrian nation.

Decades later such tribal loyalty and disdain towards outsiders could be whipped up into a frenzy of fascist brutality. Trianon might have matched borders to regional demography, but history is more complicated than the statistics imply. The region had always been turbulent, the population had always been mixed. People intermarried; many of those in the border areas were bilingual, speaking Hungarian and Slovak in the north, Hungarian and Romanian in the east, Hungarian and Serbian in the south. Had

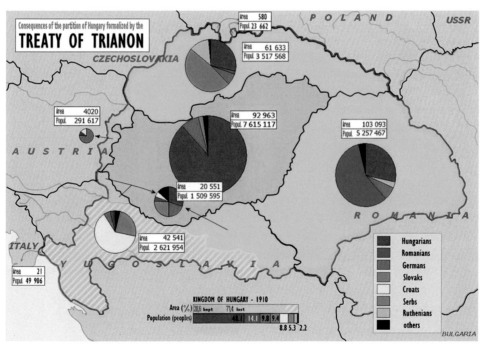

Demographic map of post-Trianon Hungary and the territories lost to the successor states in 1920.
Courtesy of Wikimedia Commons. https://commons.wikimedia.org/wiki/File:Magyarorszag_1920.png

the Hungarians treated their minorities with more respect, perhaps more mixed families would have declared themselves Hungarian, so the result of the census, and the outcome of Trianon, might have been different.

As for the Jews, they were, and still are, blamed for the country's ills, its loss of status and territory. This is why World War I and Trianon are such foundations of my story.

HUNGARY BETWEEN THE WARS

After World War I, a turbulent period followed. Uneasy stability was restored in March 1920, when Horthy – to give him his full name and rank, Admiral Vitéz Nagybányai Horthy Miklós – rode into the country on his famous white charger, to be ceremonially established as Regent. Hungary became a landlocked kingless monarchy, ruled by an Admiral. Horthy remained as Head of State until October 1944.

In 1932, the appointment of Gömbös Gyula as Prime Minister marked the radical right's ascendancy in Hungarian politics. With the support of Hitler, Hungary repudiated the Trianon Treaty, commenced a build-up of its army, and joined the Axis powers of Germany, Italy and Japan. As a result of a sequence of military campaigns, by 1941 post-Trianon Hungary's territory was almost doubled.

HUNGARY'S WORLD WAR II

Horthy's relationship with Hitler, and Hungary's role before and during World War II, remain the subject of intense debate. For example, in 2013, a statue of Horthy was unveiled at a Calvinist church in central Budapest. My cousin, the pianist Sir András Schiff, commented on this: 'A new statue of Admiral Horthy, Hungary's war-time ruler and Hitler's ally, symbolises a refusal to face up to the country's darkest history'. A more recent example is Prime Minister Orbán Victor referring to Horthy as 'an exceptional statesman'.[27]

Horthy's siding with Germany was popular in the country. Hitler fed Hungarians' national ambition to reclaim some of the lands lost in Trianon, and many Hungarians readily, even eagerly, embraced the Nazi ideology of antisemitism. Thus, Hungary entered World War II on Germany's side. Propaganda of my childhood boasted of the heart-warming and rewarding friendship between Hitler and our glorious leader Horthy. The language and the phrases were repeated a few decades later, proclaiming eternal friendship between Stalin and Hungary's glorious leader Rákosi. Here are examples of the irredentist slogans which my father had to explain to his child.[28]

---

27   His contentious legacy: A wartime leader still divides Hungarians. In *The Economist*, 8 November 2013. https://www.economist.com/europe/2013/11/08/his-contentious-legacy

28   Irredentism: nationalist movement with the aim to re-occupy territory considered 'unfairly' lost.

CSONKA MAGYARORSZÁG NEM ORSZÁG	Broken Hungary Is No Country,
EGÉSZ MAGYARORSZÁG MENNYORSZÁG	Whole Hungary Is Heaven

A more specific message was also played on the radio as a jingle:

MINDENT VISSZA!	Restore to Us Everything!
POZSONYT VISSZA!	Restore to Us Bratislava!
KASSÁT VISSZA!	Restore to Us Košice!

This verse demands the restoration to Hungary of Košice and Bratislava, the largest cities in Slovakia today.

Horthy with Hitler, reviewing the military parade in honour of Horthy's visit, Berlin, 1938.
Hungarian National Museum Historical Photo Department

This next text is the text of a song which was pumped out on the radio at all hours. How wonderful to be musical: I still remember the tune, and here is the start of the lyric:

SZABADKA, ZOMBOR, UJVIDÉK	Subotica, Sombor, Novi Sad
HONVÉDSEREG VIRÁGRA LÉP	Hungarian Troops March on Flowers
VISSZATÉRT SZÉP DÉLVIDÉKÜNK!	Our beautiful southern provinces have returned!
VISSZAADTA HORTHY NÉKÜNK!	Horthy has given them back to us!
VIGYÁZOTT MIREÁNK!	He took good care of us!

I omit the next verse, which sings of the flame of pride burning in the bosom of all Hungarians, now that Horthy restored (some of) our 'sacred' borders.

The map shows, with dates, the new borders achieved for Hungary by Horthy.

These territorial gains were ultimately obtained at the cost of entering the war. In 1941 the Hungarian army became part of Operation Barbarossa, the German invasion of the Soviet Union.

At first joining the war brought advantages for Hungary. The 1942 European map shows the Axis powers' spectacular success at that time.

However, soon the move proved disastrous. The German army was buckling under the overwhelming size of Soviet forces and the cruel severity of the Russian winter. Hungarian military was inferior in all respects, utterly unequal to the task. The largest and best equipped Hungarian army was virtually wiped out in the Battle of Stalingrad in 1943. Thereafter, the Hungarian army ceased to exist as an effective fighting force. By early 1944, the Soviet army was on the rampage. It was clear to everyone, except to Hitler himself, that the war of the Axis was lost.

19th March 1944 is a memorable date for all Hungarians: the date of Hitler launching *Operation Margarethe*, the occupation of Hungary.

Hitler had military, ideological and political reasons when taking the step of overrunning a country which fought the war on his side.

The Eastern Front was withdrawing rapidly towards Hungary's borders. To take full control of the defence of the East European flank, the German army *had* to occupy Hungary.

Hitler was obsessively convinced that Jews were evil and saw himself as the saviour of mankind against the Jewish menace. He was frustrated with Hungary, a country where Jews were deprived of their civil rights and lost many of their young men, but even in

the spring of 1944, when most of Europe's Jews were already dead, some 750,000 Jews were still alive. Operation Margarethe was to implement the 'Final Solution' of Hungary's 'Jewish problem'.

Hitler's third and most important motive for direct intervention was that Hungary was no longer a trustworthy ally. Horthy appeared willing to reach an agreement with the Allies, Hungary was about to commit 'treachery'; the country had to be occupied.

Wehrmacht troops invading Hungary on the morning of March 19th 1944 faced no resistance, and finished the occupation of the country within a day.

In the summer of 1944, Hungary turned into a battlefield, and war raged until April, 1945, when the Soviet occupation of Hungary was completed.

German army marching in Szeged, Hungary, March 1944
Hungarian National Museum Historical Photo Department

HUNGARY'S JEWS

Uniquely in Europe, in the spring of 1944, most of Hungary's Jews were still alive. They appeared to have a charmed life. What was the background? And how could it happen that in the last months of the war most of Hungary's Jews were murdered? Our historian offers a summary, but this is my story, the tragedy of those I loved and lost. I narrate it slowly, offering personal details, looking for my own explanations.[29]

THE OLDEN DAYS

The 1700 Census shows 4071 Jews living in Hungary. Some of those Jews must have been similar to the Yiddish-speaking, ghetto-dwelling shtetl Jews of Poland or Russia. Even the poorest provincial ghetto-dwelling Jew was literate, their education strictly focused on the Old Testament which they read in Hebrew and discussed in Yiddish, their mother tongue. They wrote Yiddish in Hebrew characters. These practices largely remained unchanged in Russia, Poland and Lithuania, and emigration later transferred them to the United States and Israel, where they are maintained in Hasidic communities to this day.[30]

Two such cases occurred in my own family.

My father's sister Margit married Salamon Milchior, a Polish Jew, deserter from the Polish army who lived in Paris most of his life. He had scholarly knowledge of the Old Testament, was an avid reader of Yiddish newspapers and literature, and attended every performance of the Yiddish theatre in Paris, but spoke neither Polish nor French, and could only read and write Hebrew script.

Another example was my husband's first cousin Hölzler István, product of the Hungarian higher education system, an atheist in his youth. He married the beautiful daughter of an orthodox rabbi from northeast Hungary, emigrated to the USA after the 1956 Hungarian Revolution, and got sucked into a strict Hasidic community in New York State. That is where his extensive family now lives a shtetl-style life within high walls.

In Hungary, changes started in the late 18th century. The social and legal reforms of the Habsburg Emperor Joseph II granted a measure of civil rights to Jews throughout the Austro-Hungarian Empire. Further developments took place during the first half of the 19th century, when the Hungarian liberal nobility fought for reforms, which included the extension of the rights of Jews. In the final moments of the Independence War of 1848-49, Kossuth's liberal government gave Jews equality before the law. Jews won full social and political rights after the Austro-Hungarian Compromise of 1867. Given a chance of social equality, most Hungarian Jews became integrated and adopted Hungarian language

---

29   *HISTORIAN'S VOICE: The History of Jews in Hungary in a nutshell*
30   For example: Chaim Potok, *The Chosen*. London: Penguin, 2009; Shulem Deen, *All who Go Do Not Return*. Minneapolis, MN: Graywolf Press, 2015.

and culture. Turning their backs on the Yiddish language and strict religious practices, they grabbed opportunities of liberalisation, and absorbed the culture of their country of residence. By the end of the 19th century, the large majority of the Jews of Hungary were Hungarian speakers. By 1910, more than half of Hungary's doctors and lawyers were Jews. Significantly, 58% of the country's printers were Jews, dominating the trade of the literate.

In early 20th century, the Jewish population of Hungary grew in number and in political, economic and cultural influence, playing an increasing role in many spheres of secular life: industry, finance, politics, science, technology, literature, music and sport. Nevertheless, as the *HISTORIAN'S VOICE* records, Hungary was never exempt from antisemitism.

HUNGARY'S JEWS IN WORLD WAR I AND BETWEEN THE WARS

At the time of World War I, Jews made up just over 5% of the country's population, and took part in the war just like non-Jewish Hungarians. They were patriots, like my father-in-law, fighting enthusiastically alongside their fellow countrymen in all ranks of the army. Ten generals of the Austro-Hungarian army were Jews.

The people of Hungary resented the fact that 'only' 10,000 Jewish servicemen died in that war, as against some 500,000 non-Jews. Some historians offer a possible explanation. Unlike the majority of their non-Jewish counterparts, Jews were literate German speakers, so they performed administrative and logistical tasks, as opposed to combat duties.

The historian Sebők László assigns particular significance to this period in the history of Hungary's Jews. I translate his comment:[31]

> "During the war (WWI), antisemitism gained strength. This is when the ideology of antisemitism infiltrated all spheres of Hungarian society, penetrated the national psyche, and established itself for the future as an integral part of public opinion."

Matters deteriorated further after Trianon, establishing the foundation of anti-Jewish laws, ultimately leading to the virtual destruction of the Jews of the country. A simplistic explanation for the upsurge of antisemitism would be that after World War I the country was devastated and bankrupt, and Jews were convenient scapegoats. Braham offers a more logical explanation. Before Trianon, Hungary was a multi-ethnic country whose population spoke eight different languages and pursued seven different religions. After Trianon, the country lost most of its linguistic and religious minorities, and became predominantly

---

31   László Sebők, *A magyarországi zsidók a számok tükrében*. http://www.rubicon.hu/magyar/oldalak/a_magyarorszagi_zsidok_a_szamok_tukreben/ (accessed 19 October, 2019)

Hungarian speaking and Roman Catholic, but retained its proportion of Jews, who still amounted to some 5% of the population. In this more homogeneous country Jews were more conspicuous, more resented.

As one of Horthy's earliest acts as Regent, Hungary passed a law which violated the human rights of Jews. The *'Numerus Clausus'* of 1920 aimed to restrict the number of Jews entering higher education. The law caused misery for Jews, and would have caused immeasurable harm by depriving the country of the intellectual contribution of many of its ablest citizens. However, the Numerus Clausus was not fully effective. Ten years on, the 1930 Census registered that although Jews represented only 5.1% of the population, they still supplied about half of the country's professional workforce (doctors, lawyers, graduate engineers, scientists, bankers); had the commanding role in the financial activities of the stock exchange, and virtually dominated intellectual life. A phenomenon with which all Hungarians were familiar at the time was that Jewish children tended to excel in all intellectual pursuits, being the best, or among the best, of every class. Could this be attributed to their bookishness and scholarly tradition, to their innate ability, or to their diligence and ambition, such as Asian pupils display now in the English schools? I don't know the reason, but the fact remains, and is reflected in the figures of the census.

HUNGARY'S JEWS IN WORLD WAR II

The war devastated my family in two phases. First, we lost almost all our men, and then the rest became victims.

On Hungary entering the war in 1941, young Jewish men were called up into *munkaszolgálat*: Military Labour Service in the Hungarian army.[32]

I agree with every word of a survivor:

"Perhaps the most pitiful victims of World War II were the Jewish labour battalions. Other soldiers sent into action at least had the consolation that their life was the responsibility of their commander who could not recklessly risk that life. In contrast, what the commanders of the 'Jewish labour battalions' had responsibility for was the destruction of the Jewish personnel in their charge."[33]

The second phase came in 1944, when the war was nearing its end. In 56 days almost half a million Hungarian Jews were murdered. Even for Hitler, it would have been a record.

---

32   See *HISTORIAN'S VOICE* in Chapter 2: *Military Labour Service in Hungary*
33   Tolnai László: *Kőszegi végállomás*. Vörösváry kiadó, 1947. The author's translation

FIRST PHASE – *MUNKASZOLGÁLAT* – MILITARY LABOUR SERVICE

Trying to be fair, I have considered Military Labour Service of Jews from the viewpoint of the Hungarians. By the time Hungary entered the war in 1940, laws against Jews were well in place, and had already taken away many of Jews' civil rights. Could the government trust Jews, conscript them into the army, and arm them to fight the country's war? What if Jews would use their arms to take revenge, turn against their compatriots, fight on the side of the enemy? Alternatively, should we exclude Jews from the war, leave them at home, while non-Jewish Hungarians were fighting and dying on the battlefields? The government had a dilemma.

The Germans solved this problem by subjecting their Jews to the Final Solution. Hungarians found their own solution: they took Jews into the army, but gave them neither arms nor uniforms, and employed them on particularly risky tasks 'in the bloodiest areas of the war'.[34]

The distinguished journalist Fazekas György offers a witness account. As a young Hungarian Jew, he served in Ukraine. His 85-minute Hungarian-language television interview, screened in 2006, is utterly compelling.[35] He argues that the status of Jews in Military Labour Service was exceptional and invidious:

• Jews were treated as convicted prisoners but had committed no crime.

• Jews were an integral part of an army at war but had no weapons.

• Jews were under the command of their officers' who, rather than being responsible for their welfare, were tasked to ensure that they were exposed to danger.

• Jews were kept under secure military guard by soldiers of a country at war, but were not prisoners of war, because they were members of the same army as their captors.

• Had they been prisoners of war of an enemy country, Jews would have had the protection of international law. Jews had no law to protect them; in fact, it was the laws of their own country that condemned them to a fate which often proved to be worse than death.

Jews were imprisoned by the Hungarian army, just like political internees and other 'undesirables'. Those too wore an armband to distinguish them as a specific class of outcast; they too were despised and abused. But Nazi propaganda drummed into Hungarian

---

34   Randolph L Braham, *A Magyar Holocaust.* Budapest: Gondolat, 1981, Vol. 1: 245., summarising the 1940 demands of Henrik Werth, Chief of Staff of the Hungarian army.

35   Interview of former labour serviceman György Fazekas In *Krónika: Munkaszolgálat,* https://www.youtube.com/watch?v=F0MV8ya4L4E.

soldiers that Jews were not just undesirable human beings: they were subhuman, less valuable than beasts. Fazekas records an incident when a Hungarian officer shot a Jew dead for taking a gulp of water from a bucket intended for a military horse.

Fazekas describes work carried out by Jews in the army, such as laying mines and clearing minefields, in some cases by forming a tight wall, marching through uncleared minefields. He records Jews having no uniform and no army boots, and Hungarian military stealing from Jews any warm clothing they may have brought from home. Even without being deliberately maltreated, people would have frozen to death, or died from gangrene, of starvation, or, in the absence of adequate drinking water, of dysentery or dehydration. They were dying of disease, particularly typhus. They were dying of exhaustion because of overwork. They had no rest, no sleep. They worked all day, but to avoid freezing to death in their sleep, they kept marching overnight. Hardship was not confined to Jews, but Jews were the worst clad, worst fed, worst housed and deliberately maltreated by their fellow soldiers.

BOR

The tragedy of 6,000 Hungarian Jews killed in Military Labour Service in the Serbian copper mines of Bor is widely known. My husband's uncle Veres Pál was one of the few survivors. The extraordinary story of his escape is not included here but should be told.

Radnóti Miklós, one of the greatest Hungarian poets, also served in Bor. The story of his life and death is now the stuff of legend. He was beaten almost to death by Hungarian military thugs, because he was forever 'scribbling'. Then he was shot, and buried in a mass grave, to be exhumed 18 months later. His last masterpieces, *The Eclogues*, were discovered in his pocket.[36]

KŐSZEG AND WESTERN HUNGARY

With its 16th century castle and church, the ancient royal town of Kőszeg on Hungary's western border is among the country's tourist attractions. Kőszeg's sinister role in the history of Military Labour Service is still emerging, but we have some information already.

Nearing the end of the war, Labour Service units garrisoned in Hungary, together with thousands of women from the Budapest yellow star houses, were marched towards Hungary's western borders. Their task was to build fortifications against the soviet army. Many perished along the way, others died of starvation, or were murdered. In a 2017 lecture in Hendon's orthodox synagogue, Rabbi Grosz, of Hungarian descent, reported recent findings of mass graves of Military Labour Service victims in Kőszeg and in the nearby village of Hidegség.

---

36   See: Vági–Csősz–Kádár, *Evolution of a Genocide*, 49, 58-59.

My pianist friend Péter Frankl found, in Yad Vashem records, that in February 1944 his father starved to death in the military barracks of Kőszeg.

Tolnai László's moving witness evidence is 'a monument to the 6,000 in the labour battalion who died a tragic death in Kőszeg'.[37]

WOMEN IN LABOUR SERVICE

A 1943 parliamentary decree empowered the army to call up Jewish women. There were two categories:

- women between the ages of 16 and 50 with sewing skills,

- women between 16 and 40 for 'national defence-related labour service'.

Some Jewish women were conscripted into the army under this decree, others were picked up by Hungarian fascists during Szálasi's regime and handed over to the Germans or to the military. Some stayed within the borders of Hungary, such as my Hungarian-born Czech pianist friend Eva Bernathova. She was 20, among thousands of young Jewish women assembled by Arrow Cross militia in Budapest's racecourse, taken to a women's military labour camp at Dinnyés, and used as agricultural labourer. Thousands were taken abroad, such as Jancsi's aunts Sári, and Iboly who survived Dachau.

To honour my uncles and others lost in military labour service, and add to the record of their history, my family sponsors a research project, based in the Wiener Library.[38]

SECOND PHASE – DESTRUCTION OF CIVILIANS

After our men were taken away, those of us left behind suffered more and more hardship and indignity, but for a while we still lived in our homes, unaware that the rest of Europe's Jews were being deported and systematically murdered in their millions. Why did our fate differ from that of other European Jews? The answer must lie in Hungary's status in the war.

Even before the outbreak of World War II, Germany was a fascist dictatorship. Hitler's Nazis imprisoned, enslaved or murdered Jews and other 'undesirables'. People were persecuted and killed because they were physically or mentally handicapped, or for reasons of race, religion, political affiliation, or sexual preference. Jews were considered inferior even to these: 'vermin', the foremost enemies of mankind. With the outbreak of the war, countries occupied by Germany came under the same regime of systematic murder.

---

37   Tolnai, *Kőszegi végállomás*.

38   László Csősz, Military Labour Service in Hungary. Research fellowship, 2018-2020, The Wiener Holocaust Library, London.

Until the last phase of the war, Hungary was not an occupied country: it was Germany's ally, its army fighting Hitler's war. Hitler had pressed Horthy to follow other European countries in exterminating its Jews. Although the Hungarian Parliament had passed a sequence of increasingly oppressive laws against Jews, it was not ready to formalise a policy of systematic murder of Jewish citizens.

On the fateful day of 19th March 1944, life for Hungary's Jews changed at a stroke. With the German army's occupation of Hungary, the systematic killing of Jews could begin.[39] Braham writes: "For the 'Final Solution' in Hungary, a special commando squad of 150 to 200 men was organised under the immediate command of Adolf Eichmann."

Eichmann was an inventive strategist, a clever tactician, a good organiser, experienced in 'ghettoisation': deportation and extermination of Jews. Yet, even for him, this new task was formidable. He needed careful planning, but was determined not to waste time, so deportations commenced even before plans were complete.

Eichmann's squad was tiny, and his task enormous: some 750,000 Hungarian Jews were to be deported and killed. The HISTORIAN'S VOICE explains that Germans controlled the process on Hungarian soil, but were not directly involved. Detailed planning and implementation was the task of cooperating Hungarian authorities.

Hungary's Ministry of the Interior had direct control of law enforcement. In the capital, the main cities and the municipal towns, the Police were in charge, while in the provinces, law enforcement was the responsibility of the Csendőrség, the Gendarmerie. Horthy's new government appointed two central figures: Endre László, a staunch antisemite, became Eichmann's right-hand man in the Ministry of the Interior, and Baky László, another trusted fascist, commanded the Gendarmerie.[40]

In order to support the anti-Jewish campaign, at the end of March the Ministry of the Interior created the State Security Surveillance, Hungarian version of the Gestapo, with headquarters neighbouring Eichmann's office in the leafy hills of Buda. Among the functions of State Security Surveillance was the rounding up and elimination of any remaining foreign Jews. Besides, Hungarian law enforcement arrested politically suspicious 'anti-Nazi' elements, both Jews and non-Jews.

I remember hearing, day by day, of the suicide or unexplained death of famous people my parents knew, or knew of. All over the country, Jews unable to bear the indignities of the present and the fear of the future were killing themselves singly, in pairs, in complete families. Among the victims were the uncle and neighbours of my friend Gábor. In his dry, factual style the historian Szita reports 'a virtual epidemic of suicide', and writes of people going mad. I remember hearing this at the time, not understanding what it meant. Later, in the wagon on our way to the camps, I saw many cases myself.

---

39   See HISTORIAN'S VOICE: Eichmann's Role and Hungarian Collaboration

40   Csendőrség: Hungarian law enforcement agency founded in 1881 following the model of the French Gendarmerie. It was was responsible for maintaining law and order in the countryside, whereas the police were in charge in cities and towns. After World War II the force was declared a Fascist organization and disbanded.

The State Security Police arrested wealthy Jews of Budapest, and beat out of them the whereabouts of their hidden valuables. In the provinces, this form of 'wealth creation' was entrusted to the gendarmerie. Special institutions were rapidly established country-wide, for the express purpose of interrogating the wealthy. Jews might have had valuables on their person, might have hidden their assets, or left them with trusted Christians. The latter was of particular interest to the State Security Police: such Christians were traitors, to be dealt with accordingly.

In 1941, the Hungarian gendarmerie numbered about 12,000, increasing gradually until 1944, when the force reached 22,000. This, together with 14,000 police, amounted to 36,000 trained, uniformed men. This internal force was ready to be deployed to eliminate Hungary's three-quarter-million 'civilian' Jews.[41]

Smart uniformed gendarmes on horseback might call into mind the gallant officers of the Canadian Mounted Police. Hungarian reality was different. The brutality of gendarmes was legendary. Gendarmes tortured, murdered, and destroyed all those in their path: Jews, gypsies, minorities, striking workers, liberal intellectuals. The distinguishing feature of the gendarme's uniform was the hat, decorated by plumes of the cockerel.

German officers and Hungarian gendarmes, around 1941.

Photo: Hugo Jaeger. Getty Images

How could people survive in such a country without jokes? The wartime joke was:

No wonder there are no eggs in the shops. Cockerels are on strike.
No self-respecting cockerel would wear Gendarme plumes anymore.

---

41   For the figures and further information, see the entries *Csendőrség* and *Rendőrség* in Péter Sipos, ed. *Magyarország a második világháborúban*. Budapest: Petit Real, 1997.

The paragraph below comes from a paper on the history of the gendarmerie. The author is a Hungarian nobleman, an erstwhile officer of the gendarmerie. One almost pities his earnest effort of truthfully reporting an appalling incident, one of many, while also trying to excuse the inexcusable.[42]

> 'Around the turn of the century, some units of the gendarmerie got a few unfortunate duties, when the civil administrators, instead of remedying the problems, sent units of gendarmes, and/or army to confront striking workers and unhappy voters at the city of Élesd. Unfortunately, the gendarmes had no authority to refuse the execution of the administrative orders which made a bad impression of the gendarmerie on the population.'

This event occurred half a century before World War II, and had nothing to do with Jews, but gendarmes were fierce and natural antisemites. I will never forget those gendarmes. Even after living in England for a decade, I was still frightened to pass by a man in uniform whether a soldier, a policeman or a Salvation Army major.

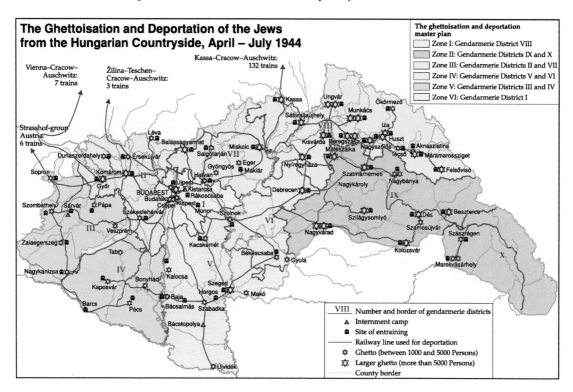

---

42   Gabriel Kiss, *A Short History of the Royal Hungarian Gendarmerie*. http://www.csendor.com/konyvtar/irasok/english/Royal%20Hungarian%20Gendarmerie%20-%20Kiss%20G.pdf (accessed 19 October, 2019)

The mentality, experience and traditions of gendarmes suited them perfectly for their new task of de-jewification of Hungary's provinces. The country, including the newly annexed territories, was divided into 10 Gendarmerie Districts (GDs), offering a ready-made framework.

The procedure was well rehearsed; Eichmann had employed it in other German-occupied countries: incarcerate Jews in ghettos, concentrate them in entrainment camps, and deport them to camps with facilities for gassing and incineration. Auschwitz-Birkenau was a mixed camp, supplying workers for industry and agriculture, but it had resources for exterminating those unfit to work. For Eichmann's purposes Auschwitz-Birkenau was convenient: it was the nearest and largest camp of its kind, but even so, facilities had to be specially enhanced to cope with the huge number and unprecedented rate of arrival of Hungary's mass of Jews. The next task was to decide the order for carrying out the process. Young Jewish men had long been taken away into the army, but Eichmann was still mindful of the possibility of uprisings in ghettos. Some 180,000 Jews lived in Budapest. They were resourceful, geographically concentrated, potentially capable of mounting organised resistance. By contrast, provincial Jews were scattered and less able to assemble a feasible force. Eichmann's plan was to deal with the provinces first. Once provincial Jews were cleared out, he could report to the impatient Hitler that *almost* all the country was free of Jews. He might then have time to deal with the complicated but focused task of eliminating the Jews of Budapest.

In early May 1944, the sequence of deportations was decided: start in the northeast, proceed clockwise, and end in the northwest. The main reason for choosing this order was that the Soviet front was progressing from the east/northeast. District VIII was about to be declared a war zone, so clearing away its Jews was urgent. But there was a further reason. District VIII had a large Jewish population, including the orthodox and Hasidic communities of Szatmár (18,000) and Munkács (30,000). These Jews were the most detested by Hungary and the Nazis of the Reich.

The administrative centre of each Gendarmerie District became the location of a main ghetto, with lesser ghettos around. District centres were sizeable cities, most with dual railway connections. Secondary railway stations could be used for deporting Jews, primary railway stations providing uninterrupted service for the Aryan population.

On 4th and 5th May 1944, Eichmann organised a planning conference in Vienna to decide details: rid Hungary of provincial Jews within 51 days, using four trains per day, each of 45 wagons. Here is the arithmetic of the plan:

Four trains over 51 days gave Eichmann 51 x 4 = 204 trains, each with 45 wagons, a total of 204 x 45 = 9180 wagons.

Did Eichmann know how many Jews were in the country, how they were distributed in the capital and the districts? I found reliable figures recently, in Stark's statistical review – a veritable goldmine. Excluding the Jews of Budapest, Eichmann might have estimated the number to be about 500,000, so 'transportation density' would have been 500,000/9180 ~ 54.5 Jews per wagon.

In practice there were fewer trains available than planned, and the task took 56 days. Szita records the starting point, date of departure and number of Jews for each train. His list shows 133 trains, each with 45 wagons, 5985 wagons in all, giving an average transportation density of 500,000:5985 ~ 84 Jew per wagon.

My family's train left Debrecen, centre of GDVI, on 27th June, with 3,842 people on board. Given 45 wagons/train, the average comes to 3842/45 ~ 85. I remember that our wagon had 87 people. This is consistent with the number recorded by my friend Gábor, although he travelled by another train.

Eichmann's aims were complex.

Foremost was the aim to implement the Final Solution.

A secondary aim was to ease the desperate labour shortage of the Reich. 'Category 1' labourers (young men) were not available, most of the young Jews having been called up into the army. However, there were young women and older men, potential 'Category 2' labourers. Some such Jews had to be directed westwards, to work for German/Austrian industry and agriculture.[43]

The tertiary aim was exchanging some Jews for 'assets'. Himmler envisaged exchanging up to 1,000,000 Jews for 1,000 British lorries. A scheme on that scale had obviously failed, but German hopes remained right to the end of the war; so, pending 'blood for goods' negotiations, some Jews were kept 'on ice'.

Esther Farbstein refers to the Nazis choosing Hungarian Jews rather than Poles or Russians, because they were secularised, and perceived to be 'more valuable and more productive elements'. She relates that the intended number had gradually been reduced from the initial million to hundreds of thousands, and finally to just above 15,000.[44]

Eichmann decided that those 'on ice' should also include 'useless' Jews: children and the very old (Category 3). This would utilise even these people. An ingenious idea: if 'useless' Jews were relatives of Category 2 workers, then families would be kept together, and workers would be happier, more productive. This is how our family was offered a chance to survive.My camp-time family had five Category 2 adults (Imre, Magda, Terka, Pici and Klári). There were also six Category 3 'useless' people: three grannies, two toddlers, and I.

---

43   See HISTORIAN'S VOICE in Chapter 2: *Military Labour Service in Hungary*

44   Esther Farbstein, *Hidden in the Heights. Orthodox Jewry in Hungary during the Holocaust.* Jerusalem: Mossad HaRav Kook, 2014.

Eichmann's men considered how best to extract resources from wealthy Jews. The controversial Jewish elder Kasztner Rezső persuaded the Nazis to allow a group of 1,685 Jews to leave for Switzerland on what became known as the 'Kasztner train'. My friend, the historian Judith Möller, insists, from experience, that Kasztner selected these lucky Jews at random, but most sources assert that these Jews *bought* their passage.[45]

For some, wealth did not buy privileges. A triumph for socialism! Many rich Jews were kept hostage under appalling conditions, tortured, often beaten to death. Other rich people were tricked into revealing the whereabouts of their valuables, and then murdered. Two members of my ghetto family had such a fate. During our times in Debrecen, there were daily arrests of prominent Jews, among them uncles of my friends the Feldman girls. I have vivid memories of people staggering home after their arrest, bruised and covered in blood, and some failing to return.

Deportations started on 14th May 1944. In the following eight weeks, up to 9th July, the number of Jews taken out of the country by train is now considered to be about 437,000. Of these, some 15,000 were sent towards Vienna, and the rest to Auschwitz/Birkenau. By the time provincial Jews were taken away, the Soviet army was arriving, and the Reich was collapsing.

Yielding to the deteriorating military situation and foreign pressure, Horthy halted the deportations on July 6th 1944. This is why a fair proportion of the Jews of Budapest survived. Some of our friends and family survived in this way, but many were lost.[46]

Here are a few personal remarks.

Pro-Nazi leaders of the Ministry of the Interior were disappointed by Horthy's decision and completed the deportation of the Jews from Deportation Zone I, that is, the towns and villages surrounding Budapest. For example, Jancsi's grandfather lived in Rákospalota, a town in the vicinity of Budapest. He and his daughter Aranka, both killed in Auschwitz, were among those Rákospalota Jews deported from the Rákoscsaba transit camp between July 6th and 8th.[47]

---

45   See *HISTORIAN'S VOICE: Kasztner Train*

46   Vági–Csősz–Kádár, *Evolution of a Genocide*, 120-145.; Paul Bogdanor: *Kasztner's Crime*. Chapter 9: The Strasshof Deal. London: Routledge 2017.

47   Rákospalota In Randolph L. Braham, ed. *The Geographical Encyclopaedia of the Holocaust in Hungary*. Budapest: Park, 2007. Vol. 2: 876

Nazis also made attempts to continue the deportations without Hungarian participation. On July 19th an SS unit raided the Kistarcsa internment camp and deported more than 1,200 detainees. Five days later, the SS raided the Sárvár camp and transported some 1,500 of the camp inmates. These two groups constituted the last major transports of Hungarian Jews to Auschwitz-Birkenau.[48]

Many of my schoolmates and friends were lost, among them my summertime playmates little blonde Lizi and the Feldman girls.

Some Jews were hidden by compassionate Christians. This is how Jancsi, his parents and my uncle Feri survived.

Jancsi's cousin Veres Tamás was eight years old in 1944. His father was in labour service in Bor, Serbia; his mother in Labour Service in Dachau. He roamed the streets of the city in the winter of 1944-45, one of the harshest on record. He found shelter in one of Wallenberg's cellars. Miraculously, all three survived.[49]

Some of my friends who survived in Budapest had found shelter in 'protected houses' of foreign embassies. Others reported having to move to 'yellow star' houses and from there to the Budapest ghetto, and in due course were liberated by the Soviet army.

Many Budapest Jews were handed over to the Germans for slave labour and taken to the western border on death marches.[50]

Then there were those, like my beloved Rózsi and 80-year-old Giza mama, who were murdered on the spot. Their neighbours told us that they had been taken away by the Arrow Cross and were seen 'marching' with a group of others towards the river. Had my parents and I stayed home rather than fleeing to Debrecen after 19th March 1944, we would have shared their fate. The Arrow Cross killed almost 10,000 Jews of the capital by shooting them dead. This mass murder took place just days before the siege of Budapest ended, while the army fought Soviet troops street by street.[51]

---

48   See: *Glossary* in Nina Munk, László Csősz and Ferenc Laczó, eds. Ernő Munkácsi: *How It Happened. Documenting the Tragedy of Hungarian Jewry.* Toronto: McGill-Queen's University Press, 2018.

49   Raoul Wallenberg (1912–1947?), Swedish architect, businessman and diplomat. As a member of the Swedish diplomatic mission and following an assignment by the American War Refugee Board, he issued thousands of protective documents to Hungarian Jews and placing dozens of Budapest buildings under Swedish diplomatic protection. Through colleagues as well as personal efforts, he saved thousands of people during the Arrow Cross regime. Soviet authorities arrested him in January 1945 and he probably died in a Moscow prison in 1947. See: Raoul Wallenberg, *Letters and Dispatches.* New York: Arcade Publishing–USHMM, 1995.

50   László Csősz, *Death Blows Overhead. The Last Transports from Hungary, November 1944.* https://blog.ehri-project.eu/2017/11/23/hungary-1944/

51   László Csősz–Laura Csonka, *Murdered on the Verge of Survival: Massacres in the Last Days of the Siege of Budapest, 1945.*
https://blog.ehri-project.eu/2017/02/08/murdered-on-the-verge-of-survivalmassacres-in-the-last-days-of-the-siege-of-budapest-1945/

Kossuth tér, a beautiful square in front of the iconic Houses of Parliament, is a few steps from my mother's shop of my childhood, the square where I used to play as a child. On the edge of the square is the famously evocative Memorial of the shoes of victims, cast in bronze. The plaque reads:

**'TO THE MEMORY OF THE VICTIMS SHOT INTO THE DANUBE
BY ARROW CROSS MILITIAMEN IN 1944-45'.**

The "Shoes on the Danube" Memorial in Budapest (2005). In the background is the Royal Castle.
Photo: Shutterstock

These days many Hungarians deny or distort the Holocaust, and nurse antisemitic sentiments, just as their parents and grandparents did. I have on file some of the handiwork of Hungary's neo-Nazis: posters, graffiti, photographs of desecrated synagogues, vandalised tombstones. Even the Memorial of the Shoes is an occasional target. Recently they stuffed a pig's leg into a shoe, and there are reports of finding them filled with dogs' excrement.

How many Hungarian Jews fell victim of World War II? We shall never know for sure. Stark provides the first estimate which appeared in February 1945, while most of the country was still at war. Numbers continue to be updated and are debated by historians. The figure of 600,000 Hungarian Holocaust victims has become 'fixed in the public mind', while currently historians consider a number between 500,000 and 550,000. If we set any such number against the 760-780,000 Hungarian Jews recorded in the 1941 census, then the loss is about two-thirds. Most survivors are Budapest Jews. Most of the victims are provincial Jews who perished in Auschwitz, and I include two of my pictures in their memory.

By luck or by miracle, many of the 15,011 provincial Jews deported to Austria survived, among them members of my family. Each survivor suffered. All of us were damaged. Nobody came through the Holocaust unscathed: not the victims, not the perpetrators, not even the descendants.

Deportation of Jews from Dunaszerdahely, Hungary to Auschwitz-Birkenau, 15th June 1944.
Memorial Museum of Hungarian Speaking Jewry, Courtesy of Rezső Steckler

HISTORIAN'S VOICE

The History of Hungary in a nutshell

Hungarians used to be one of the nomadic tribes of the Eurasian steppe, speaking a Finno-Ugric language, arriving in the Carpathian Basin at the end of the 9th century AD. Around 1000 AD, Hungarian leaders joined the Roman Catholic Church and established a feudal kingdom of Latin culture, which became one of the dominant powers of medieval Central and Eastern Europe. In the 16th century, Hungary was largely occupied by the Ottoman Turks. Two centuries of Habsburg rule followed. After unsuccessful attempts to regain independence, the Hungarian political elite forged a compromise with the Habsburg court in 1867, creating a union of Austria and Hungary, two nearly sovereign states, linked by the same person ruling both. There were also joint ministries of defence, finance, and foreign affairs.

Austro-Hungary was defeated in World War I. As a consequence, the empire was dismembered, and two-thirds of historical Hungarian territory was lost to successor states, along with more than three million ethnic Hungarians. The Trianon Peace Treaty was a great shock to Hungary. In the subsequent two decades revision of the Treaty became the ultimate aim of Hungarian foreign and internal policy. As a result, Hungary allied with Nazi Germany, a power which also aimed at nullifying the post-war treaties.

Between 1938 and 1941, with Nazi support, Hungary gained back a large part of its lost territories, but paid a hefty price. Ultimately it was on the losing side again in World War II, which left the country devastated and about a million Hungarian citizens dead, over half of them Jewish. Soviet occupation and shortly after, a Communist dictatorship followed. In 1956, a brave attempt to shake off the Stalinist yoke failed.

There had been futile attempts at establishing a democratic state after World War I and World War II. A third endeavour to create a Western-style parliamentary democracy was successful after 1989, with Hungary joining the European Union in 2004. However, like many other European countries, Hungary has recently undergone a social and political crisis, characterised by growing populism, nationalism, xenophobia, and other disturbing phenomena undermining liberal democracy.

The History of Jews in Hungary in a nutshell

Jews have been living in the area that later became Hungary since Roman times, that is, since the first centuries A.D. However, over the next one and a half millennia, Jews would disappear from the region from time to time. Thus, at the brink of the Holocaust, the majority of Jewish families in Hungary were the descendants of emigrants who arrived in the country during the 18th and 19th centuries, mostly from other provinces of the Austrian Empire, including Moravia (Czech Republic today) and Galicia (Poland). At the beginning of the 18th century, only a couple of thousand Jews lived in Hungary. The community would grow to nearly one million by the brink of World War

I. During the 'long nineteenth century', as this period is often referred to, the history of the Jews in Hungary was largely a success story, albeit overshadowed by ever growing social conflicts and anomalies.

Economic modernisation of the country and the rapidly growing market economy afforded great opportunities for Jewish entrepreneurs with financial background and experience. They were supported by the Hungarian state, led by the traditional elite, who found Jews indispensable in the modernisation process. In liberal professions (lawyers, physicians, journalists, artists, etc.), Jews contributed greatly to the development of the country and constituted a large part of the modern, urban middle-class. By the end of the 19th century this led to total legal and religious emancipation and widespread Magyarization of Jews, and to the development of a special Hungarian Jewish identity.

There were several contributors to the development of an anti-Jewish intellectual movement and social sentiment. Among these were the frustration of losers of the modernisation process, the partial survival of medieval anti-Judaism, and effects of a new political antisemitism in Europe. In Hungary, antisemitism burst to the surface with elemental force in 1882, with the so-called Tiszaeszlár blood libel case. Pogroms broke out, by the turn of the century antisemitism was reinvigorated, and by the last years of World War I it was fundamentally defining Hungarian political discourse. Anti-Jewish attitude became the ideological cornerstone of the right-wing system created after the fall of the Austro-Hungarian Monarchy. During the regime of Admiral Miklós Horthy (1920-1944), gradual radicalisation in Jewish policies led to discriminative legislation, paving the way for the genocide of Hungarian Jewry between 1941 and 1945.

Eichmann's Role and Hungarian Collaboration

The March 19th 1944 invasion of Hungary by German army troops was soon followed by SS, Police and Secret Police units, including a special detachment (Sondereinsatzkommando) of the Nazi security forces (SD) under SS lieutenant colonel Adolf Eichmann. Their task was to launch a campaign against the Jewish community, which the Nazis regarded as 'enemy number one'. Eichmann's unit included all of his experienced officers, with whom he had been orchestrating the murder of millions of people in the previous years. They acted swiftly, using their well-established methods in a coordinated manner throughout the country.

Nationwide, autonomous Jewish communities were dissolved. Following a method well-tested in a host of other countries in earlier years of the war, in the spring of 1944 the Nazi and Hungarian authorities established some 150 Jewish councils (Judenräte). These bodies became responsible for the internal and administrative affairs of the community. In practice, this task mostly involved the implementation of the orders of the German or Hungarian authorities, and the enforcement of increasingly restrictive measures against the Jews.

Despite the experience of his team, Eichmann's mission would not have been possible without the efficient and often enthusiastic cooperation of the Hungarian government, public administration and law enforcement. The Germans were careful not to remove head of the state, Regent Miklós Horthy. Instead of an exclusively military solution, they decided on a model of broad collaboration:

in exchange for the appearance of sovereignty there was a guarantee that the Hungarian Army and public administration would cooperate. This solution maintained a façade of normalcy, serving German interests. On the orders of the Regent, there was no resistance from the Hungarian Army. The Regent appointed a new government, consisting of well-known pro-Nazi political figures. Under their leadership, the overwhelming majority of the Hungarian public servants and law enforcement personnel (willingly or unwillingly) cooperated with the Nazis, with the exception of a few who had resigned or were arrested after the occupation.

Auschwitz-Birkenau, crematorium
Photo: Shutterstock

From the end of March 1944 onwards, Hungary's collaborationist government of Döme Sztójay issued a plethora of decrees. These gradually deprived Jewish citizens of their civil rights, of their assets, and ultimately, of their freedom. The first decrees were aimed at the economic and social positions and wealth of Jews. These were soon followed by other decrees restricting the free movement and communication of Jews, and the introduction of their registration, and, on 5th April, the implementation of a visual stigma, the yellow star.

Auschwitz-Birkenau, memorial plaque
Photo: Neil, 2007 (Wikimedia Commons, CC-BY-SA-3.0-migrated)

On 28th April 1944, a decree of the Ministry of the Interior ordered Hungarian municipal authorities to force Jews into ghettos: designated residential areas. Within weeks, Jews were taken from ghettos to sites of deportation. In the country, senior county officials took charge, planning the task with commanders of the gendarmerie. In cities and towns, the planning group usually included the mayor and the police commander. To implement the plans, in many cases police and gendarmerie forces cooperated and assisted each other. German authorities were not directly involved in this phase of the genocidal process.

The Kasztner Train

Following the Nazi invasion of Hungary, the underground Zionist Budapest Relief and Rescue Committee, led by lawyer Rudolf (Rezső) Kasztner and his associates, made a fateful decision to negotiate with Nazi and Hungarian authorities to thwart the deportation of Hungarian Jews, or at least to save some lives. This attempt correlated with the political maneuvres of head of SS Heinrich Himmler, who was planning to forge a separate peace treaty with the Western Allies, to prevent the inevitable total defeat of the German Reich. Himmler speculated that he could use Jews as hostages to exert pressure on the United States and Britain, and offered the lives of one million Jews in exchange for ten thousand military trucks and large amounts of goods. Allied governments never considered the 'blood for goods' offer, and the operation was a complete failure. However, with existing channels of communication, the Zionists could carry out more realistic negotiations with SS representatives. As a result, the so-called 'Kasztner train', carrying 1684 people, was allowed to leave Budapest on 30*th* June 1944. At first, passengers were placed in a special section within Bergen-Belsen concentration camp, and ultimately reached safety in neutral Switzerland in two groups in August and December 1944. It was the first sizeable group that could leave Hitler's Europe with the Nazis' permission since October 1941, when the Nazis halted Jewish emigration.[52]

Opinions about the Kasztner operation remain extremely controversial to this day.

---

52 For details about the 1944 activities of the Rescue Committee, the Nazi-Jewish negotiations and the Kasztner affair, see Braham, *The Politics of Genocide*, Chapter 29.; Yehuda Bauer, *Jews for Sale? Nazi-Jewish Negotiations, 1933-1945*. New Haven–London: Yale University Press, 1994. 172-209; Vági–Csősz–Kádár, *Evolution of a Genocide*, Chapter 8. For a bibliography of the literature on the topic, see Randolph L. Braham–Julia Bock, *The Holocaust in Hungary. A Selected and Annotated Bibliography, 2001-2007*. New York: Columbia University Press, 2008. 143-150; Randolph L. Braham, *The Holocaust in Hungary. A Selected and Annotated Bibliography, 1984–2001*. New York: Columbia University Press, 2008. 143-147.

4   A LOST CHILDHOOD

1939 – 1944

What prompted us to have a professional photograph taken? How did we find the money? I remember the studio of the photographer in Budapest's Nagymező utca, everyone taking great care choosing their clothes. Equal attention was given to the shoes, and I was disappointed that our feet were not shown. Dated 1938, the year after Terka's wedding and the year before Pici's, the picture is asymmetrical: Pici's beau Pista is absent. He and Pici would have been engaged but were not married yet, so Nanóka considered it improper to include him in a family photograph.

The author's family.
Front row: Csengeri Dezsőné (Nanóka), the author, the author's mother Magda,
the author's aunt Pici.
Back row: the author's aunt Terka, uncle Feri, the author's father Imre
Kaposi family collection

1939 was a memorable year for me, for my family and for the world. Pici and Pista got married. On the 1st September World War II broke out. On the 11th September I started school. On my 6th birthday I started piano lessons.

Co-educational schools were almost unheard of. The nearest school for girls was three blocks from the Houses Parliament, a few steps from my mother's shop. Our school building had two entrances: the right one for juniors, the left for Grammar School seniors. When starting school in September, a child had to be at least six years old. My birthday is in October, so I was almost seven when I entered that Junior school, and I graduated from the Grammar School at age 18. Much dirty water would flow down the River Danube in between.

Private education was almost non-existent. There were a few faith schools, notably Catholic and Protestant schools in Calvinist Debrecen, but in general each child attended the local junior school. The character of our school was determined by the vicinity of the Parliament. Many girls came from privileged homes, living in the large elegant flats of the district, and belonging to high society. We even had an aristocrat in our class, Báró Tornyai Marika. The father of another girl was one of the richest industrialists of the country. Their family had a huge flat by the iconic Chain Bridge, a mansion in the Buda hills, and holiday homes by Lake Balaton and abroad. Other prominent members of our class included the daughter of an MP, the daughter of a judge, two budding ballerinas of the Budapest Opera, and the daughter of an internationally celebrated academic. On the other end of the social scale, there were children of domestic servants and caretakers of buildings. A few were in between. I was one of these, and Alice was another.

Alice's father was a middle-aged post office clerk. Alice was a clever Jewish girl who was often absent, lost her books, messed up her homework. She had tangled dark hair, frequently had lice, and her clothes were not washed often enough. People avoided her. Our teacher Judit néni seated her next to me. I was not pleased but could not object.

One afternoon I was playing in Kossuth tér, the enormous garden square in front of the Parliament, near to my mother's shop. I could go there on my own. Alice was there with her father. That day we played aeroplanes: we climbed up to the pedestal of the statue of the great 19th century statesman Kossuth and took turns to jump off with outstretched arms. The girl behind me

The author's school in Szemere utca, Budapest. Entrance to the Junior School on the right, Grammar school on the left

88

got a bit impatient and pushed me: an accident. I fell, but one of my legs was trapped at the top. The edge of the marble pedestal was sharp, and great gushes of blood pumped out from the top of my thigh. Alice's father grabbed me, put me on his shoulder, and ran with me to the Red Cross Hospital in Markó utca, half a mile away, a streak of blood marking our route. I had several stitches and blood transfusions. The doctors told my parents that Alice's father saved my life.

After that, Alice's father often came to my mother's shop. He told us that his wife was 17 when Alice was born, but now she was in a tuberculosis sanatorium in the Buda hills. Once my parents allowed me to accompany Alice to visit her. We talked to her through a window. She was transparently pale but beautiful, with masses of dark hair. She died before the end of the school year.

School uniform was a black wraparound apron covering our clothing, leaving only the sleeves visible. Shirts and jumpers had to be white or black. We all looked alike, so our social status not immediately obvious, but there were tell-tale signs. For example, it was compulsory to have a milky drink every morning, and some girls did not have to pay. Everyone knew who got free milk and why.

Some girls were accompanied to school by their elegant mothers, or by their foreign nannies. Everyone lived near the school, and yet several came in their family's limousine, driven by a uniformed chauffeur. Those who, like me, had working mothers came on their own. Nobody in our family owned a car, and only a distant relative could drive one: he was a chauffeur by trade. My father had a bicycle which he used to go to work, to the concern of us all, because he was accident-prone, an indifferent cyclist with poor eyesight who often arrived home with cuts and bruises.

Social status also determined out-of-school activities. School finished at lunchtime, and girls of the 'right' sort met for afternoon tea in each other's homes. Visiting arrangements were made in whispers, but insiders made sure that everyone knew who were excluded. For a while I was not invited, and in any case, I could not have invited anyone back. Where? To our empty flat? To the room behind my mother's shop?

Birthdays of the rich girls were celebrated by lavish parties called *jours*. Some were quite spectacular, with sophisticated caterers and professional entertainers. When it became apparent that I was the top of the class, in academic terms, I was sometimes asked to such celebrations. One of these *jours* occupied the best part of a day. Festivities started at the family's spacious town home. There was a show, starring Rózsahegyi Kálmán, a famous comic actor. Elaborate food was served, the likes of which I had never seen. Then a fleet of limousines took us up to the mansion in the Buda hills. There was an orchestra, with professional dancers instructing us in ballroom dancing (we were 7 or 8!). Lots more ornate food followed, and when the party was over, everyone was taken home by limousine. I found these occasions uncomfortable, although the grownups (parents, nannies) were kind to me, even exceptionally kind. I might have realised that I was being patronised.

There were quite a few Jewish girls among the rich and the middle social tier, some almost as poor as me, but there was no Jew among the working class. This worried me, because it was consistent with some of the antisemitic propaganda of the day. But then, gradually, more of the Jews became poor because, one by one, Jewish fathers lost their jobs and businesses, or were called away to Military Labour Service.

Apart from social and academic stratification, there was also a religious divide. For Jews, there was no escape: posters, news, and radio broadcasts were full of vicious antisemitic propaganda, poisoning the atmosphere. The very timetable supported discrimination. Religious education was compulsory, and religious lessons were slotted into the timetable for the Catholic majority. The rest were labelled *másvallású*, 'other religionists'. While the Catholics had their daily religion classes, we outcasts silently waited outside in the unheated corridors.

There was a wood-burning stove in the corner of our classroom. The teacher's table was on a low platform called the *cathedra,* with a blackboard behind. Desks were arranged as three columns of linked pairs, each desk with a folding top and an inkwell. We had set places, and in first year we had to sit bolt upright, one arm behind the back, the index finger of the other hand on our lips signifying silence, one girl precisely behind the other. Except for those in the front row, the blackboard was impossible to see, but one became familiar with each hair on the head of the girl in front. I always enjoyed learning, and was eager to go to school, but the keenly anticipated institution proved a disappointment. A few girls could read as well as me, and several spoke a foreign language – learnt from their German, French or English nannies – but the majority had only just began familiarising themselves with the shapes of letters and numbers. Being used to the style and rhythm of my father's and uncles' explanations, my time at school was filled with tedium and boredom, waiting for the teacher to get going, and for the girls to catch on.

To fill the time, I played games in my head. This must have shown on my face, and I was often caught out not paying attention. Punishment for a first offence was standing in the corner, or next to one's desk, for the rest of the lesson. Repeated offences yielded an Intő: a 'Warning' written into our punishment record book, to be acknowledged by a parent's signature. I made sure not to pile up sins to the point where I would get an Intő – what would my father have said! – but my lapses of concentration earned me poor marks in 'Behaviour'. On the other hand, my results in homework, tests and examinations were always excellent. A little joke about this survives in the family, deeply rooted in fact. If I took home a mark of 98% in any subject, my father never failed to ask me, gently but firmly: "What went wrong?" He was the centre of my universe, and he was satisfied with nothing short of perfection.

My teacher in the first two years was Judit néni, middle aged, smartly dressed, coolly intelligent, fair-minded. She understood the social dynamics of the class, and was sympathetic towards children, more than most adults of the age (except of course my father and my uncles). She did not go as far as deliberately making rich girls sit next to poor, or

Jews next to ardent Catholics, but tried to soften sharp divisions. I liked and respected her. She must have had a tough time, being an enlightened teacher in an increasingly intolerant country.

I don't remember the teacher of the third year, but my school record would show that I did well. On the other hand, the teacher of the fourth and final year of junior school remains memorable. I only just recently found a class photo with her the centre. I would never forget her cold grey eyes, her face with skin the colour and texture of dough, her dry grey hair in a mean little bun, her wobbly bottom in a shapeless grey skirt. I know her surname too: she came from a famous noble family, the spinster sister of a noted politician. We were meant to call her Jana néni, but that was irrelevant, because she gave me no chance ever to address her. She told us that she was in love with Hitler, whose pictures lined the walls. She made it clear that she did not like Jews, but even among Jews, she singled me out for special treatment. During the whole of that year she never asked me a question, never talked to me, never looked me in the face: ignored me, as though I did not exist. Today her treatment of me might be considered child abuse.

I did not understand the situation at the time, but looking back on it now, I can see that having me in her class would have been a real challenge for her. She firmly held to the ideology that Jews were a race of sub-humans to be despised; but she had a Jewish girl in her class who behaved well, was popular, and kept producing 100% or near-100% work, meeting or exceeding expectations.

That final year at junior school was a special challenge, spurring me on to do my best, not because of Jana néni's treatment of me, but because I was working for my

The author in 1942, Budapest. Photo by the author's uncle Laci.

Kaposi family collection

91

future. The country's anti-Jewish laws excluded most Jewish pupils from grammar school and higher education, and some over-zealous institutions went even further than the law's demands. The year before mine, the senior school in the other half of the building accepted just one Jewish girl. She had been the top of her class all along, just like I had been the top of mine, excelling in the last year, exceeding her own high standards. This paragon helpfully warned me that nothing less than a perfect school record would do: any flaw of a Jewish candidate's performance would be an excuse for refusing admission to the seniors. I worked like never before, conquered boredom and my fear of the ogre teacher, paid attention all the time, achieved straight top marks in all subjects, and won all the prizes. I too was a paragon, the undisputed star of the class. My picture, taken by uncle Laci, reflects my state of mind at that time.

How about the rest of the family?

We struggled to make ends meet, but for a while we managed. The right-wing government's anti-socialist policy had long since ruined my brilliant father's chances of a decent job, the anti-Jewish laws had already displaced the young professionals of our family and prevented Pici from graduating from the Academy of Music, but my mother still had her shop, earning a living for us all. Gradually matters got even worse. The men lost their mean little jobs, my father and Pista replaced delivery boys in my mother's shop, and in desperation, Feri embarked on a whole new enterprise.

What gave this young lawyer the idea to make bodies of fountain pens out of bakelite? How did he get the equipment? How did he acquire the skill? One day he installed a lathe in the already cramped gloomy room behind my mother's shop. He brought along big bunches of bakelite rods on his shoulder, cut them into appropriate lengths, turned them on the lathe inside and outside, polished them with ever-finer emery paper, and last of all with an oiled cloth until the variegated colours of the bakelite emerged and the pen bodies shone. He then cut into each piece a spiral, so that the body and the lid of the pen could be twisted together. I loved to watch, and was allowed to wrap the finished pieces in tissue paper, before packing them into boxes. Feri kept busy, but made almost no money. Then the war disrupted our lives altogether. In 1939 Feri was called up into the army as an officer, soon to be dismissed, but recalled to Military Labour Service in 1940 with my uncles and all other young Jewish men. Two years later my father and other Jews in their 40s and 50s were called up as well. Feri was already serving somewhere when his little daughter Éva was born in October 1941.

The author's cousin Stern Éva in 1943, Budapest

Kaposi family collection

92

My mother and Rózsi were the last members of our family who still had jobs, but finally even they were dismissed. Now we had no income at all. There was much crying, but for a while there was a bright side because, for the first time in my life, my mother was at home, and had time for me. We also had a lot of space, now that our two-roomed flat was the home of just the two of us. Our maid, all-purpose Bözsi, had long gone, the men were in the army. Terka, Pici and Éva were in Debrecen, sheltering with Nanóka whose shop was still open for a while. There was talk of my mother and me joining them, but I was at school, so we had to stay in Budapest. My parents had a few lengths of textiles from Nanóka's stock stored at the bottom of the cupboard, saved as investments, and my mother tried to sell those. We were not going hungry; we had a small stock of food preserved in the larder.

I was 10 years old. I was frightened, and had urgent questions for my father, but he was not there to answer them:

- We had no income. The drawer in the cupboard and the shelves in the larder were emptying fast. What would happen when they became empty?

- We heard of bombing of foreign cities. What does 'bombing' mean? Would Budapest also be bombed?

- We heard that the army was winning the war, moving ever deeper into Russia. When would they come back?

- Why was it that the more we heard that our army was winning the war, the more alarmed my mother seemed?

- My uncles, father, other Jewish men went to war without weapons, so they could not fight. If they were not fighting, why were they in the army? And if they were not fighting, why were some of them dying? Might my father and uncles soon be among the dead?

- People now hated the Jews more fiercely than ever before. Was any of it my fault?

Although most papers were full of hate and propaganda, the Esti Kurir, a liberal evening paper, was still published.[53] Its editorial office was near our home, on the next corner of Vilmos császár út. Pages were displayed on the outside wall of the editorial building, under a sheet of glass, even before the paper was distributed to the shops. I craned my neck among a small crowd of eager adults, trying to read the latest edition.

We also tried to get news from the radio. Hungarian and German stations were readily available, but they were full of hate and propaganda. In 1942 we still tried to tune to the BBC and Amerika Hangja, Voice of America, although reception was poor, the signal

---

53 *See HISTORIAN'S VOICE: Hungarian Press.*

usually blotted out by deliberate disturbance. It was also dangerous; listening to 'enemy' stations was 'treason'. We hid the radio under the duvet, burying our head alongside to avoid our fascist neighbour overhearing. By 1944, radios belonging to Jews were taken away.

Clutching at straws, trying to avoid anti-Jewish discrimination, some tried to convert to Christianity. Although godless, my family regarded such converts with disdain. There were lots of rumours, some of which I could not understand, such as the Germans rounding up unmarried young women, putting them into 'breeding camps' to replace personnel lost in the battlefields. It seemed safer for women to be married, but young male Jews were away, and the law forbade Jews marrying non-Jews. Young girls married old Jews, complete strangers whom they met for the first time at the registry office.[54] My beautiful 20-year-old second cousin Édi nominally married the elderly, bizarrely named Elefánt Herman.[55]

What happened to my schooling?

It was 1943. Having met all the requirements for admission, I confidently applied to the senior, grammar school section of my school at Szemere utca. Disaster struck. The school's reply was brief and to the point: I was rejected; the school was now a 'pure Aryan' institution. As a junior, I walked past the entrance of the senior school every day for four years. It was so near, and yet unreachably far.

My mother panicked, thinking that nothing could be done. My uncles, father and aunts were away, but Rózsi was there – intelligent, resourceful, and loyal, as always.

We never knew of the existence of a Jewish Girls Grammar School in Budapest. Rózsi tracked it down. We had no grounds to expect anything from that school; none of our family had been member of any synagogue, and we had no contact with the Jewish community. Now we learnt that it was a smart school, with excellent reputation. It used to be housed in beautiful buildings in elegant Abonyi utca, near the Városliget, but that had been requisitioned by the Hungarian army, so the Girls Grammar School had been shoehorned into the already overcrowded old Jewish Boys' Civic School in Wesselényi utca, the poorest school in a poor Jewish quarter of the city. The student populations of the two schools shared the shabby building. The only place available for first-year girls was the small school kitchen. It was packed with desks from wall to wall, people climbing over each other's desks to get to their places. The door was taken off its hinges and the whole space was occupied by desks, the teachers addressing their classes from the doorway. I was one of many able Jewish girls denied a place in a state grammar school, and parents from all over the city,

---

54   See *HISTORIAN'S VOICE: Rumours.*

55   Certain Jewish family names derived from the emblem of the family shop or workshop. In this case, 'Elephant' must have been the name of an inn or tavern owned by one of the ancestors of Herman Elefánt.

perhaps all over the country, were begging the school for a place for their daughters. My application was late, because we thought that I had a place in Szemere utca. There were 60 Jewish girls already enrolled in the first-year class in that little kitchen.[56]

Of course, I was refused. My mother just wrung her hands, but Rózsi swung into action as only she could, making a nuisance of herself everywhere, calling in favours, digging up old acquaintances, sending letters, sitting in people's waiting rooms. She found a girlhood friend, a beautiful Jewish actress who in her youth had been the sweetheart of Kosztolányi Dezső, a great Hungarian poet. She was now married to Szigeti Jenő, a mid-ranking Jewish actor. Jenő interviewed me and decided to do his bit for me. He concocted some pretence about the importance of my family, with bogus near-truths, such as my father being the protégé of senior Piarist priests, and the Csengeri family being wealthy landowners. He said we must never ask him what he said to the school and to leaders of the Jewish community, but the fact was that a week after the start of the school year, in September 1943, there were 61 girls in the school kitchen in Wesselényi utca, the new girl having to squeeze in third into a desk for two.[57]

I cannot remember learning anything at that school, but I recall being taught by a famous mathematician, and by Baracs Amália, a charismatic teacher of languages, whom I met decades later in London's Golders Green.

Most of all, I remember the warm feeling of making two friends at school. We visited each other in turn, having tea on Sunday afternoons. Like other mothers, my mother was with me; we too could serve tea in our flat, although it may have been some herbal concoction rather than tea. At last I had arrived on the social scene!

One of my newfound friends was dark-haired Hollós Éva. I met her again years later at University. We both became electrical engineers, we both married wonderful young men called Jancsi, and we four became good friends. Grünspan Zsuzsa was my other friend: thin, pale, and very clever. After the war, I attempted to find her, but never could.

And then yet again, as a few times before and many times after, just when things were bad but stable and almost pleasant, everything collapsed.

It was a sunny day in early spring, our turn to host the Sunday afternoon tea. Éva arrived with her mum, but Zsuzsa and her mother did not come. Then Concierge Mr Hajdu made one of his rare appearances on our doorstep, reporting that German troops were marching across Budapest. The date was 19th March 1944. It marks the end of my childhood. I was 11 years and 5 months old.

---

56   Civic school: Secondary school for those failing grammar school entry.

57   The school was still there 15 years ago, even more tatty than before. Jancsi and I visited it. By then, the kitchen had become a tiny surgery, and I was astonished to find that the school doctor was my erstwhile classmate beautiful Judit Borgida.

HISTORIAN'S VOICE

Hungarian press

The Esti Kurír (Evening Courier) *was a Budapest newspaper between 1923 and 1944. Edited by the prominent left-wing liberal politician Károly Rassay, it was very popular among the urban middle class, including many Jews. Surprisingly, despite its oppositional tone and the increasingly hostile political environment, it survived until the German invasion in March 1944, when it was banned and Rassay deported to a concentration camp.*

Most of the other politically 'undesirable' liberal and left-wing papers fell victim before the war to the right-wing Hungarian government's policy of oppressing intellectual and political life and silencing opposition. In June 1938, the government adopted a new press law, which required special state license for press products, and applied a 6% quota for Jewish participation in the press. These steps had both political and financial motivation: the pro-government press could get rid of most of their competitors.

Before World War I, the largest and most influential Hungarian newspapers belonged to the media portfolio of 'Est Lapok', established by the Jewish Andor Miklós, 'the Hungarian Robert Murdoch'. In 1939, the company was nationalised by financial machinations, and the papers of the portfolio were soon turned into right-wing mouthpieces. These developments had fatal consequences. From this time on, the bulk of the Hungarian population had access only to information provided by government media, characterised by an increasingly nationalistic and antisemitic tone. This is one of the explanations why most non-Jews in Hungary were indifferent to the persecution of their Jewish neighbours, or were hostile to Jews.

Rumours

The author here refers to an unsubstantiated rumour, based on news about 'Lebensborn', an infamous state-supported Nazi programme, aiming to enhance the birth rate of the so-called 'master race'. It forced mothers to give birth even to unwanted or illegitimate children, to be raised by Nazi families, thus producing racially and ideologically 'perfect' citizens. The Nazi worldview considered Jews as 'subhumans' (Untermensch), so they were not included in the Lebensborn programme. There was another rumour, which might indeed have induced some Jews to contract purely formal marriages. According to theis rumour, Jewish girls could have been dragged away for German military brothels.

The number of marriages actually increased at this time mostly because the wave of call-up summonses induced many young couples to confirm their relationships before parting to face an unforeseen future. Some wedding photos survive of smiling young couples wearing Stars of David.

5   CAMPS IN HUNGARY

Spring, 1944

For lucky people, camps are happy places: holiday camps, sports training camps, education camps. I relate my journey through several camps in Hungary and Austria. All of them were prisons.[58]

After the occupation of Hungary by the German army on Sunday 19th March 1944, we lived for a while in a series of camps. The first of these was Nanóka's beloved home in Debrecen, which became part of the ghetto, housing and imprisoning an increasing number of displaced people.

My father was not much of a soldier, half blind and suffering from a chronic and frequently bleeding stomach ulcer which in due course killed him. His Military Labour Service unit was garrisoned in a nameless corner of Hungary, and on the day of the German occupation he was at home on sick leave. This is how he survived. Our first miracle. After the war he searched for his former comrades, but found none of them.

My mother, a strong intelligent woman, usually panicked in a crisis, but this time she was calm. She recognised that the arrival of the Germans meant grave danger, and for her, danger meant that the family had to be together. Nanóka, Terka, Pici, tiny Éva and most of our extended family were in Debrecen. My mother was determined that we should join them without delay, taking Rózsi and Giza mama with us. Rózsi was like an older sister who sheltered my homeless parents when they first arrived in Budapest, started my mother on her path in business, and fought for my grammar school place.

My mother threw a few essentials into suitcases. My father took some valuables to Christian 'friends' for safekeeping. These possessions were lost forever. Meanwhile I ran to Rózsi to tell her that she and Giza mama must travel with us to Debrecen. I returned in tears, alone. My pleading was unheeded. Rózsi and Giza mama were adamant: they had to

---

58   See *HISTORIAN'S VOICE: Camps in Nazi time*

stay in Budapest, to await the return from the war of Rózsi's husband and son. Their men never returned from Military Labour Service, and Rózsi and Giza mama were shot into the river in Budapest.[59]

We started for Debrecen on the 20th March. The railway station was swarming with soldiers, police, travellers. Trains were packed, our identity papers were scrutinised again and again, my father's leave certificate examined. It turned out that this was the last day when Jews could still travel to Debrecen.

When my parents and I arrived, Nanóka, Pici, Terka and Éva received us with open arms. Now we were seven in Nanóka's little two-roomed flat which had neither bathroom nor toilet.

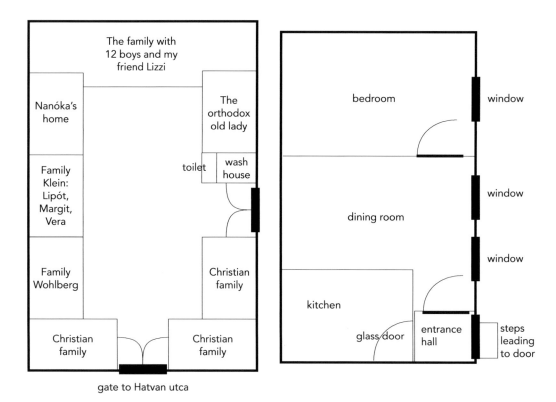

Floorplan of Nanóka's home, and the courtyard of the building, Debrecen, 42 Hatvan street

59   See *HISTORIAN'S VOICE: A paradox*

SCHOOL

It would have taken more than a world war to change my father's priorities. There was no Jewish girls' school in Debrecen, so the day after our arrival my father marched me to the Jewish Boys' Grammar School, and asked – nay, told! – the Headmaster to admit me. This was an outrageous idea, there had never been a girl student in that school before. My father was a shy and gentle man. How did he find the courage? Perhaps this Headmaster had once been one of his pupils at the Piarist school.

This school was a splendid institution, scholarly and patriotic, its very existence a tribute to the determination of Debrecen's Jewish community and the support of the city's liberally minded Protestant Bishop Baltazár. Teachers were erstwhile professors and other academics whom the anti-Jewish laws deprived of their university positions, so standards were extraordinarily high. School discipline was strict, and first-year boys – perhaps even older boys – were often caned, not viciously, but enough for them to resent it. A girl in the class was a novelty for boys and masters alike, all of them male. They called the boys by their surname, but they addressed 11-year-old me formally as Klein kisasszony, 'Miss' Klein. This was the only time anyone called me Miss.[60]

By the end of the week my classmates had enough of this sex discrimination. They gave me a caning. Not viciously, but enough for me to remember. Male pride was restored, I was now accepted.

School did not last long. In the words of Headmaster Kardos László, 'the school was killed in April 1944, one the most heroic and tragic incidents of the cultural history of Hungarian Jewry'. I remain the only girl ever to attend that school.

A SHRINKING WORLD

Eichmann wasted no time. A small section of his Sonderkommando arrived in Debrecen on Monday 20th March 1944. A handful of Germans was sufficient to mastermind the destruction of the Jewish community of Debrecen and district.[61]

Portrait of Szeszler Tamás and his little brother György in June 1944, Budapest.
Private collection of Georg Sessler

---

60   Béla Síró, *A debreceni zsidóság szellemi arcképéhez.* http://www.multesjovo.hu/hu/aitdownloadablefiles/download/aitfile/aitfile_id/1146/ (accessed 19 October, 2019)

61   See *HISTORIAN'S VOICE: Debrecen after German occupation*

None of our family were members of any synagogue, but neighbours told us that the Germans immediately imposed a Jewish Council to manipulate Debrecen's Jewish community. They entrusted leadership to Rabbi Weisz Pál. He was widely admired by Jews of the city; a scholarly man, an inspiring orator. The congregation learnt later that their beloved rabbi turned his newfound power to his own advantage.[62]

By governmental decree, from 5th April Jews had to wear a yellow star: colour, hue and size (10cm diameter) strictly specified.

At first, Jews appeared on the streets with limp scraps of yellow rags. The police chased them home, demanding regulation stars.

My father had taught me how to construct hexagons, using a compass. I cut six-pointed stars of the prescribed size out of thin cardboard. Next, Nanóka and I cut slightly larger stars of some yellow felt from her stock of textiles, and she and I tucked and sewed the felt around the cardboard. We made stars for each member of the family and sewed them to our outdoor clothing. Everyone admired our smart designs, and soon we were producing yellow stars by the dozen, the fruits of our labour freely available to all. These stars earned me a handsome sum decades later, when Nanóka, the real star of the star factory, was long dead. In London, in 2006, my mother was nearing the end of her life, suffering from dementia. One day a lady came from Britain's 'Jewish Care' organisation, asking how they might help. The lady was surprised to hear that my mother and I had been in the camps and asked whether we had worked in the ghetto. I said of course not. How did we spend our time, she wanted to know? When I mentioned making yellow stars, she perked up, asked a lot of questions, filled in a questionnaire, and told me to sign it: she knew of a German fund which 'compensated' Jews who worked in the ghetto. I received a cheque for some £800. Other survivors (although not my husband or I) had received 'restitution' money. Can a lost childhood be restituted? Can people be compensated for fear, pain, grief, degradation?

On 5th April, motor vehicles were confiscated, and telephones disconnected. This did not affect our family – we had neither cars nor phones – but soon a series of regulations followed, including restrictions to travel, or to visit pubs, restaurants or places of entertainment (who wanted to?).

Hostage-taking started in the first hours of the occupation and continued in the first half of April. First came rumours, but later we heard of prominent members of the community being taken away, among them the much admired Kardos Albert, founder of Debrecen's Jewish Boys Grammar School.

From 16th April, new decrees and bylaws appeared: confiscation of Jewish assets and property. Jews were ordered to deposit at specified collection centres their bicycles, radios, silver, jewellery, other valuables, military medals and uniforms, fur coats and

---

62   See *HISTORIAN'S VOICE: Debrecen's Jews on the Kasztner Train*

hats, hand-carts, grand pianos, electrical goods, ladders, tools, stainless steel pots, kitchen mortars and heavy metal objects. This prompted Nanóka to visit a few trusted Christian acquaintances: customers, business associates, erstwhile employees. They willingly agreed to save some of her jewellery, silver candlesticks, trays and cutlery, her fine china, her household linen and bales of textiles. In her orderly way, Nanóka listed what she left with whom, and guarded her list throughout our journey through the camps. She need not have bothered: she never saw a single item again.

Entrance door of a patisserie in Budapest, 1944
"It is strictly forbidden to bring dogs into these premises"
"In accordance with the Decree No. 300/1944 of the Ministry of the Interior, those obliged to wear the distinguishing yellow star may neither purchase nor consume products at this patisserie"
"We close at 7"
Courtesy of FORTEPAN/Tivadar Lissák

On 21st April, Jewish shops were closed by order. Some non-Jewish shops displayed placards such as:

ZSIDÓT NEM SZOLGÁLUNK KI!
WE DON'T SERVE JEWS!

Luckily our helper Boriska brought us food – for good money of course, paid by Nanóka. Her story is soon to come.

GHETTO

On 28th April, a governmental decree was issued on establishing ghettos over all of Hungary. The Mayor's Office was responsible for the operation in Debrecen. Ghetto boundaries were published.[63]

Debrecen ghetto
Hand drawn by László Csősz, based on the map of Anikó Gazda
(source: László Gerő, ed. *Magyarországi zsinagógák*. Budapest: Műszaki, 1989. 146.)

---

63   See *HISTORIAN'S VOICE: Ghettoisation in Debrecen*

102

On 9th May, a ghetto registration office was set up at the police station in Hatvan utca 23. There were two sections: a 'large' and a 'small' ghetto, divided by Nanóka's own street. Jews had six days to comply, to take up residence within the ghetto. Jews moved to the ghetto on 15th May, but until 6th June food could be brought in, post and messages could be passed, and a few Jews could still work outside, albeit under police guard.[64]

On 2nd June, Debrecen was bombed by the US air force. The ghetto area was not damaged, but to house citizens who became homeless, the small ghetto was cleared of Jews. On 7th June the ghetto was sealed tighter than a prison. Jews were locked in, and gentiles were shut out. No more post, no inflow of goods, no outflow of rubbish. How did Jews cope with medical emergency? The ghetto had plenty of doctors and nurses, but no hospitals, and no medical supplies.

Segment of the Debrecen ghetto fence. In the background: the building of the Jewish community.
Hungarian National Museum Historical Photo Department

---

64   I later heard that in this period distant members of the Csengeri family had the task of providing communication and supplying food for some inmates of the ghetto.

Just before the shutters came down, the post brought notification of the death of Pici's husband Pista. My father opened the envelope, and it was his task to give Pici the news. Pici's world collapsed; she lost her sparkle, she never recovered her vitality, her love of life, her natural easy charm. Part of her personality died, and those who did not know her before the war never realised what a jolly, vibrant person she had been. She told me years later that she never forgave my father for giving her news of Pista's death.

Some Jews lived outside the area which became the ghetto, and some gentiles had homes marked as ghetto, as in case of Nanóka's building. The swap-over was a complex multi-phase process.

Jews outside the ghetto had to leave their homes. The obedient majority carefully locked their doors, expecting soon to return. The local authority intended to transfer Jewish goods from these homes to municipal depots. Instead, looting started immediately. Others found it hard to leave their homes. We heard of suicides and frightening rumours of a family who hid in their cellar and, when discovered, were shot.

After Jewish homes outside the ghetto were vacated, gentiles who had lived in the ghetto area could move out. They had the choice of thousands of empty Jewish homes, but not all were happy. For example, the gentiles in Nanóka's building asked permission to remain in their homes. However, their request was refused.[65]

Following the air raid, on 3rd June the Small Ghetto was emptied of Jews and the area of the Large Ghetto was also reduced. The ghetto was already overcrowded, so many newly dispossessed Jews had to camp in makeshift tents in streets or courtyards. Nanóka's courtyard serves as an example.

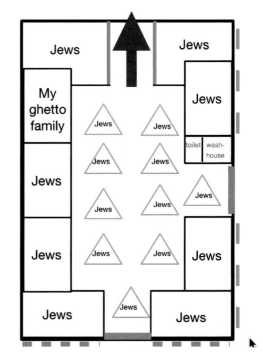

Nanóka's courtyard, Debrecen, 42 Hatvan street as ghetto in May-June 1944

---

65   The letter, along with other petitions of gentile residents to remain in their homes was filed by Debrecen's Mayoral office. National Archives of Hungary, Hajdú County Archives (MNL HBML) IV. B. 1406/b. 22730/1944.

Nanóka's building was on a corner, with both streets on the ghetto boundary. Since gates and windows facing the streets were boarded off, access for the Jews of the courtyard was by a path broken through the home of my friend Lizi.[66]

What happened to our family?

The first to arrive from another part of town was Terka's mother-in-law Máli néni. A silent, dignified lady in her 70s, she lived alone; her three married sons were in Military Labour Service in Ukraine. She turned up on Nanóka's doorstep, carrying a little bundle. Nanóka's little home was already overcrowded with seven of us, but of course we welcomed her, and this set the pattern.

Next came cousin Klári, with 3-year-old Gyurika in her arms. The picture captures the child's lovely smile but cannot do justice to his beautiful blue eyes. Klári's mother, my aunt Mariska, lived hundreds of miles away in Újpest, and would die in Auschwitz. Klári's husband never returned from Ukraine.

Left: Máli néni (Stern Mártonné)
Right: Our toddler Gyurika with mother Klári and grandmother Mariska
Kaposi family collection

My step-grandmother Szeréna also staggered in. Her sons were in Ukraine. In her mid-70s, she barely managed the walk from distant Cegléd utca. This might have been a chance to repay her cruelty to my father when a boy, but of course we took her in.

---

66   For further details see *HISTORIAN'S VOICE: Debrecen's Ghetto*

Ilus came last, holding 5-year-old Gabika by the hand. Just before leaving their home in smart Piac utca, the post brought news of the death of her husband in Military Labour Service. Ilus was too distraught to think of packing, so they arrived almost empty-handed. I will soon tell their story.

Now 13 of us were in Nanóka's little two-roomed flat. This is how our camp-time family became formed.

The grownups were crying, grieving, and anxious, but we were not yet hungry; Nanóka's larder fed us all, and I enjoyed not being an only child, now that I had a baby sister and two little brothers.

Name in story	Official name	Age
Szeréna	Klein Sámuelné	about 75
Máli néni	Stern Mártonné	over 70
Nanóka	Csengeri Dezsőné	about 60
my father	Klein Imre	43
Ilus	Dr Friedmann Imréné	34
my mother	Klein Imréné	32
Terka	Dr Stern Ferencné	30
Klári	Frankl Miklósné	29
Pici	Deutsch Istvánné	28
Agnes	Klein Aranka Ágnes	11
Gabika	Friedmann Gábor	5
Gyurika	Frankl György	3
Éva	Stern Éva	2

Our ghetto family, the Csengeri Clan

An innovation: Jewish Police appeared on the scene. Burly officious middle-aged men, veterans of World War I, wearing armbands, symbols of their office. They had two thankless tasks: to locate and hand over to the police at the ghetto gate nominated people, and to insert people into already overcrowded homes.

The ghetto was a silent place. No traffic, no children's laughter. I don't even recall arguments. The only sound was sobbing, perhaps because the father of a family had been taken away and returned bruised or failed to return at all. Then, suddenly, a brief respite: walking through a narrow alley, one day I heard wonderful piano playing. It had to be live music – Jews had no radios. Pici helped me to track down the pianist and the piece: Schneider Hédi was playing Bach's Italian Concerto. Hédi survived the war, and became a well-known concert pianist. I will always love the piece.

Uncertainty is a powerful psychological weapon. We had no information. There was an atmosphere of dread. Rumours had it that we were soon to leave, but when, and where? It was almost a relief when, on 16th June, the order came that in five days we would move from the ghetto, each person allowed to carry one item of luggage. Our destination was unspecified, but at least we now had a date.

Jews started to pack suitcases, bundling pillows and duvets into bedsheets. The picture could have been taken in Debrecen.

Nanóka foresaw that suitcases and bundles would not do, so she prepared her family's journey to the unknown in another way. She figured that our toddlers had to be carried, so adults' hands had to be free of luggage. She and Terka sewed for each adult and for me capacious rucksacks of stiff red and white striped canvas, originally meant for deckchair seats. Nanóka did not forget the grandmothers. She rolled blankets into sausages, filling each with soft items: towels and underwear. These neat packages were strapped up with belts or harnesses, such that each grandmother could carry a roll on her back.

Next, Nanóka packed our rucksacks. Overcoats would have been too bulky, and T-shirts, sweatshirts, or anoraks did not exist yet. So, she packed jackets, shirts, pullovers, cardigans, and shawls (how useful these proved to be!). There was a cap for my father and headscarves for the women, little children and me. She added other necessities: thread, needles and scissors, aluminium mugs, cutlery, a ladle (which soon proved a blessing), soap for washing ourselves, and kitchen soap for washing clothes. In went salt, sugar and some non-perishable foodstuffs, such as salamis and smoked sausages. There was also an enamel pot with a handle; blue outside, white inside. It was strong without being heavy, large enough to hold a ladleful of soup for each. At first the pot had a lid, soon lost. It was filled with roux (goose fat mixed with flour, lightly fried, basis for soups). This valuable asset of the whole family was entrusted to my rucksack.

Deportation of Jews from Dunaszerdahely, Hungary to Auschwitz-Birkenau, 15th June 1944
Memorial Museum of Hungarian Speaking Jewry, Courtesy of Rezső Steckler

I packed a small, thick notebook. Biros had not been invented and fountain pens would have been useless, but I had pencils, rubber and pencil sharpener. My plan to write a diary was not a secret, but it was my private project. Throughout our camp life I wrote into my diary most days, and then I lost it just before our journey home. I regret the loss to this day.

On 21st June, gates were broken open all along Hatvan utca, at the northern boundary of the ghetto, a fleet of horse-drawn carts, oxcarts and trucks lining the street. Like everyone else, I had heard of the brutality of gendarmes, but being a city girl, I never met a gendarme before. Here they came, an army of them, herding Jews onto the carts, shouting, cursing, wielding truncheons, kicking old people with hobnailed boots. The wisdom of my grandmother's planning was immediately apparent. Wearing our rucksacks, we could carry our toddlers and help our grannies. People thought our cheerful red and white rucksacks ridiculous, but we could hardly have managed without them then, and we would have been lost without them later when, weakened by malnutrition, we had to march for endless miles. Our family of 13, with three old ladies and four children, was not a very viable unit, but Nanóka's foresight helped 11 of us to survive.

Those rucksacks also taught me a lifelong lesson. During my professional life my employers provided me with travel by air or first-class train. I wore smart clothes and high heels, but I always carried a rucksack for essentials. Now that I am old and retired, the high heels are gone, but the rucksack remains, reminding me of my beloved Nanóka.

The line of carts, bearing the Jews with their pitiful bundles, started to move along Hatvan utca. A triumphant crowd jeered us along the way, some brandishing Arrow Cross insignia. The Jews in the carts were shocked, some in tears. They had expected sympathy from people of this Protestant city who had themselves experienced discrimination from Hungary's Catholic majority.

We also expected solidarity from Csermák Boriska. She was an attractive widow whom I had known all my life. Before she married a tenant farmer of a nearby village, Nanóka employed her occasionally to help with spring cleaning. She had been orphaned young, and Nanóka taught her domestic skills, supported her when her husband became a drunkard, helped her assemble her daughters' trousseau, gave her presents for family occasions, and even paid some of the funeral expenses when her husband died. Boriska's son took over the farm, Boriska herself selling the produce in Debrecen's farmers' market. When food became scarce, she brought us eggs, cheese, and butter. Nanóka paid her well. It was she who helped us with shopping when Jewish shops were shut, and Jews were no longer welcome in the shops of gentiles. Just before the ghetto was sealed, Nanóka asked Boriska if she would look after some valuables for us. Together, they repeatedly filled Boriska's basket, covering it with a crisp white cloth. Gently flirting with the police to divert attention from her enterprise, she smuggled out many of Nanóka's treasures. We admired her spirit. – Boriska was one of the first we noted on our way out from the ghetto. She stood by the roadside, waving a pair of my grandmother's silver candlesticks, shouting: 'Now these are mine!'

Until that day I loved my birthplace Debrecen; thought of it as home, an anchor in my native land. People sometimes refer to me as a *Hungarian* Jew. I always object. From a child, I was told that I was not Hungarian. Hungary had rejected me, and citizens of my native city even ruined the memory of my grandmother's home which had been my favourite place in the world.

COLLECTION CAMP

Our destination turned out to be the *Serly Brickyard,* on the western edge of the city. At the start of the war the brickyard stopped being operational, so it could serve as collection camp not just for the Jews of Debrecen, but also for neighbouring towns and villages. There was a railway line, some office buildings, an array of drying sheds, and an enormous yard. There were also latrines – I save my readers the details. I remember the place clearly and could draw the layout.

A few select Jews were housed in the office buildings. We thought they were the lucky ones, but those buildings proved airless and unbearably hot. We, the majority, were accommodated in the drying sheds: tiled roofs on stilts, without sides. There was also an overflow, people for whom there was only room in the open air, in the sun.

Women's hair was hacked off. When my beautiful blonde plaits were cut off, Terka cried. Gendarmes came with ever new demands, new threats and ever-increasing brutality. We had to stand for hours in the blazing sun, questioned about the hiding places of our money and gold (what money? what gold?). Well-to-do members of the community were taken away for interrogation again and again. They returned with bruises, injuries, signs of torture, and some failed to return. People were bodily searched for hidden valuables. When nobody had anything of value any more, gendarmes inflicted extra misery by taking away people's glasses, trampling them underfoot. My father and I wore glasses. I was young enough to adjust; I learned to read without them, but my father had only one working eye, and needed glasses of pebble thickness for the other. He was clumsy and accident-prone even *with* glasses. Without glasses he struggled and suffered many accidents. One of these almost cost him his life.

Our Ilus was one of those taken away for questioning. Her husband Friedmann Imre was the son of Nanóka's older sister Róza néni. Imre had been a successful Debrecen lawyer, my father's friend. His wife Rácz Ilus was a beautiful willowy woman, a famous porcelain designer whose china fetches good prices today on the internet.

A well-to-do couple, they had an elegant flat in the main street of Debrecen, their spacious rooms overlooking the street. This living area was linked by a corridor to workrooms in the back, housing Ilus's studio with kiln, drawing boards, and paints. Six young ladies sat at little tables in a line under the windows of the corridor, painting with thin brushes Ilus' designs onto ornamental bowls, vases, figurines and tableware. I loved to watch them at work. As a wedding present for my parents, Ilus made an exquisite black, red and gold coffee service. The paper-thin cups, lined with gold, are my favourites. In the picture one of the cups is upside-down, showing the marking of the porcelain, and Ilus' initials in gold. Miraculously, I still possess this sample of Ilus' art.

Left: Coffee service, wedding present for the author's parents made by Ilus.
Photo by the author, 2019.
Right: The author's mother's cousin Futó (Friedmann) Imre and his wife the artist Rácz Ilus.
Kaposi family collection

Ilus returned from the interrogation ordeal unharmed, but distressed. She had been offered an escape by train to Switzerland if she revealed the whereabouts of her hidden jewellery and valuables, paying the 'capitation fee' set by the gendarmes. She had the resources to pay for herself and her son, but not for the rest of the family. She asked my father's advice. My father said the decision must be hers alone, she must do what she thought best for her and her child. Ilus cried, hugged us, and returned to her interrogators to pay her dues.

With several other 'wealthy' Jews, Ilus and Gabika were taken out of the brickyard, and never seen again. We looked for them after the war, hoping that they might have been among the fortunate few who left the country with the rabbi's party. Not so. I loved all three members of this little family, and I have a picture of Imre and Ilus. No picture remains of Gabika.

Now our camp-time family was reduced to 11.

ENTRAINMENT

Deportation from the brickyard started on the 24th June. Daily, a train left the railway line by our drying sheds, most wagons bearing a plaque: *'6 horses or 40 men'*. Later I learnt that our train left on the 27th, with 3,842 people on board. It turned out that our destination was Auschwitz-Birkenau. 87 of us travelled for four days and five nights in a wagon like the one shown in this picture, without food, water, or the prescribed sanitation facilities.[67]

The first challenge was to get to the train. Jews struggled, crossing rail tracks, carrying their luggage and babies, propping up their old. Gendarmes divided us into groups, herding each group to a wagon. At first, they just yelled and cursed, but soon resorted to other measures. Did they think that a beaten or kicked Jew moved faster?

The next task was climbing into the wagon. There was no platform, and the steps were high.

There was crying and screaming; people pushed too hard from behind; many fell, some fainted.

Those who climbed up first sat down, but there was no room for everyone to sit. Gendarmes shoved more and more people into each wagon. Newcomers fell over or stepped on those sitting. People screamed. We thought matters would be better once we were all in the wagon. How wrong we were. It is not a cliché that conditions in the wagon were unbearable. Some could not bear it. Several went mad, and some died. That journey was the worst experience of my life.

---

67   See *HISTORIAN'S VOICE: Deportation*

Cattle car in Auschwitz Birkenau
Photo: Shutterstock

The sliding door of our wagon left a gap, the door chained and padlocked on the outside. That gap proved to be a great advantage for us, over my friend and others whose wagon door shut tight.

Now we were locked into our wagon. Chaos reigned. Someone took pity on the oldest members of our family, clearing room on the floor for Szeréna and Máli néni, who took Gyurika and Éva in their laps. The others, including Nanóka, stood.

Luggage and bundles had been thrown in at random. Once some semblance of order was created by placing the belongings of some families around the walls of the wagon, and once small children were put in adults' laps, there was just about enough room for everyone to sit. Those fortunate enough to be near the wall could lean against it. The rest had to lean against each other's hot sweaty bodies.

Being the youngest and the only able-bodied man, albeit half blind, everyone expected my father to take charge, sort out the mayhem. This was bad luck for our family, and foreshadowed later events. My father did take charge calmly, weighing up needs, asking people to move so that adjacent places could be occupied by members of a family. He was dignified and obviously fair, so nobody argued, but I was quietly fuming. Why was

112

our family the last to be considered, why did he allocate others to good places around the walls, leaving for us the worst? I did not ask, he did not explain, but he expected me to understand that this is what any honest leader would do.

JOURNEY

At last, for a short while, the exhausted Jews were at rest. We were relieved when the train began to move.

This was the continental summer; the outside temperature must have been well above 30°C. The air inside the wagon was hotter, and so dry that breathing hurt the throat. We still had food in our bags, but nobody could eat. Nanóka had brought along some water, but the supply was soon exhausted. When the train stopped at a station, as it often did, we begged for water through the gap in the door, but nobody responded. Someone had the idea of bending the iron bars over the window so that 'water beggars' could hold out a cup to a pipe which dribbled distilled water, intended for the steam engine of the train. This required people hoisting up to the window someone strong enough to bend the bars. Jews were unwilling to collaborate, but when the enterprise succeeded, I was the one whose hand was small enough to poke through between the bars. Only once was I lucky enough to capture a few drops of water intended for the steam engine.

There was an oil drum in the wagon, stood on its end, near the door. The top end of the drum had been hacked off, so a person could perch on the edge. That was the toilet. There were problems. People were shy to do their business in view of 86 others. The old could not squat over the thin high rim of the drum; they stood on nearby luggage, but owners objected. A pedestal had to be improvised.

The next problem was getting to the drum. People had to climb over each other, disturbing those who had escaped into sleep. Jews started to bicker again, and my father became very busy trying to cool tempers and maintain the peace.

As the drum filled up, it smelled worse and worse. Least fortunate were those near the drum, like our family. A worse problem than the smell was that, after a day, the drum was almost full, threatening to overflow. Who but Nanóka would find a solution? She fished out our ladle from someone's rucksack. My father organised a rota, with somebody standing by the door, ladling out the contents of the drum through the gap. My father took the first turn, and thereafter nobody objected to doing their duty. He exempted the old and the children and, since I was still a child, I never had to perform drum duty. You think we had a hard time with this toilet business? Imagine other wagons, where the door was shut tight, without a gap through which to ladle out the s... and also, probably, no ladle either…

Night followed day and day came after night, again and again, so we could count the passage of time. The train was moving sometimes, we had no idea where, but it was clear which end of the wagon was towards the direction of travel. That is how we knew that our train travelled one way for three nights and two days, and then the direction was reversed; what had been the front became the rear. We moved in this new direction for two nights and two days.

As I understand it, ours was the only deportation train that departed from Debrecen and did not reach Auschwitz, its initial destination. The changes of directions made the difference between life and death for the grannies and children of our family. It is a 'miracle' that my family of 11 survived that hellish journey of five nights and four days, and the ordeal that followed. Had Ilus and Gabika not been tricked by Debrecen's gendarmes, they might have survived with us.[68]

HISTORIAN'S VOICE

Camps in Nazi times

According to the estimate of the US Holocaust Memorial Museum's experts, Nazi Germany and its allies established more than 42,000 camps and other incarceration sites between 1933 and 1945.[69] Here is a classification, by function.

- **Internment camps** *were detention facilities run by the police or the military, where foreign citizens, refugees or political prisoners were confined. About a dozen major internment camps already operated in Hungary before the war. After the Nazi occupation in March 1944, new internment camps were established throughout Hungary, primarily for Jews whom the German authorities started to arrest within hours of the invasion. During the mass deportations of later months, Hungary's internment camps were emptied, and their inmates were deported to Auschwitz.*

- **Labour service camps**, *or briefly 'labour camps' were for unarmed military labour service personnel in the Hungarian army.[70]*

- **Ghettos** *were designated neighbourhoods, separate streets or individual houses isolating the Jews of a city or a region.*

---

68   See *HISTORIAN'S VOICE: Survival*

69   USHMM Holocaust Encyclopedia https://www.ushmm.org/wlc/en/article.php?ModuleId=10005144

70   See *HISTORIAN'S VOICE* in Chapter 2: *Military Labour Service in Hungary*

- *Collection camps* or *transit camps* were makeshift temporary detention facilities set up in disused industrial or agricultural establishments, such as farms, brickyards or lumberyards. They were situated in the outskirts of towns, and equipped with railway lines, suited to entrainment and deportation of victims to Auschwitz or other camps. In some cases, victims were taken directly to these camps from their homes, but more often they were first forced into ghettos, and then several ghettos were emptied into collection camps.

- *Concentration camps:* the concept goes back to the period before World War I, when colonial powers used these kinds of facilities for detaining political enemies or displaced members of the indigenous population. One of the earliest examples are camps operated by British Forces during the Boer War in early 20th century. German Nazis established the first 'Konzentrationslager' right after taking power in 1933, confining their political enemies, but soon such camps were used for imprisoning various elements of society not fitting into Nazi worldview: 'undesirables', such as the disabled, homosexuals and various ethnic, religious and 'racial' groups, primarily Jews.

- *Forced labour camps* or *slave labour camps* were camps, where inmates had to perform hard physical labour in mines, constructions sites, factories, farms or branches of the war industry, generally under grave living and working conditions and inhumane treatment. Certain camps were situated at the workplace, but in many cases, prisoners were in 'Aussenlagers', taken or marched to work on a daily basis.

- *Distribution camps* (Durchgangslager) were transit camps for receiving transports of deportees, and after a short period of time transferring them to slave labour camps. Strasshof in Lower Austria was the most important such camp for transports arriving from Hungary in 1944.

- *Death camps* or *extermination camps* were designed for the sole purpose of systematic and industrialised killing of people. Belsec, Chelmno, Sobibór, and Treblinka (in Nazi-occupied Poland) were such camps, where all the victims were gassed or otherwise murdered upon arrival.

- *Mixed category camps.* Several camps served multiple functions. Among these was Auschwitz-Birkenau, the main destination of the Hungarian Jews. Arrivals underwent a selection process on the infamous railway platform, the 'Judenramp'. An estimated 20 to 30%, declared fit to work by SS physicians, were taken to forced labour, and the rest, mostly the elderly, sick, mothers and children, were gassed right away. Labourers were distributed among surrounding farms and industrial enterprises, many being worked to death, or dying later of starvation.

A paradox

Agnes, the narrator of this story, survived in the provinces. Rózsi was murdered in Budapest. Paradoxically and tragically, the larger picture was quite the opposite: those in the provinces had much less chance of survival than the Jews of Budapest.

Debrecen after the German occupation

Eichmann's right-hand man in Debrecen was SS captain Siegfried Seidl, who later also gained notoriety as commander of the Theresienstadt ghetto. He quartered himself in the luxurious apartments of the Arany Bika hotel in the main square, near the Jewish quarter. His forces would arrest quite a few potential resistors or the politically unreliable, primarily Jews, and would take other 'preemptive measures' of control and intimidation. By early April 1944, hundreds of prominent Jews – community leaders, businessmen and intellectuals from Debrecen's military district of three counties – were taken to a makeshift internment camp in Szentgyörgypuszta, near Debrecen. They were subjected to forced interrogation, even torture, with the main purpose to extort as much money and valuables from the victims as possible.

Next, Nazi and Hungarian authorities established Debrecen's Jewish council to implement orders and enforce restrictive measures against the Jews. This unwanted and tragic task fell upon Pál Weisz, the rabbi of the Status Quo congregation.[71]

Debrecen's Jews on the Kasztner Train

Debrecen's Jews chosen to be rescued on Kasztner's train included Rabbi Pál Weisz and other leaders, as well as local Zionists and prominent figures of the community, such as wrestling champion Károly Kárpáti, gold medalist of the Berlin Olympics, who infuriated Hitler by defeating a German rival, and Mór Mannheim, teacher of the local Jewish secondary school, who was the author of the first modern Hebrew textbook and dictionary. Together with family members, the privileged group included 357 people.[72]

Ghettoisation in Debrecen

The ghettoisation meeting ordered by the Ministry of the Interior took place in the city hall on 8th May 1944. Debrecen's conservative mayor, Sándor Kölcsey, did not oppose the measures, but was trying to achieve relatively more humane arrangements for the inmates, including larger living space, freer movement, and avoidance of sealing the ghetto. However, the radical right-winger Lajos

---

71   HISTORIAN'S VOICE on the Holocaust in Debrecen is based on archival research in the following record groups: National Archives of Hungary, Hajdú County Archives (MNL HBML) IV. B. 901; IV.B. 1406; VI. 4; XXV. 1.; XXV. 22.

72   See also HISTORIAN'S VOICE in Chapter 3: The Kasztner train

Bessenyei, former director of the Calvinist secondary school, freshly appointed Prefect of Hajdú County and Debrecen by the pro-Nazi government, insisted on adhering fully to the Ministry's harsh directives. A debate followed, involving even more radical propositions, such as the total relocation of Jews outside of town, leading to a decision that the ghetto for Debrecen's 7500 Jews should be set up south-west of the city centre.

The historical process of Jewish integration was reversed. Jews were pushed back into the historical quarter with its outdated 19th-century buildings where they had first settled a hundred years before. By the 20th century, most middle-class Jews had moved to modern apartments in the main square and along the major roads where the new synagogue was also built, leaving the old quarter to Orthodox and Hasidic Jews. In 1944, all Jews were back in the old ghetto. The centre of Debrecen became 'free of Jews' (Judenrein).

The 'large ghetto', bordered by Hatvan, Széchényi and Szepességi streets, included two old synagogues, and had some 50% of the homes in Jewish hands. Another designated area, the 'small ghetto', lay between Hatvan and Csokonai streets, engulfing most of the Hasidic homes and prayer rooms.

Local designers adhered to the principle that the ghetto quarter should avoid busy junctions, major routes and public buildings, so as not to hinder city traffic and day-to-day life. 'Moral' considerations were also taken into account: churches and educational institutions were excluded from the ghetto area, and even from the very sight of the ghetto. That is why the border of the ghetto was carefully 'gerrymandered', leaving out public buildings, such as the school at the corner of Reáltanoda and Hatvan streets. Initially, 4 square metres of living space was to be allowed for each person in the ghetto: three to four people sharing a room.[73]

In the morning of 2nd June, the US Air Force attacked Debrecen. This proved to be one of the deadliest air raids in wartime Hungary. At least 120 people died, hundreds were severely injured, close to 300 buildings were totally destroyed, and hundreds more were damaged, some 5000 people becoming homeless. The bombing primarily aimed to destroy the railway station and the industrial area in the southern part of the city, so the city centre, including the ghetto, was spared. After the air raid, Jews from the ghetto were forcibly taken to collect the corpses and clear up the rubble. To ease the housing problem, the 'small ghetto' was liquidated, its Jewish inmates were crammed into the large ghetto, and the living space allowance of Jews was reduced.[74]

73   Vági–Csősz–Kádár, *Evolution of a Genocide*, 84-87.
74   National Archives of Hungary, Hajdú County Archives (MNL HBML) IV. B. 1406/e. 153/1944., XXXV. 1. F.

Debrecen's Ghetto

Debrecen's local authorities treated the Jews in a relatively humane way, compared with more brutal methods elsewhere. At first, the ghetto was not strictly fenced in, and Jews were allowed to move in and out. However, soon pro-Nazi central authorities forced their local subordinates to close off the ghetto and impose strict regulations. Only a few had special permission to leave the ghetto for performing forced labour or other important duties. Non-Jews were forbidden to enter the ghetto. All the professional, cultural and personal bonds linking Jews and non-Jews were cut. Local police guarded the ghetto from the outside. A Jewish police force, armed with batons, was recruited from veterans of World War I. This body was under the command of a decorated lieutenant.

In the crowded ghetto nobody had any privacy. 10-12 or even more people were forced to share one room, washing or dressing behind makeshift panels. Shortage of food soon worsened the situation, since most ghetto inmates had only brought with them provisions for a week or two. The mayor's office failed to provide the necessary resources; instead, neighbours shared, and the Jewish community tried to offer support.

The government seized nearly all Jewish property, regarding it 'national wealth'. Local police and gendarmerie were ordered by the Ministry of the Interior to find hidden assets of Jews by conducting body cavity searches and interrogations under torture. Despite the risk of punishment, several non-Jews hid valuables or took property for safeguarding. Some did so for altruistic reasons, some in exchange of money or services, but some out of sheer greed. Most assets taken by non-Jews were pilfered or were destroyed in the war, and very few survivors would get back their private belongings.

Transit camp in Debrecen

The Jews of Debrecen and Hajdú county spent about one month in the ghetto. On 16th June, Hungarian authorities began transferring inhabitants of the ghettos of the district to a central collection camp in the Serly brickyard in the outskirts of Debrecen. Liquidation of ghettos was preceded by an administrative meeting in each of the six deportation zones in Hungary. The leaders of county and city administration and law enforcement commanders from a particular region were all required to join these meetings, where they received instructions from the representatives of the Ministry of the Interior and Eichmann's Sondereinsatzkommando. State Secretary László Endre outlined the details of the deportation. On average, the trains would consist of 45 cattle cars, into each of which 70 Jews had to be crammed. Each cattle car had a bucket of water and an empty bucket for the deportees' bodily needs. For the journey, the local public administration had to secure a two-day ration of bread, that is, 80 dekagram (1.76 pounds) per person. The doors of the cattle cars had to be locked with a chain.

According to an administrative report, a total of 13,084 people, 7411 of them from the city and 5673 from other Hajdú County ghettos, were crammed into the transit camp in Debrecen. A few Jews could find shelter in the buildings of the brickyard; most were forced to stay in the open, or in *drying sheds without walls. The camp lacked even basic sanitary facilities, except for some makeshift latrines. The scarcity of water and food supplies made the situation barely tolerable after one or two days.*

A gendarmerie cadet detachment from another city marched into Debrecen to round up the Jews and guard the collection camp. Unlike most of the policemen in Debrecen, these young men, affected by wartime propaganda and anti-Jewish sentiments, and not influenced by connections to local Jews they had not known, usually handled the Jews in the transit camp mercilessly. They would beat people with rubber batons, and routinely robbed and humiliated their victims. For example, they would force middle-class Jewish women to clean the latrines and demand elderly men to salute them. The Germans closely supervised the process, but they left the task of guarding the camp to the Hungarians, apart from a handful of SS-privates patrolling the gates. For several days a special inspection team of the gendarmerie brutally interrogated and tortured Jews who were accused of trying to hide their personal belongings sequestered by the state. The inspectors combined medieval methods and modern technology: they would beat the soles of people hung upside down (a technique used under the Ottoman occupation) and would send electric currents through their bodies. Some Jews were killed during these actions or committed suicide.

Deportation

The victims were deported from Debrecen between June 25th and 28th, 1944. Sources concerning the number of transports and the people in them are inconsistent. The intended destination of the transports was the extermination camp at Auschwitz-Birkenau. However, about half of the victims, close to 7000, escaped this fate, and were sent to labour camps in Austria. Methods of deportation were cruel. Theoretically, the nationwide conferences regarding administrative preparations for deportation of Jews specified mayors' responsibilities: providing food, water and sanitation facilities for deportees. In practice, 70 or more people were crammed into overheated boxcars without any food and adequate water. Several children and elderly people died during two to four-day long journeys. In Auschwitz-Birkenau, most of the deportees were declared unfit to work, and were murdered in gas chambers upon arrival. People selected for work, mostly young women, were sent to various forced labour camps, where many of them also perished under inhumane treatment.

In the labour camps in Austria, the chances of survival were much higher. Many fell victim to bomb raids, illnesses, hardships, and sporadic executions, but they were not systematically killed. That is why a larger proportion of Jews of Eastern Hungary, including the regions of Debrecen, Szeged and Szolnok, survived the Holocaust, compared to other Jews of the provinces.

Survival

About half of Debrecen's Jewish women, children and older men survived the Holocaust.

As discussed before, most young and middle-aged Jewish men had been drafted for labour service before or right after ghettoisation, and therefore they were spared deportation to Auschwitz or Strasshof. However, their lives were still at stake: many of them fell victim to the events of war or antisemitic violence. Here is an example.

Right before the Soviet occupation of Debrecen, some groups of labour servicemen were trying to hide, unwilling to leave the city with the retreating German and Hungarian troops. One of these groups, composed of Jews from Debrecen and the surrounding region, was reported by a non-Jewish neighbour. As a result, on 13th October 1944, Nazi soldiers and Hungarian field gendarmes arrested and executed 60 people at the Apafa shooting range in the outskirts of the city. One week later, surviving labour servicemen could walk freely on the war-damaged streets of Debrecen.

After the war, Debrecen had a Jewish community of 4500, including Jews who subsequently moved to the city. Many of them moved to Budapest, or left the country in the late 1940s and after the Hungarian uprising of 1956, for the newly-established state of Israel, the United States, and Western Europe. Today about a thousand Jews live in Debrecen, making it the second largest Jewish community in Hungary.

6 CAMPS IN AUSTRIA

1944 - 1945

STRASSHOF

Our train stopped, as it had done countless times through our interminable journey. Four days and five nights with almost no water. People were dazed. Some were raving. I thought I was hallucinating when the wagon door opened. Someone barked: *wie viele Tote?!* How many dead?! A relief: we were not in Hungary anymore. In our wagon there were two dead.

Where were we? We learnt later that this was Strasshof, near Vienna. I recently visited Auschwitz-Birkenau and found it similar to Strasshof in many ways. Both were large camps divided into sections, surrounded by electrified barbed wire at high voltage. Both had armed guards, and long narrow makeshift buildings arranged in a matrix, tightly packed with two- or three-layered bunks. Both had a railway line, but here was the difference: Strasshof was a transit camp, with the railway running through. Auschwitz-Birkenau was essentially a death camp where the railway line terminated.[75]

It turned out that deportation trains bearing 'Jews on ice' (those used for slave labour, pending exchange negotiations between the Germans and the Allies) were sent to Strasshof from Szeged, Szolnok and Debrecen, as shown on the map. As far as I can ascertain, ours was the only train originally destined for Auschwitz, but diverted midway, eventually arriving in Strasshof. Esther Farbstein quotes from a rabbi's arrival in Strasshof:

> 'There were eighty-seven in my wagon [from Debrecen to Strasshof]. The wagon was locked from the outside on Monday evening, and on Thursday *at 10am* we reached Strasshof, near Vienna. Thus, we travelled without food and water, and in every wagon people died of *starvation*, thirst, and the tremendous crowding, and many went out of their minds with anguish ... Towards evening, we entered the camp. On Friday, evil Ukrainian guards there, may their names be obliterated, came to the barracks and beat Jews with sticks to make everyone go to the bathhouse.'[76]

---

75   See *HISTORIAN'S VOICE* in Chapter 5: *Camps in Nazi Times*

76   Esther Farbstein, *The Forgotten Memoirs: Moving Personal Accounts from Rabbis who Survived the Holocaust*. New York: Shaar Press, 2011.

The rabbi's journey took three days; it was shorter than ours. He must have been on the train that went directly to Strasshof. Even so, we shared much of the rabbi's experience of the journey: thirst, hunger, overcrowding, madness and death. He may have been too delicate to mention the hellish sanitation. However, I query some of the rabbi's details, marked in *italics*. He could not know the time of arrival; no Jew had a watch. Some staff were Germans, but the guards were not. Nobody died of starvation – dehydration kills first. In my experience guards were brutish, wielded batons and roared in inhuman voices, but I don't recall beatings.

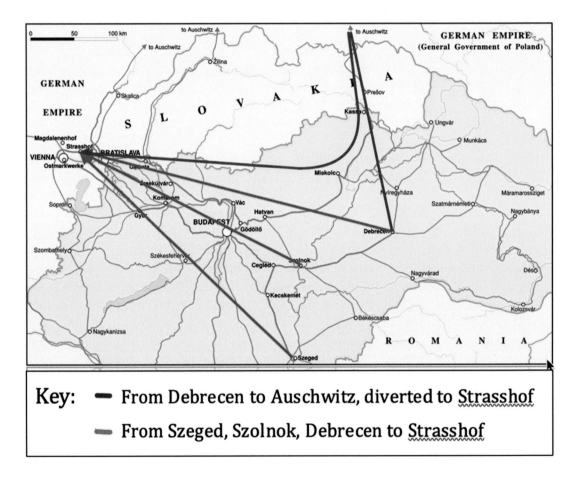

Key: ━ From Debrecen to Auschwitz, diverted to Strasshof
     ━ From Szeged, Szolnok, Debrecen to Strasshof

And another quote:

> 'In the Strasshof camp, law and order was enforced by Ukrainians. They gained this distinction by voluntarily joining the German army as it advanced through their country and following the army in its retreat. ... The intellectual level of these people does not compare with that of any human being. Their incessant roaring spelt

constant danger, and their hooked truncheons symbolised their power over us. They used this weapon frequently, whenever we failed to read their minds and did not do as they wished. What they usually demanded were items of our meagre clothing, including the headscarves of women.'[77]

Here is what I remember.

On arrival, we climbed out of the wagon in blazing sunlight. Seeking shade, Terka climbed under the wagon with Éva in her arms. My father dragged them out in a blind panic. In a few moments the train pulled away.

Next, men and women were separated. There were no young men, and children were with the women, so the women's group was much larger. A short distance from the railway line stood a complex of interlinked cavernous barracks. I don't recall us being given any food or water.

We had to strip naked. The staff in charge were uniformed men. Parading in front of a succession of men was distressing for everyone, particularly for religious women, brought up always to cover their head and most of their body in the presence of men. These women were violated in their humanity and in their beliefs.

Our dazed crowd was shunted along all day and all night by taciturn guards who subjected us to a relentless process.

At the first stage, groups of about a hundred were pushed into a room with a matrix of showers overhead. I realised years later that this resembled the gas chambers of extermination camps, but here soap and warm water were dispensed. Afterwards, guards rubbed us down with harsh disinfectant, paying particular attention to any part with hair. We continued naked.

Next, several parallel registration queues were formed. Uniformed guards at trestle tables shoved a long questionnaire before us, in German. Pici was mandated to interpret; meanwhile the rest of us were jerked along, anxious lest we lose touch with her.

We were photographed, fingerprinted, weighed, measured. Height, vital statistics, even shoe size was recorded, and a sequence of operatives took our blood pressure, registered our blood type, and examined us in various ways, some quite distressing. We were also given a card with our 'designation number'. I lost mine, but here is the card of my friend Gábor, who felt that replacing our name with a number was part of the process of stripping away our humanity.

---

77   Memoirs of Rabbi Zwi Kohn of Derecske. Quoted in Szita, *Utak a pokolból*, 44.

Strasshof identity card of Lefkovics (Lacko) Gabor
Courtesy of Mr G Lacko

Many fainted during this routine. I was in a haze, my high temperature duly recorded. In my feverish state naked old women with wrinkled faces, sagging breasts and bloated bellies appeared as terrifying witches. They haunted my dreams for years. Whatever caused my fever, by the next morning it was gone. Throughout our camp days I was briefly ill on this and on two other occasions.

The process was brutal, but it was sensible. After our nightmare journey we were filthy, perhaps even diseased. We needed to be examined, our bodies and clothes washed and disinfected. Arriving in a country of which we were not citizens, we had to be registered and our details recorded. If only women had administered to us rather than uniformed men; if only they treated us as human beings.

At sunrise it was all over. At the last barracks our disinfected clothes were waiting in neat bundles. When the doors opened, there stood our men. My father had been almost out of his mind. Years later he told me that through his secret contacts with socialists, he had known about the extermination camps, and thought he would never see us again.

Our barracks had three layers of bunks. Food was tasteless brown bread and *Dörrgemüse*, a foul-smelling soup of dried vegetables. None of us would ever forget it.

Compounds for different kinds of prisoners were divided by barbed wire fencing, but only the outer boundary was at high voltage. Adjacent to us were prisoners of war. They were willing to be friendly, but we had no language in common. German, French, English, even Greek failed. At his wit's end, my father thought of trying Latin. This got them going: they were Italians. Pici also became involved. With goodwill, the two sides understood each other.

Our new friends told us that this place was called Strasshof, it was near Vienna, and the guards, Ukrainians, were brutal. When they saw our toddlers ('bambini!') they smiled and poked a few pieces of edible bread across the wire. It had been a long time since we saw anyone smile.

We now had a clue about our whereabouts, but we still had no idea why we were there, or what would happen next.

By sunset on our second day, I gathered enough courage to wander to the edge of our compound. Before me stretched a meadow, a carpet of poppies. I thought I had never seen anything so beautiful. It made me think of beautiful and ugly things, of good people and bad. How some people were cruel and mean, how my father was fair and generous. I thought it was good that I loved my family and would do my best for them, but it was bad that I was jealous of fellow victims, envying anyone who had a bite more food, or a better place in the barracks. I thought that next time I felt mean and jealous, thinking of this beautiful poppy field might overcome my bad feelings of jealousy so that I could be less like those cruel people and more like my father.

Were these naïve thoughts? I was only eleven.

After a few days, loudhailers started to howl that 50 Jews were needed for working in a flour mill, 200 should volunteer for metal work, 90 for building work, etc. Seeing how bewildered I was, my father addressed me almost as before. Reasonable, he said: the war had deprived Germans of their workforce, so they needed labourers. It had been like this towards the end of World War I, when the harvest was rotting on the stem while people were starving, factories stood idle while shops lacked goods, and armies were short of weapons and ammunition. He discussed it with Nanóka; they agreed that agricultural work seemed better than factory work –we would have fresh air and might be nearer to food.

Did we choose or were we press-ganged? With some 40 others, next day we found ourselves on an open truck, travelling to a farm. It was a short journey. It was also a terrible choice. Farm work almost broke us.

MAGDALENENHOF: WE ARE FARMERS

Our truck drove through featureless countryside. Climbing a hill, it deposited us in a farmyard at the foot of an enormous metal structure.

Bisamberg is not much of a *Berg* (mountain), only lying 190 m above sea level, but it is the highest spot in the Vienna district. Magdalenenhof was the largest farm of Lower Austria, state owned. For almost half a year we worked on that farm, and 'camped' in the farmyard. Adjacent to the farmyard, a huge radio transmitter tower dominated the landscape, visible from miles away, surrounded by barbed wire and guarded by soldiers. Some fifteen kilometres north of Vienna, today Bisamberg is a busy market town, and Magdalenenhof is a smart hotel/restaurant.

I thought I had a sound memory of the farmyard and its transmitter tower. My confidence was shaken when the satellite map showed no trace of that tower. Did I fall at an early hurdle of writing this story? Perhaps I was not a fit chronicler; after all, events occurred three quarter of a century ago, and I was only 11 at the time.

Near the point of giving up, I found a clue: the street running east-west on top of the map was called *Senderstrasse,* Transmitter Street. Investigating the history of radio broadcasting in Austria, I found that Lower Austria's medium-wave transmitter *used* to be located at Bisamberg, but the withdrawing German army blew up the transmitter station and its mast on the 13th April 1945.

The farm Magdalenenhof at Bisamberg, with its medium-wave transmitter towers in 1940.
Picture postcard. Private collection of László Csősz.

So far, I have only found record of Szita mentioning our camp. His brief outline of Magdalenenhof mostly agrees with my experience. Magdalenenhof was a large state-owned mixed farm with arable land stretching from its hilltop farmyard in three directions. Crops included cereals, corn, and vegetables, but the farm also had cultivated forests and famous vineyards. There were silos and grain stores nearby, and caves, used as wine cellars.

Our hayloft home was crowded, and the roof was so low that even I could not stand up. We slept on straw which soon turned to dust. There were cockroaches, mice and rats. The hayloft protected us from the rain, but it was stiflingly hot in the summer, damp and severely cold in late autumn. We were concerned about our old and young, who stayed in the hayloft all day while the adults were at work.

At first there was no electricity in our hayloft and, because of fire risk, candles were not permitted. This made life difficult for workers who started out in the dark and returned in the dark. After some weeks we discovered that there was an electric cable, and at our request a dim lightbulb was dangled from the ceiling. How privileged we felt!

Washing was difficult. The 'washroom' had only a couple of cold-water taps. It was too dark to wash before work, and we were too exhausted to wash after. There were a few showers, but they rarely worked, and almost never had hot water. One never knew when the showers might come to life, or when the water might stop suddenly. Nanóka washed our clothes in the daytime while the adults were at work. We came in for plenty of mocking from the Kohn family, our fellow inmates: 'The snooty/posh/stuck-up Csengeris are washing their hair/underwear/shirts/babies again!'

My memory about some of our fellow travellers is vague, but some notable people are etched in my memory.

The Schwartz family, headed by Nanóka's sister Irén néni, had seven members: one granny, four adults (including uncle Lipót) and two children: Vera the Menace, and Gabi, a sickly boy aged six.

The Székely family of four, all tall and strikingly good-looking, comprised mother Elza, about 50, son László, 20, teenager Magda, and my 'uncle' Jani's wife Manci, 25.

The religious and malevolent Kohn family of six, all adults, constantly bickering among themselves, and picking quarrels with others.

Other families, with four children between them, all younger than me.

Máli néni had two daughters-in-law in the camp: Terka and Székely Manci. If she joined the Székelys, she would have had four adults to support her, whereas our family had five adults to look after three grannies and three children. The matter never arose; Máli néni belonged to us, member of the Csengeri Clan.

On arrival, we were told that this was a work camp: those who worked hard would be treated well and given food; those who didn't work would do without. In fact, nobody was treated well. People worked until they dropped, food rations were small, the food was always poor and sometimes inedible. People were perpetually hungry, everyone lost weight, women stopped menstruating, what hair they had fell out. Families with children and grandparents had the toughest time, having to share working members' food rations. From this viewpoint, our situation was worst. I suggested that we claim that I was not 11 but 14, the official working age. The others objected a bit but gave in readily enough. The farm administrators had our personal details, they must have known that we lied about my age, but labour was scarce; this gave them another pair of hands, and it gave us an extra portion of food. Throughout our stay at Magdalenenhof, I worked as an adult. Nobody made any concession for me, and I expected none.

Life was harsh. Many people behaved shamefully; hurled abuse at each other, stole from fellow inmates, took advantage if they could. Age, education and social status were not deciding factors in determining conduct. There will be an example later of a child acting heroically, whereas a distinguished medical professor abandoned human and ethical standards, selling his soul for a mess of potage. I now understand that great stress can make people aggressive, intolerant, and might even cause serious illness, such as heart disease or diabetes.

Sometimes I envied and almost hated fellow sufferers who had a whole food ration to themselves. I had two remedies: remembering the poppy field, and thinking of my beautiful two-year-old cousin Éva, the personification of all that was precious and important. The commitment to save her became a source of physical and spiritual strength, an inspiration, the key to surviving and remaining human. The dignity, intelligence and generosity of my grandmother and my father, two exceptional human beings, set the tone for our family. In the crowded ghetto, in the unspeakable conditions of the wagon, in the fear and uncertainty of Strasshof, in the gnawing hunger and dawn-to-dusk slave labour of Magdalenenhof, there never was a harsh word among us; none of us quarrelled with anyone within or outside the family. We remained ourselves, we did nothing to make us feel ashamed, then or afterwards.

The Managing Director of the farm was the *Oberverwalter*. A powerfully built man, he lived with his beautiful wife and three tall blond teenage children in a spacious house in the farmyard. Once I spent a day in the home of this family. Obervervalter was a competent manager who worked his staff hard, but we never thought him deliberately cruel. He must have realised that a few of us sneaked out of the compound on some Sunday afternoons, but since this did not interfere with our work on other days, he pretended not to notice. I will relate another occasion when he prevented an SS murdering a Jew.

Second in command was the aloof *Verwalter,* Herr Pavlicek. I learned later that he was an underground socialist who risked his life supplying information to my father about the progress of the war and the wartime fate of Jews. I never knew how the two of them communicated. After our arrival in England, Jancsi and I tried to locate him, but without success.

Verwalter and Oberverwalter were much too grand personages to have direct contact with us Jews. Day-to-day supervision was entrusted to *Herr Practikant* (Mr Intern), an agronomist student apprentice, aged about 20: an SS officer who looked like a model for the Aryan race. He was knowledgeable, strong, and relentlessly, gratuitously cruel. He skilfully demonstrated each new task and kept constant check on the quality and speed of our work, barking out commands, issuing frightening threats. Here is an example: at the start of the grape harvest, he screamed that we must not eat a single grape. I was hungry enough to try. The shot into the ground, an inch from my foot, came immediately. Also instant was his warning that next time he would not miss. We believed him. Starved as we were, we never ate a single grape.

A fat Austrian woman, malicious and incompetent, was in charge of domestic arrangements, and cooked our food. Evening-time watery soups were tasteless, and she even managed to ruin Sunday lunch, the only two-course meal of the week: soup, followed by some kind of pasta, such as dumplings of potato gnocchi, a well-loved Austro-Hungarian dish. The dough should be made with butter-rich potato purée, dumplings should be about 1½ inch in diameter, filled with fresh fruit (plum or apricot), flavoured with cinnamon sugar, and thoroughly cooked inside without being soggy outside. This woman's dough was a gooey mess, her unfilled dumplings the size of a child's fist, to be shared between two. On cooking, these dumplings turned into a sticky glue on the outside, while staying raw within. My mother was convinced that she stole some of the ingredients; after all, Austrians were hungry too.

Many local people worked on the farm, women and old men tending the animals, driving carts and agricultural machinery. We had no dealings with them. There were also foreign workers, mostly Ukrainian farm labourers, the original temporary inhabitants of Strasshof. They were young, strong, well-fed. We had the misfortune to encounter them sometimes.

Inmates in slave camps talk of ten, twelve, fourteen-hour working days. How could they tell? Who had a watch? We worked from before sunup to past sundown. This meant waking and going to the fields in the dark, arriving when the sun just began to rise, staying at work until the light faded, then stumbling homewards in the gloom, arriving back to our hayloft in complete darkness. It would have been heaven to sit or lie down for the short break at lunchtime; we craved rest even more than food, but getting up again was hell, so many chose to stay upright all day.

'Lunch' consisted of bread which we were supposed to save from 'breakfast', and a mug of 'coffee', a tepid brown liquid. Evening meal was a bowl of 'soup'. Again and again, Nanóka was a blessing for us. A country girl, she taught us which wild berries were edible and which poisonous, which tree bark hid a trickle of sap, which weed had a nutritious root. Her knowledge benefited the whole troop of workers and even those back at base, because on our way 'home' we collected what we could for those in the hayloft.

Our first job was picking peas, and our last was reaping sugar beet. In between, we lifted potatoes and carrots, harvested wheat, barley, rye, fruit, grapes and sweetcorn. We aired grain in the loft, prepared the ground for planting and sowing, and much more besides. Since the farm was at the highest spot in the landscape, we started by going downhill to the field, carrying our tools: spade, rake, pitchfork, wooden hammer, whatever. The way down was almost pleasant, but we measured every step, already afraid of the way home, uphill, dragging our feet, carrying our tools, which by evening felt like they weighed a ton. To this day, I am anxious when descending any hill or staircase, anticipating the climb up. We were weak, inexperienced, but we were needed, because the farm was always in a rush to save the crop.

I will never forget our very first task. Half the field was in the shade; pea pods stank, slimy and rotten on the vine. On the sunny side the pods were dried to a crisp, peas hard as bullets; some spilled to the ground. That crop was useless, even as animal feed.

Next day we were commandeered to more promising fields of peas. We were each given a large sack. A scale stood at the end of the field. When your sack weighed 10 kg, Herr Praktikant chalked up one sackful to your record, and gave you a new sack. At the end of the day the person with the most sackfuls got a few cherries. The prize inevitably went to the Székely women but hope of it kept your mind on the job all day.

The field was edged on one side by trees. We soon learned why the Székelys took a beeline for that side. Peas in the shade were green and heavy, so half a sackful weighed 10kg. Elsewhere in the field peas were dry; the sack could be bursting full and still not weigh 10kg. We never managed to get those cherries for Éva and Gyurika, because they were the reward for the best workers, and those were always the Székelys.

It was early July, the height of continental summer. Working the fields was hard for all, but for some it was almost unbearable. Lipót's daughter Édi fainted on most hot days, but she had to persevere, because her food ration was essential for the Schwartz family, with two children and a granny. Two of our own family, Klári and Terka, were also liable to faint in strong sunshine. They soldiered on, the rest of us trying to shield them from the heat, or at least keeping them out of sight of Herr Praktikant. A few months later the weather turned wet, and finally icy. Each season offered its own challenge.

The Székely family were undoubtedly the most glamorous members of our group, the women stunningly beautiful, the handsome young man a tragic figure. They were always polite, and singled out Máli néni (Manci's mother-in-law) and our Éva (Manci's niece) for their smiles and concerned attention. Their women were the most skilful and strongest workers, and were also manipulative; they knew how to play the system. They made informed choices before anyone else realised that there were options at all, and found the easiest tasks, the best tools. Herr Praktikant soon figured how to use them to advantage. The output of the Székely women was set as the standard for all. We pushed ourselves harder and harder, but it was hopeless; none of us could equal their work rate. Let me emphasise: the Székelys did not behave badly – not *exactly* – but they were ruthless. They were shrewd and not stupid, and must have known that they caused us misery. I thought them hypocritical. They did their best to befriend us years later when we met two of them in England, but it was too late.

For one of us, fieldwork proved not just hard but unbearable. Székely László was obviously ill, as he kept collapsing. We learned later that he had tuberculosis. Perhaps that's why he escaped conscription. After a few days at Magdalenenhof, I overheard Herr

Praktikant suggesting to Oberverwalter that he shoot László because he was a constant nuisance. Oberverwalter was not a murderer. He said one need not shoot László, just stop him working. The farm would lose practically no output and would save a food ration.

László survived Magdalenenhof but died soon after arrival at our next camp. His death is recorded in Yad Vashem. Can his desperate condition explain, and perhaps even excuse, the conduct of his mother and sisters?

Original Record No.:	OW-III/1.
Last Name:	Szekely
First Name:	Laszlo
Gender:	Male
Age:	22
Permanent Place of Residence:	Debrecen,Hajdu,Hungary
Place during the war:	Wien - Favoriten (Ostmarkwerke Gmbh),Camp
Place of Death:	Wien - Favoriten (Ostmarkwerke Gmbh),Camp
Status in the source:	murdered
Connected to Item:	M.34.1 -
Source:	M.34.1 -
Type of material:	List of murdered persons
Item ID:	6963966

Record of the death of Székely László.

Yad Vashem Archives

Now about work. Fields were long rectangles. We were lined up at one end, and worked a strip lengthways, then we turned around and worked another strip in the opposite direction. Some fields were so long that one could not see the other end. They made me feel that there *was* no end; that our task, like that of Sisyphus, was eternal.[78] My father should not have taught me that legend.

Farm machinery was unsophisticated. There was no combine harvester. Large fields of wheat were harvested by a mechanised cutter which spewed out sheaves, to be fed into the threshing machine. Carrying and lifting the sheaves was hard, but the feeder had the worst job. The thresher created a cloud of dust, and flying bits of hay got into the eyes, hair, mouth, lungs, every pore. Standing on the thresher in blazing sun was dangerous; the

---

78   In Greek mythology, King Sisyphus was condemned forever to roll an immense boulder up a hill which kept rolling back, so his task was endless.

dizzy feeder might have fallen into the machine. Even Herr Praktikant acknowledged this, and every few hours the feeder – usually my father or one of the Székely women – was given a brief rest.

The thresher discharged the grain into sacks in waiting oxcarts and dropped out blocks of compressed hay. We carried the blocks to muscular Ukrainians, who built from them enormous rectangular haystacks. After the first day such a haystack was the size of a bungalow; at the end of the second day it was two floors high. Haystack builders made a staircase on the side on which we carried up more hay bricks, so the house could be built higher and higher.

The harvest had to be completed quickly to take advantage of the dry weather. To save time, we slept on that haystack for two nights, working from *before* sunup to *past* sundown. This was exhausting but sleeping in the open was magical. The air was warm, the hay made a soft bed, the freshly cut hay had beautiful scent, and the August sky was full of the brightest stars. The memory of those nights gave me strength in the bad days and nights that followed.

Some fields were too small for machine cultivation and had to be harvested by hand. A Ukrainian cut the wheat with a huge scythe, and a Jewish woman followed, tying the wheat into sheaves. My sheaves were uneven and I was slow, so my towering young Ukrainian soon left me behind. At first, he just swore at me in Russian (or Ukrainian?), then he took off his belt and beat me. Did it make me faster? He must have complained to Herr Praktikant, because next day I was assigned to some other job. I feared punishment, but none came. Perhaps just this once Herr Praktikant was reasonable.

After harvest, fields were ploughed by tractor. Grooves were deep, and the clay soil dried into lumps hard as rock. The solution was *Schroll schlagen*: pulverising the rocks with big long-handled wooden hammers. You worked a groove back and forth several times. The first pass would expose the damp inside of the rock to the sun, and the part-lump dried by the time you came back to it. After three or four work-overs, the field became smooth, ready for planting or sowing. The hammer was heavy, and wielding it was backbreaking. The handle caused bleeding calluses. Our eyes and pores were filled with dust. Some thought this was the worst of our jobs. Not so.

Autumn rain never stopped us working. If the rain was just moderately heavy, most outdoor jobs could still be carried out. When it was raining really hard, we were moved to indoor tasks. It was not an easy option. Airing grain will give an idea.

Grain was stored in huge piles alongside the wall of the barn loft. The top layer dried naturally, but the bottom retained the moisture of the fresh grain, and after a few weeks it began to rot. The rotting grain smelt foul, the air was hot, humid and dusty. With a great flat wooden shovel shaped like a half ellipse, you threw the grain in a high arc from one side of the loft to the other, exposing the damp grain to the air. Bits of the grain got in your eyes, hair, and lungs. If it continued to rain, the next day, or the day after, you shovelled the grain back again. The job was tiring, and you exhausted yourself coughing.

Your palms bled, your arms ached, your back was stiff and painful. For once, being small was an advantage. Lofts had low ceilings, so shovelling bent half-way made the hard job backbreaking. While the others were unable to stand upright, I almost could.

As I said, I was ill on three occasions in the camps. I had high fever each time, and we never knew why. My first illness was on arrival to Strasshof. The second happened on a sunny day at Magdalenenhof.

I was too ill to work on the field. I heard Herr Praktikant saying to Oberverwalter that precedent should not be set; if I could not do fieldwork, there were only two options: I could stay in the hayloft, food withheld, or I could do some job sitting down. Oberverwalter sent Herr Praktikant on his way and took me into his house. I was too ill even to be terrified. Oberverwalter told me that my job was to assemble the week's provisions list, and go with an oxcart to Klein Engersdorf, the nearest village, to bring back the farm's shopping. In his own dining room, he put before me a list of requirements for the farm, gave me a price list, and told me to prepare the priced shopping list. – This was the home of a normal family; wife and children coming and going. They took no notice of me; gave me no drink, no food. The sums were easy – I had done this kind of thing in my mother's shop – but the list was in German. I had a good grasp of the everyday language, but here some terms were unfamiliar. Still, when I finished, Oberverwalter checked my list, and was satisfied. He counted out a pile of paper money and told me to ensure that the shopkeeper gave me the correct goods, weights and change. He then hailed over a huge Ukrainian with an oxcart, and we were off. I was familiar with the environment of the farm on the shallow sides of the hill where we had worked, but Klein Engersdorf was in a new direction, down a steep slope, along an unpaved road full of stones.

The shopkeeper showed no surprise at his new customer. The transaction went smoothly, the oxcart duly loaded with the requisite goods. Trouble started on the way up. The ox was not keen on pulling the loaded cart up the steep rocky road; the Ukrainian swore and put me off the cart. I was ill and afraid that the cart would slide back or tip over, spilling the provisions which were my responsibility. The journey was a nightmare. Still, the man, the ox, and I managed. Obervelwalter mumbled something like 'well done' and sent me back to the hayloft to sleep off my fever, although it was not yet evening. He even gave me a few coins. Braham and Szita report that Jews were not *allowed* to have money in the camps. Wrong. Had there been such an edict, Oberverwalter would have breached it when giving me those few pennies, and he was not a man to transgress a regulation. – I was the only Jew ever to set foot in that house. I never saw Obervelwalter's wife and family again.

Autumn brought the grape harvest. We bent or squatted between the vines, cutting the fruit into baskets, which were then collected by Ukrainians who circulated with great wooden barrels on their backs. Remembering my incident with Herr Praktikant's gun, none of us dared to taste the grapes. The harvested grapes were trampled in rectangular containers by Jews wearing thigh-high rubber boots. It sounds fun. It was not. Just another hard, hard job.

Sometimes our grandmothers were commandeered to work on some nasty task, like picking out the few not-so-rotten potatoes from a big pile of slimy ones in the cellar, or standing knee-deep in the huge heap of manure in the middle of the farmyard, loading manure on oxcarts with a pitchfork. Fair's fair: on those occasions the grannies were given part of a food ration.

The weather was getting frosty. Our clothes were unsuitable. Even if we *had* winter overcoats, we would have been unable to work in them. Nanóka's wisdom became manifest yet again. She had packed a light woollen shawl for each, and she taught us how to twist it round our torso securely, keeping arms free. I have a couple of similar shawls now, and I sometimes put them on, Nanóka-style. We had no gloves, and we could not have worked wearing them. Nanóka also taught us how to improve blood circulation, thrashing arms about rhythmically, crossing them over the torso, hitting the body as far towards the back as possible. Her method helped, but it was no solution. Some of us, myself included, acquired frostbite.

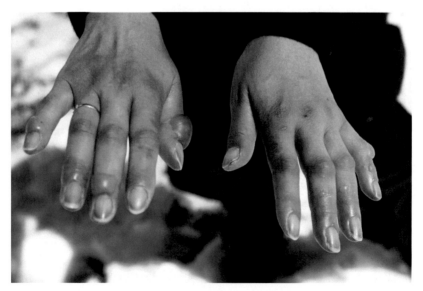

Frostbite, a freezing of living tissue.
Encyclopedia Britannica, https://www.britannica.com/science/frostbite/images-videos

Sores and swelling returned to fingers, toes and heels for years. In the Hungarian winters my hands looked like those in the picture. Mild winters are one of the many gifts England offered me.

SUGARBEET HARVEST

Looking back on our time in Magdalenenhof, we all agreed: harvesting sugarbeet was the worst job of all, a horrible experience second only to the wagon.

The beet is a beast, a giant root weighing two pounds or more, with huge bushy leaves.

It is the combination of the beet, the soil, and the weather that almost beats you.

Sugarbeet likes clay, so plenty of it was planted in the clay soil of Magdalenenhof. To bring out the sugar, the beet must be bitten by frost. Sugarbeet harvest was the last item on our farming calendar.

It rained for weeks, with frost at night. Now sleet had come. To reach the field, we must get down the hill, carrying a huge pitchfork and a razor-sharp sickle. The path is icy and stony. You slip at every step, fall dozens of times, cut your hand on the stones, your hand is bleeding. At your next fall you might hurt yourself with your pitchfork or your sickle. Each of your boots carries on its sole a great ball of frozen clay which sticks to the ground at every step (the story of the boots is coming). When the boot comes away from the clay, it makes a sucking sound, like a sloppy kiss. It is still dark, the working day is yet to start, you are only half-way down the hill, and you are already exhausted. At last you reach the edge of the field. It is vast. You must not allow yourself to think it endless; you tell yourself that the end is lost in the freezing fog. Herr Praktikant stands you between two rows of beets and gives you a huge sack. You put down the sack and the sickle, and tackle your first beet with your pitchfork. It is cemented into the ground by the clay and the frost. You heave and heave – you must lift out the beet without damaging it, Herr Praktikant is watching. You win at last; the beet comes out, with a great lump of frozen clay stuck to it. Surely the next beet will break your back? You put your weight on the pitchfork. Wisely, they selected the heaviest pitchfork for this task. You haul, and here it is, out at last: the first two you have conquered. You grab the leaves of your beets, one in each painful stiff hand. The leaves must not slip out of your grip. You bang the roots together to beat off the clay. Where did you put the sickle? There, hidden under the bushy leaves. Must not step on it, must not grab it by the blade. Got it! You hack off the leaves with your sickle, locate the sack, and throw in the beets. Your first success. Meanwhile the half-frozen clay you shook off from the beets sticks to your clothes, you are stiff as a golem.[79] Herr Praktikant yells, you are falling behind, the Székely women are yards ahead, their sacks half full already. You attack your next beet, trying not to look at the Székelys, nor at Herr Praktikant, not even at the endless field, but you *must* look up: what if Terka or Klári have fainted? No, they are struggling, but are still upright. You never thought tiredness could be like this.

---

79   *Golem:* by Jewish tradition, an animated being, magically created entirely from inanimate matter.

Must not think that the day will never end, best not to think of anything at all, not even about the day's end when you must climb up the slippery stony path, holding your sickle and your fork, dragging your feet with its ton of clay. There is no past, no future, just the present. Your hands are throbbing with pain, your face is covered with mud, but at least the sleet washes away your tears.

EQUIPMENT

Was it at Strasshof or at Magdalenenhof where the German Reich equipped their labourers for their tasks? Each worker received a grey blanket and a pair of boots.

Even Nanóka could not work out what the blanket was made of. It was tightly woven and durable, not warm, but useful for covering the straw in our hayloft. Until recently I still had mine; my grandchildren used to play on it in the garden. It had served me for over 70 years. Jancsi thought it deserved a place in some archive, so after he died I donated it to Yad Vashem, the World Holocaust Remembrance Centre in Jerusalem. My granddaughter Molly urges me to retrieve it; she regards it as her heritage.

The boots were heavy, with thick wooden soles and uppers made of something like papier maché. They were all size 42. Luckily, not even my father needed a larger size; those with bigger feet had to cut out a hole for their toes. All women in my family had small feet. Nanóka's feet were size 33, but this did not matter, because being officially old and off the workers' list, she was not entitled to boots or blanket.

At first the boots were useful in the fields and on the way up and down the Berg; the uppers stood up well to the rain and sleet, and the toes could be filled with crumpled paper. The heels were the problem. We all had uneven gait; the outside of the heels wore off, and we were fearful that we would soon walk bare-heeled on the ground.

Klári found the solution: change our boots around, wear the left boot on the right foot and the right boot on the left. At first this was uncomfortable, but soon the offside started to wear down, and the boots became more balanced. They lasted all our time in Magdalenenhof.

BENEFACTORS

Magdalenenhof was surrounded by barbed wire. On arrival Herr Praktikant said in plain German that Jews could only leave the compound under supervision of armed guard, and anyone leaving the camp or the work detail without permission would be shot.

The order was unenforceable. We could easily have slipped away while doing our business in the bushes during the working day, and nobody guarded me with a gun when I went shopping with the ox and the Ukrainian. But where could we go? And how could we go anywhere, with three grannies and two babies?

One could not escape, but one could slip out in search of food. For once, my family was more enterprising than the Székelys, or anyone else, because several of us (Pici, Klári, Magda, Szeréna and I) spoke German. Vienna was within walking distance, albeit a *long* walking distance. It was visible from the top of Bisamberg, and we were free on Sunday afternoons. We were hungry. Our babies were hungry. The temptation was irresistible.

Our first trip took us down to Vienna, and it almost led to disaster. It was my fault.

We had a bit of money, given me by Oberverwalter. We still had our town shoes, and Nanóka could still make us look reasonably presentable. She had packed into my rucksack my little red-checked two-piece suit (I am wearing it on this photo with my parents). Under normal circumstances I would have outgrown these, but I had lost weight, so the suit fitted me still. Soon after lunch (?), Pici, Magda and I sneaked out towards Vienna.

Our first stop was a grocery shop, surprisingly open on Sunday afternoon. It had almost nothing to sell, and of course we had no coupons. We blew our fortune on a box of matches and a jar of mustard.

Scared but thrilled, we continued towards Vienna. We came to a suburban square, fairground in the middle, tavern on the corner, a band playing Hungarian gypsy music. We stopped by the door, hearing music the first time since the Italian Concerto in the ghetto. The violinist glanced in our direction, downed his fiddle, and marched towards us with a stern expression on his face. We ran away, but he caught up with us, took off his jacket and threw it over my shoulder. He drew us to a side street and asked, in Hungarian, whether we realised that I was wearing a yellow star. I had not worn my suit since the ghetto; it had one of our smart stars stitched to it, and none of us had noticed. I took off my jacket, thanked the gypsy musician, and, shaken, we started for Magdalenenhof. I was still wearing *his* jacket. The man walked a short way with us, asked where our camp was, and told us his name: Bokor Imre.

None of us saw gypsy Mr Bokor again, but he remained in contact with Pici through exchange of brief notes. From that Sunday, throughout our stay in Magdalenenhof, he hid small parcels of food somewhere agreed with Pici: half a loaf, a tin of sardines, a piece of sausage. Most wonderful was a little tin of condensed milk, a novelty for us. Everyone tasted a drop, and then we fed the syrupy liquid spoonful by spoonful to our babies. You should have seen their little faces. – After the war, Pici and I tried to find Mr Bokor, but never could.

Klári also acquired a benefactor: Frau Doleschal, an elderly woman, a sort of bag-lady. She was intelligent, educated, a fierce Royalist, devotee of the Habsburgs, and hater of Hitler. She had two goats and some chickens, and lived with her animals in a hut somewhere near the Magdalenenhof estates. One day she saw us going to work, figured who we were, and signalled to Klári, who was nearest, pointing at a small parcel containing a couple of boiled eggs and a piece of goat cheese. Klári visited her once on a Sunday afternoon, reporting back to us the squalor of the place and the generosity of its inhabitant. When Frau Doleschal heard about our toddlers, she redoubled her efforts, sometimes bringing us a little goat's milk, walking long distances to find us at our different places of work.

The author with her parents in April 1943, Budapest.
Kaposi family collection

My father had the occasional bit of news, and he also had a few coins from time to time. The source was *Verwalter,* underground socialist Herr Pavlicek.

I never acquired a benefactor, but I did manage to bring home contributions. At first, I went begging for food to Langenzersdorf, a nearby village. Villagers were getting used to me: one gave me a piece of bread, another an apple, but then a Nazi noticed me. He threatened to set his dogs on me if he ever saw me again. Thereafter I confined myself to stealing fruit from orchards, or corn from fields.

The sugarbeet harvest marked the end of our contribution to Austrian agriculture. One evening Herr Praktikant announced that next morning we would be leaving the farm. Reveille was before dawn, as usual. We never saw Obervervalter or Verwalter again, and had no chance to thank our benefactors. The weather told us that it had to be late November or early December. I worked out recently that we left on 2nd December 1944, destination unknown.

With all our possessions, we climbed onto oxcarts, and rattled down Bisamberg. At the edge of the farm, some 15 km north of the boundary of Vienna, we climbed down from the oxcarts, and SS officer Herr Praktikant formally handed us over to three soldiers.

JOURNEY ACROSS VIENNA

Our armed jailers may have been Wehrmacht or SS, German, Austrian or Ukrainian – I don't remember; but I recall that it was early morning when we started out on foot from the edge of the farm. We walked for hours, wearing our rucksacks, my father carrying Gyurika, the women taking turns to carry Éva. We struggled, but the rest of the Jews struggled even more, with their suitcases and shapeless bundles. There was an armed guard at front, another at the back, and a third hovering between the two, trying to close up the more and more unruly snake of exhausted Jews. It rained heavily, and then it turned to sleet. We realised that we were heading for Vienna.

We were crossing the Danube when air raid alarms sounded. Our guards had no idea how to cope with 40 Jews in an air raid. They looked for a public air raid shelter, as much against the sleet as against the possible bombing, but found none, so they shepherded us under the bridge. Bombing was coming nearer. The guards were clearly frightened; they nudged us out from under the bridge and propelled us down the first side street, as unfamiliar to them as to us. Had we all been young and enterprising, this would have been a great opportunity to escape, but where could we run, and who had the energy?

We ended up in the staircase of a block of flats. The locals must have been down in the shelter. We squatted on the floor, the grownups pulling us children under their own bodies for protection.

This was not our first camp-time air raid experience. There had been a dramatic raid in Magdalenenhof, a bizarre event which might have ended in tragedy. I was in charge of a child detail, the five oldest children of our group directed to scrape out any remaining carrots from an already harvested field. The target of the raid was the radio transmitter, but a bomb hit the edge of the stables. The horses escaped and stampeded across the field where my troop of tiny workers squatted. No child was hurt. A miracle?

We experienced many air raids later, in our next camp. I was never afraid. It may have been my famous lack of imagination. During raids everyone was calm, even the babies. Everyone, except my mother. She could not control her panic, and during raids she grabbed me, hugged me tightly, and buried my head in her lap. I tried to calm her; she made me feel that I was the adult and she was the child.

Back to our journey. When the raid was over, it was almost funny to see our guards trying to regain their dignity and initiative. Remembering our destination, they led us back to the bridge under which we had sheltered a short while before. The bridge was not there: it had taken a direct hit.

This air raid episode was yet another of our 'miracles'. I thought I remembered it well, but to turn memory to fact, I had to find proof. This section is an example of how I validate details of my story.

FIRST QUESTION: WHERE?

Our starting point was Magdalenenhof, north of Vienna. Our next camp turned out to be OstmarkWerke in Favoriten, Vienna's District X. These two are on opposite sides of the Danube, so we had to cross a bridge.

The obvious route on foot is across a bridge: Florisdorferbücke. The nearest alternative further north would make the route three times as long, and a crossing further south would be 25% longer. They must have taken us through **Florisdorf**.

SECOND QUESTION: WHEN?

A moderately fit walker would cover such a distance in four hours. My memory tells me that it took us all day, and we arrived at night, no later than the day after our starting date.

The sugarbeet harvest was our last job. We left the morning after. Weather reports showed no significant frost before late November, and heavy snow in mid-December. That sets the bounds of the date of us leaving Magdalenenhof.

I consulted historical records. During World War II, Vienna and its district had been bombed 52 times. Bombings in the relevant period are listed below.

- **19th November 1944:** bombing **Winterhafen**, some **170 km west** of Vienna. *Too early and too far.*

- **2nd December 1944**, bombing **Florisdorf**, 10 km from Magdalenenhof, on the northern edge of Vienna. *Possible.*

- **8th December 1944**, bombing **Moosbierbaum**, **45 km west** of Vienna. *Too far.*

- **11th December 1944**, bombing **Moosbierbaum**, **45 km west** of Vienna. *Too far.*

- **18th December 1944**, bombing **Florisdorf**. *Too late.*

The date had to be the **2nd December 1944**.

THIRD QUESTION: WHAT WAS THE MOTIVATION?

There was an oil refinery at Florisdorf. It had been bombed 12 times during World War II, including on the 2nd December 1944, **QED**.

HAPPY BIRTHDAY?

The day-long walk gave me time to realise that all three of us children had birthdays in Magdalenenhof. Gyurika turned four on 20th August. Since 5th October, Éva was a big girl of three. On 20th October I became twelve. The adults loved and cherished us, but it had not occurred to anyone to celebrate our birthdays. This was not a time for celebrations.

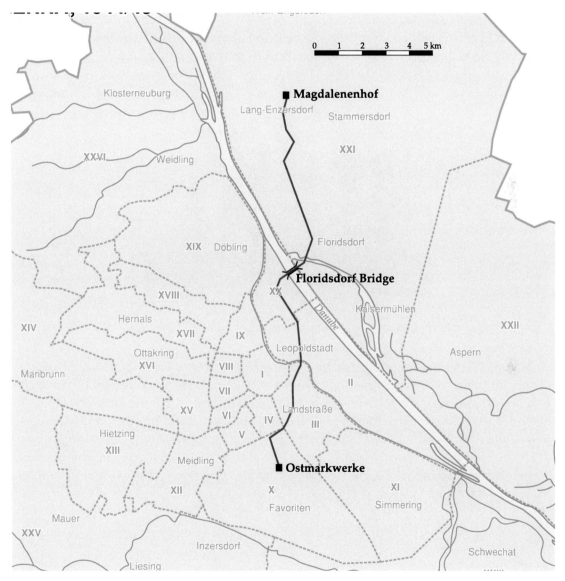

Walk from Magdalenenhof to Ostmarkwerke (Arsenal Strasse, Favoriten, District 10 of Vienna)

OSTMARKWERKE: WE ARE FACTORY WORKERS

We arrived at our new camp in the small hours. We learned later that this was Ostmark-Werke, an armament factory known as *Arsenal*. It must have been one of the last manufacturing resources of the German army, others having been destroyed or occupied by the Allies advancing from the west, or by the Soviets from the east. The dominant product of the factory was the Flakvierling 38 Anti-Aircraft Gun, by far the most numerously produced German artillery weapon throughout the war. My friend and comrade Gábor is an important character in this part of my story. A boy of 13 at the time, he was a born engineer. In his memoir he describes how he learnt about the manufacturing process of the gun, its high-technology design for the age, and its strategic significance.[80]

The Flakvierling 38 Anti-Aircraft Gun
Bundesarchiv, Bild 1011-635-4000-24. Photo: Walther, 1943

OstmarkWerke was huge, built on the site of an old factory, all but one of the 19th century factory buildings replaced by modern structures of low, single-story design, sunk into the ground, camouflaged by gardens on their roofs. Only one of the old redbrick buildings remained, five-floors high, utterly conspicuous. Buildings were numbered; this old relic was *Bau 12*.

The ground floor of Bau 12 was occupied by metalwork machinery, and the first floor housed stores. Assembly took place on the fourth and fifth floors. Sandwiched in between, the second and third floors accommodated the Jews.

---

80   Gabor Lacko (formerly Lefkovics): *Mein Kampf*, 2006, private publication.

Most of the Jews who arrived directly from Strasshof were housed on the second floor. The Magdalenenhof contingent joined the overflow on the third floor, where half the area was unused. Having plenty of space was no advantage: bunks were jammed together, and the cavernous empty floor area allowed an icy draught to blow through our living quarters.

We slept on two-tier bunks pushed together, with two people sharing each 'bed'. Two to a bed was a tight squeeze, but at least we warmed each other. Our family of 11 would have been entitled to 5½ beds, but that would have meant one sharing with someone other than family. We chose having only five beds, three sharing one bed; some of us were quite small. A narrow gap separated one bunk pair from the other. It proved essential for washing arrangements.

It was wintertime. There was no heating. Bomb blasts blew out the glass, so soon there were no windows. People tried to replace window-panes with pieces of cardboard. Gábor, a scrawny thirteen-year-old, rose to importance in the community, cobbling together small stoves from stolen bits of scrap metal. We all did our best to steal pieces of wood to make a fire in Gábor's stoves.

We had no winter clothes. Gábor, the same youngster, turned cat burglar. He risked his life stealing bits of blackout curtains from bombed-out factory buildings. My grandmother made up the curtain bits into makeshift garments for the most in need.

WASHING

A problem. Cold water was usually available from taps in the toilet, but warm water was precious, a rarity, to be put to a carefully managed series of uses.

Gábor reminded me recently how we obtained a small tin basin, just big enough to stand a little child in. It was his handiwork. He stole, from bombed-out factory buildings, tin lampshades, turned them upside down, and sealed up the bottom. The 'basin' formed the top of the little stoves he himself had constructed. While there was fire smouldering, the water in the basin would get slightly warm.

Nanóka planned a precisely choreographed sequence of washing. First, we washed one of the toddlers in a fresh bowl of water. Next, a grownup would wash in the used water. Then we washed the clothes of the child, and then of the adult, and we used what water was still left to wash the floor between and below the bunks. The place was cold and draughty. Washing took place in the narrow corridor between bunks, shielded by curtains made of grey blankets. To the mild amusement of neighbours, the whole procedure was repeated with a different cast each time. For the purpose of washing, I was classed as a child, except I got on with the process myself. Each child was washed every third occasion we had warm water. I suppose five warm-water events were needed before the rota came around to any given grownup.

WORK

Everyone between 12 and 60 had to work, and those 16 and over were classed as 'adult'. The adult work force – mostly women – worked night shifts in the modern underground buildings, operating metalwork machinery: drills, lathes, milling machines.

I was the youngest of the 'children's work gang'. The oldest was strong handsome Hoffmann Pista, aged 15. The gang included two important personalities, both aged 13: cat burglar/engineer genius Gábor, and Kárpáti Bandi, another exceptional boy. Geszti Zsuzsa, a girl of 15, was also member of the gang.

Work was not easy but compared with Magdalenenhof it was almost a holiday. Children worked as porters, facilitating the assembly of that famous gun. The backbone of the gun was a large pressed-steel chassis on which the operating parts were mounted. Here is the process from our viewpoint:

- Trucks delivered a pile of raw chassis, typically 100 pieces, to the entrance of Bau 12, together with gun parts. Child porters carried the bare chassis to the workshop.

- An adult work team, mostly Czechs, prepared the raw chassis for assembly, drilling holes and filing down raw edges. Now the chassis was ready to take the parts.

- Child porters carried the prepared chassis and the gun parts upstairs to the fourth or fifth floors where the assembly line mounted the parts on the chassis.

- Child porters carried the completed work piece back down those four or five flights of stairs, and lined them up, ready to be taken away by trucks.

- Trucks were just arriving, delivering fresh raw chassis and parts, taking away the completed assembly. The cycle started again.

The staircase was narrow, and stone steps steep. Child porters worked in pairs, one holding the chassis lower down the stairs, the other above. Chassis were some 1 square metre in area, weighing 20–25 kg. Carrying the boards upstairs was hard, but at least the chassis was bare. Coming down should have been easier, but the loaded assembly was much heavier. A reliable partner was of the essence. If the child above let go of his end, the board would come tumbling down on top of you. If you were the one above and your partner below dropped his side, the object would pull you down on your partner and the pair below.

Strong and helpful Pista always chose the weakest partner and the hardest job. Others might have been well-meaning but feeble or clumsy. One such, a nice boy with two left feet, was Kárpáti Bandi, a geography genius who knew the map of Europe in minute detail. Whenever anyone had information about the progress of the war, people would crowd around Bandi, who could explain how the front was shaping up, and could sketch a map for the anxious audience.

We struggled but were loyal to each other. There was only one slacker: flabby Zsuzsa, who often arrived late or not at all, leaving her share of the job to the rest. She learnt her attitude from her grandparents, medical officers of the camp. After the war, Zsuzsa visited Terka in Budapest, asking her to testify to the good conduct of her family: someone had filed a case against them. Terka gave her a cup of coffee with homemade biscuits and signed the testimony but told her never to return. My lovely aunt had no desire for revenge.

SOCIAL LIFE

When we arrived at OstmarkWerke, we found a well-established camp society. With us newcomers, the camp contained some 300 Jews.

In a few weeks the Magdalenenhof group became absorbed into the society, but I remained an outsider. The children's work gang had been formed, friendships and work pairs had been established. I was the youngest and the weakest, and I was from Budapest. All the others came from provincial cities of Debrecen, Szeged or Szolnok, and knew each other from school or synagogue. They were not exactly unfriendly, but I remained alone. I did admire Gábor and Bandi, and sometimes had the benefit of being teamed up with Pista. I managed.

FOOD

The camp community had an officially appointed leader: Elek, a large, jovial man, older than my father. Among other responsibilities, he was in charge of designating bunks to families, and overseeing food distribution. Unlike the malevolent Jewish Police in the ghetto, he did not abuse his position.

There were three other important functions: bringing the food to the camp, distributing the food, and clearing out the latrines.

Soon after we arrived to OstmarkWerke, Senior Jew Elek became friendly with Lili, a member of the Schwartz family who had been with us in Magdalenenhof. Lili was the wife of my mother's beloved cousin Gyuri. Unbeknown to us all, she was by then a widow: Gyuri had been killed in munkaszolgálat.

The romance between Elek and Lili blossomed, and soon they moved to shared bunks. This did not please other women in the camp; perhaps they also had designs on Elek. It certainly distressed Lili's mother-in-law, Nanóka's sister Irén néni, who was still hoping that her son Gyuri would return. Lili's dalliance with Elek met with stern disapproval from my straight-laced family.

As the token of his devotion, Elek appointed Lili Food Distributor for the camp, the most coveted task of all. Lili was the mistress of the ladle, and the ladle meant food. We were chronically hungry. Food was always scarce, always bad, at times quite ghastly. It was some semblance of vegetable soup, sometimes with tiny scraps of meat in it.

Unlike in Magdalenenhof, in OstmarkWerke everyone, even toddlers and grannies, had their own food ration. Each family sent along someone to collect their share, the number of ladlefuls of soup equalling the number of members of the family. Lili had no problem giving full measure to a single person, or to small families of two, three, or even four. But the Csengeri clan, with 11 members, was the largest in the whole camp, and Lili must have felt that 11 ladlefuls for a single family was altogether too much.

It was my job to fetch the soup. I stood before Lili day after day, holding out my blue pot, watching her filling the ladle for the count of one, two, three, but then I saw with an aching heart how each subsequent ladle was less and less full. I don't think she ever gave full measure for all 11 of us. I asked the grownups to talk to Lili. They never did, perhaps because they disapproved of her. I even suggested splitting up the family by surname: 1 Csengeri (Nanóka), 3 Stern (Terka, Éva, Máli néni), 4 Klein (Imre, Magda, Szeréna and I), 2 Frankel (Klári, Gyurika), 1 Deutsch (Pici). It never happened. By then my father was too weak to plead the case, and the others had other preoccupations. So we remained the largest and hungriest family of all.

Was Lili's treatment of the Csengeris chance, negligence, or carelessness, or was it deliberate? Who will ever know? Lili and Elek died long ago. After the war, Lili's son Gabi grew up to be an excellent doctor, staunch supporter of Terka and Pici, and a friend of my cousin Ági. He died recently, in his late 70s.

CAULDRONS

It was the task of two skinny 16-year-olds to bring the soup cauldrons upstairs, and put them before Lili. I chanced to meet one of those cauldron-carriers recently, in London. I know his name, but we shall just call him Boy 1. Aged 90 by now, he is blessed with a good memory. He helped me by confirming many details of this story, even adding a detail of his own. He said, proudly, that he and his mate Boy 2 had always stopped on the way up with the soup cauldron, sticking their hands in to fish out from the bottom scraps of meat or vegetable before delivering the remainder for distribution. When I appeared surprised, he said with a smug smile: 'You had to be streetwise to survive'.

Those cauldrons may have had another use.

Quite often all 300 of us had food poisoning, usually brought on by the dreadful Dörrgemüse. The extraordinary demand for toilet facilities coincided with, or precipitated, failure of the water supply. Emergency cauldrons were installed in the lavatories, the same kind of vessels – or perhaps the very same vessels – as those used in food distribution. The boys who carried up the cauldrons of food also had the job to carry down the cauldrons from the toilets. Our guards had a sense of humour.

CULTURE

Jews being 'people of the book' should refer to the Torah. There were some religious people among us, but I don't recall anybody having any sacred books. Yet, somehow someone had salvaged a fragment of a poetry book, just a few pages of Babits, a great Hungarian romantic poet whose verses are like music. We treasured the book, learnt the poems, and recited them to the community. Some knew other poems by heart. There were a few, like me, who knew folk songs and opera arias, while others knew bits of popular music. A few even had a gift for making up short songs called *juppajdés*, recounting the gossip of the camp. Occasionally, on a Sunday evening, air raids permitting, we would hold little performances. These events were important, signifying that we were still human beings.

HEALTH

Air raids were ever more frequent and fiercer. We spent less and less time at work, longer and longer in bomb shelters. Adults worked in different buildings, and the raid might have caught them in different places. Buildings were often hit, and when a raid was over, we would anxiously assemble, relieved that everyone had survived.

It happened once that, after a raid, my father could not be found. The building where he worked had been darkened for the raid; he had poor eyesight and no glasses; he did not notice an opening in the floor and fell down into a deep cellar. Eventually he was found, unconscious. We ran for help to Professor Geszti, the appointed medical officer of the camp, a famous lung specialist whose wife was also a doctor. They had special privileges: a glass cubicle as surgery, and a small private apartment shared with their daughter and granddaughter, our workmate Zsuzsa. The Gesztis had the reputation of being greedy and unhelpful. This was the first time we needed their attention.

When asked to see my unconscious father, Professor Geszti demanded 'the requisite number of bread rations'. What did he mean? He explained that his usual tariff was a certain number of bread rations (I don't remember how many), and since we failed to produce the 'payment' up front, he would only come if we pledged double. We promised whatever he asked, so at last he consented to see my still-unconscious father. My father's injuries – cracked ribs and bruises – were not severe: after an alarming hour he regained consciousness, and after a few days of amnesia he even regained his memory, but the incident taught me a lesson. Professor Geszti, aged 60, with an international reputation, failed to live up to being an honourable person, what the Yiddish call a *Mensch*. My half-blind father, my semi-literate grandmother, and my skinny 13-year-old cat burglar friend all passed the test with flying colours.

Some time in the winter our Éva, a lovely three-year-old, became ill, and was taken to Vienna's Jewish hospital. She had inflammation of the middle ear. Terka was not allowed to accompany her. They had to open up her skull to drain the pus from the ear.

Esther Farbstein describes the Jewish hospital as a 'place of kindness'. Instead, we heard of overcrowding, several sharing a bed, bullying of small children by older children, operations without proper anaesthesia. When my little cousin returned to us, she was cured of the infection, but did not speak, did not cry, did not recognise anyone, was not even interested in food. Her recovery took many months. She grew up to be a beautiful young woman, became a linguist, married and had a wonderful son, but her life was not as happy as she deserved. She died young.[81]

In our final days at OstmarkWerke, our Gyurika too fell ill with pneumonia. Not surprising: it was the bitterest of winters, the camp had no heating, and his nutrition was poor. The surprise was that he survived. He too was taken to the Jewish hospital, but, perhaps because he was more severely ill, or because the war had reached a new phase, his mother Klári was allowed to accompany him.

Gyurika had never recovered fully from that pneumonia. The disease led to tuberculosis, and soon after the war he caught polio which paralysed him on one side. He was seldom well enough to attend school, and could never go to university. He remained an invalid all his life, physically weak and psychologically damaged, a casualty of the war. After the 1956 Hungarian revolution he emigrated to Israel and got a job in one of the country's largest banks, as a gofer. He worked his way through the ranks, becoming the bank's Chief Auditor. He never knew his banker father, my beloved uncle Can't Swim, but he inherited his father's talent.

A TALL TALE?

OstmarkWerke was a strategic military target. By the end of January 1945, daily raids were persistent. Sometimes we spent complete days in the cellar under our camp in Bau 12. Once our building was firebombed. The fire on the top floor was minor and we soon put it out, so our camp on the second and third floor was still as habitable (or as uninhabitable) as before. Not so the rest of the factory. One by one, each beautifully camouflaged underground building was reduced to rabble, and only the tall 19th century edifice Bau 12 stood intact, the one which housed the Jewish camp. A tall tale, or a miracle?

The management battled to maintain some semblance of production, but by the end of February they had to admit defeat. In the wrecked OstmarkWerke the Germans had 300 idle Jews on their hands. Surely, they considered administering to us the Final Solution. Thousands of Jews who had arrived with us at Strasshof were killed when their 'employers' did not need them anymore. My family escaped such a fate – just another miracle.[82]

---

81   Farbstein's account puts more emphasis on religious services than on medical matters. She states that Vienna had one of the only two Jewish hospitals established under the auspices of the Reich, the other being in Berlin, and indicates that the hospital was located in Malzgasse, Leopoldsville, Vienna.

82   Kinga Frojimovics–Éva Kovács, Jews in a 'Judenrein' City: Hungarian Jewish Slave Labourers in Vienna (1944-1945), *Hungarian Historical Review* 4, No.3. (2015) 705-736.

VIENNA: WE ARE NAVVIES

OstmarkWerke was a ruin, and so was the rest of Vienna.

They found us a new occupation. In the mornings they piled us into open lorries, threw in some shovels and wheelbarrows, drove us to some wrecked building in Vienna, and commandeered us to clear up the damage. Come evening, they took us 'home' to Bau 12 of OstmarkWerke.

Former Nazis clearing rubble after the liberation of Vienna, 1945.
Camera Press, IWM, London

We laboured on churches, palaces, ministries, museums, schools and dwelling houses, even on the opera house. But what impression could a bunch of skeletal Jews make on those ruins, equipped with a few shovels and wheelbarrows? And while we cleared the bomb damage here, bombing continued there. The city was being destroyed faster than we could clear it of rubble. The undertaking was hopeless, but it was good while it lasted. Our armed guards had lost their resolve, so it was easy for enterprising child workers to sneak

149

away for a few minutes. Those of us who spoke German could beg food from locals, but the Viennese were hungry themselves. A better method was to offer help to people who dragged along possessions saved from their bombed-out homes or carried loot from the ruins. Most people chased us away and some threatened to hand us over to the SS, but a few accepted our help, and gave us a bite of food as payment. I managed to obtain some scraps most days. Once I helped a lady who led me upstairs to her blue-tiled kitchen and put before me a plateful of *krumplis nudli*: a kind of pasta I loved then, and I still love now. I asked her to please wrap this food up. She said well, if I was not hungry … I said of course I was hungry, but might I take it away? I had a little sister back at the camp. She said no, it was dangerous to let me take food away; I had to eat it right there. I did as she bid me, almost choking on this lovely food, crying while eating it.

Then one evening came one of those sudden announcements that we would be leaving the next morning. Destination unknown.

STRASSHOF REVISITED

The journey out of OstmarkWerke is a blur, but I remember that arriving at Strasshof was almost like going home. Barracks with bunk beds, cramped but not overcrowded. Windows with glass. German guards, thankfully no Ukrainians. Barbed-wire fence at high voltage. In the huge camp there would have been other captives beside us Jews, but we had no strength to explore. I can find no map of the Strasshof camp, but the arrangement is easy to describe: a matrix of single-storey barracks for thousands of people, butting on to railway tracks.

Not having to work would have been a relief, but food was almost non-existent. If they fed us at all, it was the dreaded foul Dörrgemüse. People were dying of starvation. One of the dead was Judge Hoffmann, father of my gallant OstmarkWerke workmate Pista. My own father was a skeleton. By the end of the war he weighed 35 kg. He, rather than Éva or the grannies, was the most vulnerable member of our family. Klári and Gyurika had not returned from hospital, so now we were nine.

We shared our living quarters with Jews from Szeged, among them a young lady doctor whose name I cannot recall. During the night when biting hunger kept us awake, she would gently talk us to sleep by reciting recipes, like soothing little children with nursery rhymes. I had a problem with her recipes involving boiled potatoes. Why mash or manipulate those precious potatoes, why slice them or mix them with other ingredients? My dream was to have a whole boiled potato all to myself.

The day after our arrival, trains started to take Jews away. One-by-one, lines of barracks were emptied, trains leaving, destination unknown. The wagons were similar to those in which we travelled from Hungary. There was no cursing or brutal pushing; these guards were not Hungarian gendarmes.

Meanwhile new kinds of air attacks started. Not high-flying British and American aircraft like the ones that had bombed Vienna and the OstmarkWerke, but Soviet planes flying so low that we could almost make out the pilots' facial features. They were not bombing, but machine-gunning people, shooting into the barracks through the windows.

About half the camp had been emptied when, one day in late March, it was our turn. I was glad that our stay in Strasshof was over, hoping that at our next camp we might get some food, and would be free of Russian air attacks. We boarded the train with something resembling optimism. Unlike our dreadful journey from Hungary, these wagons were not crowded, everyone had a place to sit, some could even stretch out. Our guards locked the doors of the wagons, and we were ready to start.

And then came the worst air raid in our experience, Allied planes bombing from on high. Bombs came raining down in the immediate vicinity; they were falling all around us, debris bombarding our wagon. The noise was deafening, the ground shook. I recall trying to comfort my mother, but this time everyone was screaming with fright. When it was over and our guards pushed the wagon door open, we just sat there, paralysed.

A year or so ago I talked about this part of our shared experience with my friend Gábor. Of course he remembered this event, and then referred to a further detail which I had forgotten, but his words awoke vivid memories. When the doors were opened, we could hardly climb out, because one of the wheels of our wagon was up in the air, over the edge of a crater. The bomb must have missed us by a couple of feet. Bombing also missed the barracks full of Jews who were to travel on subsequent days. Instead, bombs fell *next* to our wagons, *between* the railway line and the barracks, and *further along* the railway line, just a few yards beyond our train. The air attack did not just stop us travelling that day; it destroyed the railway line altogether, so no train could leave Strasshof thereafter. A miracle.

Only after the war did we learn the significance of this air attack. Had the railway been usable, we would have followed previous trainloads of Jews to Theresienstadt. From there, some were taken to death camps, others were force-marched to indefinite destinations, most dying along the way. This is how thousands of the 15,011 who arrived in Strasshof in June 1944 found their death in March 1945.

Surviving that air raid in the wagon, we returned to our Strasshof barracks. Mealtimes came, but no food arrived that day, the next day, or the day after. Slowly, it dawned on us that, since they released us from the train, we had seen no guards. Even before, guards were only in evidence at mealtimes, perhaps because they did not need to guard us: weakness, hunger and the high voltage fence did the job. People started to suspect that the Germans might have gone altogether!

Then, hunger made someone desperate enough to throw himself at the high voltage fence – and nothing happened: there was no voltage in the fence. Perhaps there had never been any voltage. Near the end of the war, Vienna had been starved of electricity. A handful of guards might have held captive thousands of starving Jews and other prisoners, tricking them into believing that they were surrounded by a high voltage fence. Perhaps we could have left the camp in search of food some days before, and perhaps Judge Hoffmann and many others would not have died of starvation.

Once the myth of high voltage had been dispelled, those strong enough started to climb across the fence into the potato field on the other side. The potatoes had been harvested the previous autumn, but a few could still be dug out of the ground with fingers. Some enterprising people even went beyond the field, approaching nearby houses in search of food.

Then people discovered several marooned trains apart from the one in which we would have travelled to our deaths. Resourceful Jews prized open a wagon and found a barrelful of sugary red liquid which passed for jam. By the time I got to the scene with my trusty blue pot, some people had already filled their food bowls, and were running back to their barracks for more containers. I dipped the blue pot into that red goo.

After this, there was no stopping the hungry Jews. They broke open wagon after wagon of the stranded trains, discovering precious supplies of four sorts of food: soya beans, salt, sugar, and of course 'jam'. There were other goods too, in wooden crates. Some said they contained paintings and carpets, perhaps even silver. We had no interest in the treasures; what we wanted was the wood of the crates to make fire for cooking. It took all Nanóka's ingenuity to make a camp-fire and combine the unpromising ingredients into palatable food, but she was in her element.

The unexpected appearance of food felt like another miracle.

We should have been happy to have lost our Nazi guards. There was a whole wagonload of food at hand – peculiar food, but source of protein and carbohydrate. This could have been a chance of slowly regaining some of our strength. Instead, Russian air attacks were almost continuous. They must have thought that this was a military camp. Someone suggested that we put some white sheets on the roof of our barracks. Some even tried to create a giant yellow star. In any case, after a day or two the air attacks stopped, and soon our Russian liberators appeared in person, in droves. A few of the stronger Jews threw themselves into their arms. They liked this so much that they took away some young women to their own quarters. These women returned later, battered and bruised. In the daytime the Russians were relatively safe; they liked children and gave them some bread. Come the evening however, they were predatory, and women were in danger. I was 12. I knew that women and girls had to hide from the soldiers. I did not understand why, but I saw that women picked up by Soviet soldiers returned severely damaged, almost like the rich Jews who had been beaten for their money by Hungarian gendarmes.

Weak and lacking energy, we were dazed and could not think straight. It took us a day or two to understand that we were no longer prisoners, could decide what to do. How long ago was it that we could make any decision about our life and destiny?

The camp began to empty; people were leaving, and we realised that we should escape from the Russians as soon as possible. Our natural destination was Budapest, to be reunited with the young men of our family. We did not know that almost all of them were dead.

Putting the decision into action seemed impossible. We had no means of transport. My father was emaciated, our toddler had to be carried, and our three grannies needed help. The four of us young women – Magda, Terka, Pici and I – were unequal to the task.

Then two things happened: one good, one bad. The good: someone discovered that one of the bombed-out trains contained a wagonload of wheelbarrows and lengths of straps. We could put Éva and Szeréna, the weakest granny, into two wheelbarrows, and we could take turns pushing them along, with straps around our necks. Finding those wheelbarrows may even count as a minor miracle. The bad: I fell ill, my third illness in the camps. It was like the others, but worse: high fever, loss of consciousness. The lovely lady doctor from Szeged – the one with the recipes – was at hand, but could not help; there was no diagnosis and no medicine. She said the family should give up any plan of moving until my fever subsided. Having said this, she herself left.

I recovered in a few days. By then, everything was packed into rucksacks and blanket rolls. Everything – except my diary. I looked for it thoroughly, but I was still very weak. I hoped to find it inside one of the rucksacks, but I never did.

'HOMEWARD'

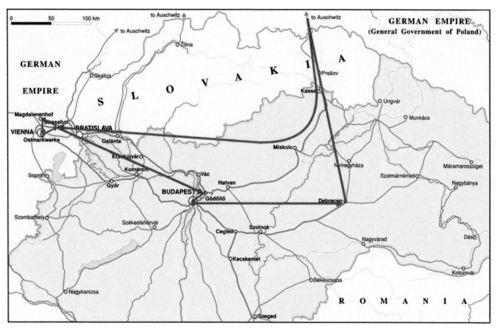

Our journey to and from the camps, starting from Budapest on 20th March 1944, arriving back on 29th April 1945

The map indicates my family's route from our home in Budapest through the camps in Hungary and Austria finally back 'home'.

How did we navigate our way from Strasshof to Budapest? We had no map. The weather was gloomy, so there was no sun to serve as guide. We just followed our instincts and the route of the Soviet army, moving in the opposite direction.

It took the best part of the month of April. We walked through one deserted village after the other. The locals had fled from the Russians. This must have been a wealthy area: houses were sizeable and neat, kitchens well equipped, carpeted sitting rooms with comfortable furniture. It was pointless to look into these houses: the inhabitants took with them every scrap of food, or any food they left behind had already been taken away by Jews passing through before us.

The journey only survives in disconnected memory fragments, each accompanied by visual details. If I could draw, I could turn these memories into a picture book. However bizarre they may seem, these story fragments contain the truth. Here are some memorable incidents.

STEW

Krémer Zsuzsi had been a school friend of Pici's. In a previous life her mother had been an elegant lady, and Zsuzsi's father an important personage, the District Engineer of the county. I still remember their imposing house near Debrecen's Great Forest. Zsuzsi and her mother were with us at OstmarkWerke and Strasshof, Mrs Krémer retaining her dignity throughout the hardships.

We were still near Strasshof when, one evening, Mrs Krémer sidled up to Nanóka, saying: 'My dear Ilonka, I have something to show you, but please don't think badly of me. I must show you what I found.' Nanóka was not sure what to expect when Mrs Krémer led her behind the pigsty of one of the houses; there on the ground was a great mound of steaming beef stew with vegetables and buckwheat, a one-pot meal freshly cooked, still hot, obviously dumped by Russian soldiers whose unit had moved on before they could eat their dinner.

Mrs Krémer's discovery was shared among some 30 hungry Jews, their first proper meal since leaving their home. We squatted around that food mountain, stuffing handfuls into our mouths. People kept telling each other to eat slowly, chew well. But for our few days on sugary soy bean soup, this sudden feast of rich food might have killed us, but it was just what we needed. When we could eat no more, there was still a lot left on the ground, so everyone filled whatever vessels they had. Our blue pot came in handy. We had food for a few days.

CHICKENS

Staggering along with our wheelbarrows, we considered bedding down for the night in one of the empty village houses. Bad idea. The Russians, generous in the daytime, were a menace at night, rounding up young women. They would start on houses, go on to haylofts and end at the barns. Nanóka's solution was practical, if uncomfortable: night after night, four of us young women slept curled up in stinking chicken coops.

The chicken coop reminds me of another incident. It was daytime; Mrs Krémer's beef stew was long gone, we looked as hungry as we were, and a Russian soldier tried to be helpful. A chicken, left behind by its Austrian owners, ran out of a farmyard just as we were staggering along. The Russian got hold of the bird by the head, and whirled it around a few times above his own head. The head of the chicken remained in his hand, and the headless animal ran along for a few yards. He picked up the chicken and gave it to Nanóka, gesturing that she should cook it. We were hungry, she would have been able to clean the chicken, and there were plenty of kitchens where she could have cooked it, but we did not have the time or the spirit. Onward we ambled, hungry. I don't recall what happened to the headless chicken.

HORSE AND CART

Wheelbarrows were useful at the start, but they soon proved too much for us. Our progress was slow, and it did not improve when my father tried to take a turn at pushing. Along came a young Russian. He darted into a farmyard and dragged out a cart. He picked up each of the grannies and Éva, threw them into the cart, piled in the wheelbarrows and our bags, and then ran after his unit which was fast disappearing at the far end of the village.

The cart was easier to push than the wheelbarrows. Four of us women pushed the cart from behind, while my father at the front tried to steer it in the right direction.

We only just began to get the hang of this mode of locomotion when another unit of Russians loomed up. Another helpful young soldier split off from his unit, shook his head at my father disapprovingly, shouting *stari*, *stari*, Russian for 'old' – too old for the task. In fact, my father was 44 years old at the time, but looked 90. Scanning a few of the nearby yards, our second Russian knight triumphantly turned up with a great brown horse, harnessed it to the cart, and then he, too, ran off to join his comrades.

This sounds like a farce, but the funny part is only just coming. There was my father with the reins, there was the horse, and there were we all, sitting in the cart, complete with our rucksacks, but my father had no clue how to make the creature move. He tried shouting at it, and whistling to it. We climbed down from the cart and tried to pull it; my father even tried to smack it (animal lovers can relax: he had neither the strength nor the inclination to do it harm). The rest of us tried to assist by pushing and pulling, but the horse was rigid as a statue. While we were considering appealing for help to a bunch of Jews coming along, the problem was resolved at a stroke. A third Russian appeared, scooped each of the grannies out of the cart, deposited them on the ground, pushed Éva into Terka's arms, threw out the wheelbarrows and our bags, made a gentle little sound by clicking his tongue, and off went horse, cart and Russian at a gallop. We had been owners of the cart and horse for 10 minutes, maximum, and were back on the road with our grannies, toddler, rucksacks and wheelbarrows.

LOCOMOTION

We tried various means of transport. There were trucks, but Russians drove them in the opposite direction, and in any case only they had fuel. Carts and horses were out, so trains were the most promising option. We followed railway lines through muddy fields, and found trains that had stopped on the open line. It was hard to climb on, and we were terrified that the train might start while part of the family was still on the ground. This never happened, but neither did we get anywhere. The train we had just mounted would stay stationary; we would give up and climb down, only to see it start up and move away. Or we would get on a train heading eastwards, but then it soon started back towards Vienna, cancelling out some of our hard-gained progress. It was early April, windy and rainy, and nights were frosty. Some of our train journeys were on flatcars, carriages for transporting large cargo, such as armoured vehicles or tanks. It was scary, especially with a toddler, and particularly at night when we could not see how far from the platform edge we were. We did not dare go to sleep, but in any case, it was too cold; by the morning the dew had settled on everything, including ourselves.

BRATISLAVA

By chance, we found ourselves in Bratislava, the Slovak capital. Looking for overnight shelter, we heard someone suggest the nearby cinema. The foyer and auditorium were already packed with refugees of every nationality, but there was still room in the corridors. A picture of tatty maroon carpets and wallpaper comes to mind.

Next day Pici and I went scouting for food. We found nothing, but Pici started to talk in French to a skinny Slovak woman who was also looking for food. She turned out to be a pianist who lived locally. Her shabby home had only a few sticks of furniture, but there was a full-size grand piano. The two of them talked music, and even played to each other. I tried to listen, but I fell asleep on a chair. The woman was sympathetic and kind, but her home was cold, and she too was hungry.

Bratislava had nothing for us. On the third day we hit the road again.

I have a memory of Bratislava, from around 1990. Travelling through Europe by car from London with English friends, we stopped for a night in Bratislava. Our English friends were shocked at the vicious antisemitic graffiti on buildings and billboards. I would never set foot in that city again.

HOMELAND

Leaving Bratislava, we stumbled on a train of flatcars that seemed to move fairly steadily towards Budapest, our destination. We were weak and exhausted; we must have slept, and we had no idea of our route. The train had overshot our target: next morning it came to a halt in Gödöllő, a small town some 30 km northeast of Budapest, known nowadays for its University of Agricultural Sciences.

It was mid-morning. We climbed down from our flatcar, our feet touching Hungarian soil for the first time since the previous June. Facing us were our fellow citizens, dressed in their Sunday best, going to church. Many stared at us, and one of them assumed the role of spokesman. His articulation was precise, his message clear. This is what he said:

> **"Rohadt zsidók nem tudtatok ott idegenben megdögleni, hát visszajöttetek a nyakunkra?"**

Hungarian is rich in expressing emotion. Translating the man's words into much less evocative English, his greeting would go something like:

> **"Stinking Jews, could you not just rot away abroad instead of returning to ruin our lives?"**

Home at last. It was Sunday, 29th April 1945. The war was over, and I was 12½ years old, almost a teenager.

POSTSCRIPT

To check my facts, I reread the memoir of my good friend Gábor. He lived through the ghetto, the wagon, OstmarkWerke and Strasshof, and had to find his way through the Soviet lines, the Austrian villages and Bratislava, back to Hungary. It is a miracle that he, his mother and sister survived, but his account makes me realise that their ordeal was much less taxing than ours. Aged 14, 18 and 45, they were all 'adults'. Our family was blessed and burdened with grannies and toddlers.

Eleven of the Csengeri Clan survived. Yes, our existence was marginal, we needed luck, or a long series of miracles, but we did not just *hope* to survive. We *worked* on our survival, and were *inspired* to survive. Remaining true to our values and being loyal to each other was our strength. Our old people linked us to our past, and their wisdom guided us in the hardships of the present. Our little ones symbolised the future. I am the only one left of the Csengeri Clan to tell this tale, but the others would have agreed when I say with pride that we all contributed to our survival of the Holocaust.[83]

HISTORIAN'S VOICE

Strasshof

The destruction of Hungarian Jewish communities in the last phase of World War II was one of the most efficient genocidal campaigns in history. Between mid-May and mid-July 1944, the Nazi and Hungarian authorities deported about 450,000 people, mostly women, children, and elderly, from the Hungarian provinces. Their destination was the Auschwitz camp complex, where most of them were gassed upon arrival, killing at least 300,000 in eight weeks. However, some deported Jews escaped that fate. In late June, more than 15,000 people were transported to Strasshof, in Lower Austria, rather than to Auschwitz, taken there primarily for work purposes.

This process is referred to in the professional literature as the 'rescue operation' or 'putting Jews on ice'. Both terms are slightly misleading. Despite their genocidal aims, in the last phase of the war Nazis also needed to obtain Jewish manpower for agricultural and military production. Industrial and construction companies, farms and infrastructural projects all required cheap slave labour of prisoners of war and civil forced labourers, including Jews. The decision was related to negotiations between Eichmann and the Zionists, led by Rezső Kasztner. In early June, SS-Brigadeführer Blaschke, the Gauleiter of Vienna, requested from Kaltenbrunner, head of Reich Main Security Office, workers for projects of 'military importance'. Kaltenbrunner instructed Eichmann to send some transports to Vienna. Eichmann offered this on 14th June to Kasztner as a concession in their ongoing negotiations.[84]

As preparation for Strasshof transports, in camps across Deportation Zone VI Jewish Councils were told to divide residents into two groups. The process was accompanied by dramatic scenes. Directives from the Central Jewish Council indicated that primarily the prominent members of congregations and their families were to be in the 'privileged' group, along with doctors, engineers, and other specialists. The remaining slots were to be filled by those fit to work and families of labour

---

83   See *HISTORIAN'S VOICE, Losses and hopes*

84   József Schiller, *A strasshofi mentőakció és előzményei*. Budapest: Cserépfalvi, 1996.; Braham, *The Politics of Genocide*, 850-854. For Blaschke's letter on June 7 and Kaltenbrunner's reply of June 30, in which he informs Blaschke about the arrival of 12,000 Jews, 30% of them fit to work, see Randolph L. Braham, ed. *The Destruction of Hungarian Jewry. A Documentary Account*. Vols. 1–2. (New York: World Federation of Hungarian Jews, 1963). Vol. 2. Doc. no. 184. 415-416.

servicemen. Since most camp inmates belonged to the latter two categories, it was difficult to decide whom to include. Jews had no information regarding destinations, but many suspected that members of the first group would have better circumstances.

According to the testimony of Edit Csillag, a Hungarian deportee who worked for the SS office at the Strasshof distribution camp, they registered 15,011 people deported from collection camps, including Debrecen, Szeged, Szolnok and Baja. Another 1690 people travelled on the so called 'Kasztner train'.[85] From Strasshof, Jews were transferred to settlements in the vicinity, where they worked in agriculture, rubble clearing, construction, and branches of industry. There was no selection, families were allowed to stay together. Living conditions, workload and treatment varied, but by-and-large, the situation of Hungarian Jewish slave labourers was relatively bearable, compared with other Nazi concentration and labour camps. Because of inadequate provisions, illness and mass murder committed by retreating SS troops, many of these people died, but eventually an estimated 75% survived the war.[86]

Losses and hopes

In World War II, the German Nazis and their Hungarian accomplices murdered about two-thirds of the Jewish community of wartime Hungary, more than half a million people. The majority of the victims were women, children, or the elderly. There were significant territorial differences in survival rates, because Budapest's Jewish community was ultimately spared mass deportation to Auschwitz. About half of Budapest's Jews survived, whereas this rate was about one-fifth in provincial Hungary and even less in the occupied territories. In Debrecen and those few other communities partly deported to labour camps in Austria, the survival rate was around 50%.[87]

Many Hungarian Jews liberated in the camps never made it back to Hungary, or promptly left the country. With the shocking experience of having been betrayed by their compatriots, and having lost their loved ones, communities and property, they felt that Hungary could never be their home again. Others were hoping for a new beginning, and worked hard to re-build their lives and the country. They expected that the new regime would ensure stability, equality and prosperity. However, soon they had to realise that the ghosts of the past had not disappeared, and a new wave of threats and tribulations appeared on the horizon.

---

85   Hungarian Jewish Museum and Archives, DEGOB Protocols no. 3628.

86   About the Strasshof deportation, see also Judit Molnár, *Zsidósors 1944-ben az V. (szegedi) csendőrkerületben.* Budapest: Cserépfalvi, 1995. 146-151; Szita, *Utak a pokolból*, 25-41. About the fate of Hungarian deportees in Austria, see Szita, *Utak a pokolból*, 41-47, 84-117.

87   According to estimates of the Statistical Department of the Hungarian Representation of the World Jewish Congress, in the countryside regions of post-Trianon Hungary 78% of Jews perished. In Budapest, this figure was 52%. See the statistical tables in Braham, *The Politics of Genocide*, Chapter 32.

7 TEENS IN TIMES OF CONFUSION

1945 – 1950

In the month-long journey home from our Austrian camp, our emaciated and exhausted family needed all its resources to cope with moment-by-moment crises. We had no strength to examine our motives or plan our future, we just moved by instinct. We assumed that we would be reunited with our loved ones, and that our old home would be restored to us. Having been officially an adult for almost a year, I thought I would smoothly revert to being a schoolgirl once more. Those crude words of greeting in Gödöllő shocked us, but we still expected that our country would accept us, and our fellow citizens would receive us with sympathy. These proved to be unrealistic expectations. It turned out that re-entry into society was difficult. The outburst of the man in Gödöllő was not unusual, and there were plenty of obstacles along the way.

When World War II was over, the Treaty of Paris restored post-Trianon borders, Hungary losing all its wartime territorial gains. The country was in ruins. Budapest suffered the most: all bridges down, over 80% of buildings damaged or destroyed. There were corpses of people, horses, and dogs on the streets. Rats were thriving while people were starving. Water supply was suspect, and there was a threat of epidemics. Mass vaccination against typhus and cholera started in the summer of 1945. We were still weak, and all my family became seriously ill.

Flirting briefly with democracy, a free election was held in November 1945, five parties competing. The resulting coalition was led by the central-right Smallholders' Party. The Communists gained just sufficient votes for a place in the coalition government.

Antisemitism appeared dormant for a while; perhaps people were stunned, a few might have been embarrassed, even ashamed, but Nazi ideology had appealed to the instincts of Hungarians. Fascist messages had been propagated for many years by images, writing and radio for decades, its poison reaching everyone, even infecting children at school. How could it have been blotted out at a stroke when the war ended? History teaches us that anti-Jewish racism is still there, generations later, deeply rooted in the soul of the nation.[88]

---

88   See *HISTORIAN'S VOICE, Post-war Antisemitism*

In the years between 1945 and 1947, Hungary had a democratically elected government. I have little recollection about the national politics of those two years: I was preoccupied with day-to-day matters of food, home and school, but the 1947 elections brought politics into focus. As usual in a multi-party democracy, in the 1947 election polling stations were manned by representatives of each party. In our district my father was the Social Democratic Party's representative. He detected – it did not need much insight – many instances of multiple voting: people registering for postal votes and also voting in person, or voting more than once. By then the police force was already under Communist control. My father protested; the police removed him from the polling station, and he was threatened with imprisonment. His experience was shared by representatives of several parties the country over.[89]

Gaining control by fraudulent means, the Communists established a dictatorship which persisted for decades. The five leading figures of the regimes turned out to be of Jewish origin.

- Farkas Mihály was a key figure in the Communist Party, organiser of the fraudulent takeover of political power.

- The country's Great Communist Leader was Rákosi Mátyás, the Hungarian Stalin. In my teens, his personal cult permeated everything: his pictures adorned walls, his speeches were printed in all papers and broadcast on all (both) radio stations, his wise words had to be learnt by everyone and chanted everywhere.[90]

- Gerő Ernő was a popular Transport Minister after the war, credited with rebuilding the country's wrecked bridges and roads, but later he acquired notoriety as the most rigid of Communist hardliners.

- Révai József was in total charge of the country's oppressive press and cultural life.

- Péter Gábor was the most feared and most hated man in Hungary as Head of AVH (Államvédelmi Hatóság – State Defence Authority), the Hungarian equivalent of Hitler's Gestapo and Stalin's NKVD.

Oppression leads to pent-up hatred against the oppressors. Although the new Communist regime hit Jews and non-Jews alike, Jews in the leadership ignited a new wave of antisemitism.[91]

---

89   See *HISTORIAN'S VOICE, Short History of Post-War Hungary*

90   Andrew Handler–Susan V. Meschel, eds. *Red Star, Blue Star: The Lives and Times of Jewish Students in Communist Hungary, 1948-1956.* Boulder and New York: Columbia University Press, 1997.

91   See *HISTORIAN'S VOICE: Jews and Non-Jews in the New Regime*

THE FAMILY

How did my family navigate through the country's turbulent political and economic waters?

The journey from Gödöllő to our Budapest home is blotted from my memory. Most likely there was no regular public transport anywhere in the country. It was a 30km walk.

We had no key to our flat at Vilmos Császár út 58. We knocked on Caretaker Mr Hajdu's door. Mrs Hajdu opened the door. In her taciturn way, showing no surprise or emotion, she told us that she knew nothing about our men, her own husband was dead, and our flat was occupied by people who had been bombed out of their home. When we asked what we should do, she shrugged her shoulders, shut the door, and exited from my story.

In our flat we found a family of five: parents, grandparents and a boy, about nine. Our flat had been allocated to them, perhaps by the council. They were sleeping in our beds, using what was left of our belongings. These tired and defeated people were not aggressive; neither they nor we had the strength or the inclination to argue. As there were more of us than of them, it was fair that we should have Terka and Feri's room because it was slightly bigger than the other. We nine did not find it difficult to live in one room, nor to share the small flat with five strangers – we had coped with much worse before – but we warned them that our family would soon grow bigger when our loved ones returned from camps, or wherever the end of the war found them.

My father was a weak skeleton, and in any case his priority was to get me to school. The tale of my schooling is soon to follow. It was my mother who approached the authorities for restoring our home to us. They did not want to know; they almost laughed at her: had she not heard that there had been a war? Budapest's houses were destroyed, the city was a ruin. Go away, they told her, and count yourself lucky to have a roof over your head. There might have been charitable bodies to whom we could have turned for help with food and clothing. It never occurred to us. Were we proud, or just ill-informed? Perhaps our flatmates offered us some scraps of food, but I remember being hungry, as usual.

It took my parents weeks to recall that they had left precious belongings with neighbours and friends for safekeeping. When my mother brought herself to visit these people, she returned empty-handed. She refused to discuss the matter.

We searched desperately for Klári, Gyurika, Rózsi, Giza mama, Ilus, Gabika, all my uncles, our other relatives, friends, people who used to be part of our lives. Everyone everywhere did the same. Posters were stuck to doorways, walls, lampposts. Little slips of hand-written anguished messages were pushed through letterboxes. When newspapers started up, they were full of advertisements of people looking for people. Pleas and appeals were broadcast on the radio for years. Among my papers are two attempts of my father searching for his sister Margit through the Red Cross. The search for those loved and lost went on for decades. Jancsi's mother never gave up; she refused to accept that her elder son was lost. I have just donated to the Wiener Library a letter she wrote in 1984, shortly before she died, begging for information from anyone who might have known the whereabouts of her boy András.

The day after our return we looked for Rózsi and Giza mama. Their neighbours told us that the Arrow Cross 'marched them away' in the direction of the river. We then heard about the riverside massacres. We never found out the fate of Ilus and Gabika.

I was at school when my uncle Feri arrived. I did not witness his joy when he met his wife Terka and his little daughter Éva who had been a small baby when he saw her last. He and three of his devoted friends insisted that they had stayed alive in Ukraine because of their mutual solidarity: 'all for one and one for all', acquainting me with Dumas. While we were still in our camps, all four had returned to Hungary with the retreating Hungarian army, and they absconded. In the darkest days of Szálasi's pro-Nazi regime, Feri had been hidden by his great friend Gazda Bandi, a warm-hearted, uneducated man with a wealth of natural talents. Bandi had built his own house in Angyalföld, a working-class neighbourhood of Budapest, creating in it a brick-built cubbyhole for Feri, walling him in for the daytime, and releasing him each night, risking his own life.[92]

From time to time a few returning friends stopped by, most of them sole survivors of their families. They told their stories. As my father said, they survived because their unlikely tales were likely to be true. It was early summer when Klári and Gyurika returned from Vienna. There was great rejoicing, although Gyurika was ill with tuberculosis. Soon afterwards, the Ministry of Defence notified Klári of the death of her husband in Military Labour Service. Just a statement of fact, no expression of sympathy, no pension for her or her sick child.

Our hopes for my uncles were fading. I will never stop mourning them.

With the addition of Feri, Klári and Gyurika, our family had now 12 members, and our room in the shared home in Vilmos Császár út was beginning to be crowded.

Feri mobilised his legal friends, and managed to obtain a flat allocation for his immediate family.

Hoping to regain her home, shop and assets, Nanóka and the widowed Pici headed for Debrecen.

My step-grandmother Szeréna was admitted to the old people's home of Budapest's Jewish Hospital, where she lived happily until she was almost a hundred. She had failed to care for my father when he was a small boy, but my father took exquisite care of her in her old age; of course he did.

---

92 Alexander Dumas, *Three Musketeers*, a tale of loyalty and friendship.

All that remained of the Csengeri Clan was Klári, Gyurika, my parents and me. Everyone seemed content; only I was unhappy. I understood that our camp-time family had to disperse if we were to return to something like a normal life, but I missed companionship with the people I loved and who loved me. I did not realise that only a war and extreme hardship could form a bond as strong as ours had been.

Bewildered by faceless bureaucracy, my parents gave up hope of having our flat restored to us. It had never been much of a home; we were ready to leave it to the bombed-out family. Someone advised that we might have better luck finding a home in neighbouring Újpest, because that town had many empty homes. They did not say that those homes stood empty because almost all of Újpest's Jews had been murdered.

SOMEWHERE TO LIVE

These days Újpest is a district of Greater Budapest. At that time, it was a town in its own right. It was not a pretty place, but the 'Újpest' football team was well known the world over. The town has a remarkable history. Lőwy Izsák, a tanner, started the settlement in 1835. It became a 'Jewish colony' where Jewish craftsmen and tradesmen could settle, transport their wares downriver, and sell them in the capital. The town was formally founded in 1840, and under the leadership of Aschner Lipót, another Jew, by the early 20th century became the country's fourth largest industrial centre.[93] In 1944, Újpest had 76,000 inhabitants, of whom 12,000 were Jews. All but 10% were lost in the Holocaust – the young men in military labour service, the rest in Auschwitz. This is how the town repaid the people of its founder and its famous benefactor.[94]

To qualify for a flat allocation in Újpest, the applicant needed some past connection with the town. My parents and I had no right to a home in Újpest. It seemed that we had no right to a home anywhere, but Klári did: her mother – my aunt Mariska – had lived in Újpest before being killed in Auschwitz. My parents and I claimed to be Klári's dependents. We submitted petitions, sat in offices, wrote letters to unresponsive administrators. Promises were unfulfilled, hopes dashed. A lucky coincidence: Feri knew Benedek

---

93   Lipót Aschner was a visionary, mass producer of lightbulbs under the well-known trade name *Tungsram*. Extending his range of products and interests, he became Chairman of the World Cartel of Manufacturers, founder of a string of research laboratories which revolutionised the industry, and made his manufacturing organisation into one of the world's leaders. He established entire faculties in new branches of science, such as the Faculty of Atomic Physics at the Technical University of Budapest. See: Lajos Sipos, ed. *Újpesti történetek*. Budapest: Újpesti Városvédő Egyesület, 2001.

94   László Szilágyi-Windt, *Az újpesti zsidóság története*. Tel Aviv, LAHAV, 1975. Szilágyi's book gives a full list of Újpest's Jewish 'martyrs of the Holocaust', together with a 'repository of personal data', with photographs of prominent survivors, among them my father-in-law and most 'adults' to whom this chapter refers by name.

Jenő, a Jewish lawyer who became influential in Újpest's Town Council. Success! We were declared eligible for a home – in principle. Theoretical eligibility was still not an actual flat allocation.

It was still summer when we heard the brilliant news: we had been allocated a flat in Újpest, close to all civic and cultural amenities and to the girls' grammar school. There were two spacious sunny rooms, one for my parents and one for Klári and Gyurika, and there was a small room just for me, with a window to the garden. The flat had been occupied by Soviet soldiers who did not understand the toilet and used the bathtub instead, had made open fires in the kitchen, and barbecued on the parquet floor of one of the rooms. Klári, my mother and I set to work, and after a few days the foul smell had gone, the soot had been rubbed off the walls and ceilings, and the damaged parquet floor was covered up with one of the grey blankets of Strasshof.

Just when we were about to move in, we received both good news and bad. The good news: a young Jew of 20, presumed dead, miraculously returned from labour service, the only survivor of his family. We rejoiced in every survival. The bad news: the flat had belonged to his family; he had every right to it, and the authorities told us to get out. The young man thanked us for cleaning up his home so nicely. We wished him luck, and never saw him again.

Back we went to the authorities to beg for another flat allocation. There were delays, tears, but – at last – success! Our new flat was filthy, in a bizarre, forbidding old building among shabby squat little houses, on the northmost edge of Újpest, the nearest public transport a mile away. How different from our previous home in the heart of Metropolitan Budapest.

The building is still there. Originally intended as a convent (!), it pre-dates founder Lőwy's enterprise by a century. Constructed of grim purple bricks, it had two-foot-thick solid walls, with accommodation on two floors: a mezzanine with tall ceilings, and a semi-basement divided into small dwellings. In the early 20th Century the house had been converted into a family home and studio for Rubovics Márk, a well-known Jewish painter. His work sells today for high prices on the European art market.

We were allocated half of the mezzanine floor. I could draw the floor plan of our flat which comprised the artist's studio, two very tall but modest-sized rooms, a smallish kitchen, a tiny bathroom, and a toilet (no wash basin). Klári and Gyurika chose the studio, larger and even taller than the other rooms. My parents had a bedroom, and I slept in the living room. This arrangement lasted till the autumn, when it became clear that the studio was even more difficult to heat than the rooms. We offered it back to the council. Klári and Gyurika came to occupy one of the two rooms, and I reverted to sharing my parents' room, as before.

Before we arrived in our new home, the place had been lived in by Soviet soldiers. It was a familiar scenario. We cleaned up the flat, and brought over from Vilmos Császár út the few remaining items of my parents' bedroom furniture. We found from somewhere a narrow table and rickety stools, so we could now eat in the kitchen, but it had an icy stone floor. My father bartered with someone and obtained a rusty kitchen range (what could he have given in exchange?). It is hard to credit my own memory: for the first summer a rat took up residence inside the range. Once the rat met its fate, the range functioned well. It cooked and baked our food, warmed water for washing clothes and ourselves, and kept the kitchen temperate. It was the best place in the flat. The bathroom must have been an afterthought: a small brick-built cube on stilts, protruding into the garden, exposed to the elements on five sides: the floor, the ceiling and three walls. It had a single washbasin with a cold-water tap, and a bathtub without any water tap at all. It was useless even in summer.

We gave that bathroom every chance. Heating water on top of the kitchen range, two of us lugged a large blue cast-iron pot across the entrance hall and my parents' room, and poured the hot water into the bath. Warming another potful in the kitchen while the first lot cooled in the bath, we tried to have a bath in two potfuls – about six inches of water. It was hopeless. We washed instead in a large enamel washing-up bowl in the kitchen. Klári bathed Gyurika in the evening, and the rest of us queued up in the morning. We shut off the miserable bathroom, sealed the gaps with grey blankets (we had one each), and forgot about it altogether. Luckily the toilet was separate.

At first, we did not even dream of the luxury of a bath, but later, becoming more ambitious, we started to wish for a full tub of water. There were public baths a mile away, open once a week for men, and on another day for women. We could only afford it about once a fortnight. Later we became friendly with the Kaposi family who had a centrally heated detached house, almost unheard-of in those days. A coal-fired boiler in their bathroom supplied hot water for the bath and for the radiators of the whole house. They generously offered us access to their bathroom, but fuel was scarce and they were not well off, and in any case their house was no nearer than the public baths, so I doubt if we ever availed ourselves of their hospitality.

After a couple of years our family reduced even more. Klári met and married Zoli, a decent down-to-earth man, foreman in one of Újpest's factories, very different from her brilliant banker first husband Can'tSwim. She and Gyurika moved out of the convent, and I regained possession of the living room. My parents and I lived in that convent until my marriage. With its lack of bathroom, unheatable tall rooms, and remoteness from amenities, it was never a comfortable home. So, soon after I moved away, my parents exchanged it for a flat in town, in Népszinház utca, Budapest.[95]

95   In Communist times a significant part of real estate was state owned and homes were rented. The housing crisis led to the institution of 'home exchange': a primitive bartering arrangement, usually involving long chains and bitter quarrels.

SOMETHING TO EAT

It was the summer of 1945. We now had somewhere to live, but had no money, and nothing to eat. Rumour had it that hot soup was dispensed somewhere in the neighbourhood. I was a stranger to the town, but I was ready, willing and hungry. Taking along my trusty blue pot, I went in search of that soup. A queue was, and remained for years, a sign of food. Right enough, a mile away there was a queue. Those in queues were usually secretive, not wanting competition, but I extracted the information that this was indeed the soup queue.

We waited in front of a house on the corner of a leafy suburban street. Lovely aromas wafted out. It was a long wait, but I had time, and I had been hungry for over a year. Fences were low. The house opposite had a big oval terrace where a lady was playing with her dog. I needed all my envy-training to cope with the sight. At length the lady descended from her elegant house, and a few minutes later appeared with a ladle, behind two people carrying a cauldron of bean soup. She reassured us that there was plenty more inside, and asked everyone how much they wanted. I held out the blue pot which had served the 11-strong Csengeri Clan through the camps, and told her to 'fill it up, please'.

Years in the future, that woman became my mother-in-law. Rather than being a lady of leisure as I assumed, she had been through the hell of the war. Her elder son had been lost in Ukraine. She had offered shelter to returners from the camps who brought with them typhoid fever. Her younger son, my would-be husband, caught the disease, and she had barely managed to nurse him back from the brink of death.

Food remained a problem for years. The last year of the war disrupted agricultural production; after the war the capital was starved of meat, poultry, fresh fruit and vegetables. There was a black market for those who could afford it, but most of our food was pulses, mouldy dried lentils and beans left over in grocers' cellars from years before. One day my father brought home a pike, big enough for a meal for us all. My mother cooked it up into a fish soup (*halászlé*), with a few precious potatoes and onions – and we could not eat it. The fish had come from a branch of the Danube blocked up by wartime rubble: destroyed tanks, abandoned armoured vehicles. The water was polluted, and it was the noxious chemicals that had killed the fish.

As years passed, agriculture started up, but food shortages remained a permanent feature in Communist Hungary (an agricultural country!). We were not exactly starving any more, but food queues were commonplace, and neighbours would alert each other on the rare occasions when bread, eggs, potatoes or anything edible happened to turn up in the shops. Food shortage was even reflected in official slogans. Placards proclaimed everywhere:

Those who don't work are not entitled to eat!
Aki nem dolgozik, ne is egyék!

There were whispered bitter jokes about food being exported to the Soviet Union without recompense. For example:

Teacher in the classroom: Tommy, what are the parts of the pig?

Child: The skin, the bones and the innards.

Unable to queue for food, working people and their children had their main meal in factory canteens and school refectories. Quality was lamentable. When Jancsi and I were students at the country's famous Technical University, food poisoning was commonplace, as was finding maggots on your plate. When we were married and Jancsi and his best friend Zoli, graduate engineers both, had been employed in professional jobs, Zoli and his wife would drop in on their way home, saying: "We have two inches of sausage. Got a few potatoes? Let's have supper together."

Meat, if available, was of poor quality, and very expensive. Beef came from elderly oxen no longer fit to drag carts, or cows beyond the menopause. Meat cooked for 4-5 hours became tasteless, but still remained tough. There were no food imports, and children would grow up without ever seeing an orange. I was 24, a refugee in Vienna, when I first saw a banana. Frozen food was unknown – the food processing industry had not started up yet. Real tea and coffee were luxuries, appearing only after the 1956 revolution, sent from abroad by emigrants. When a fruit or a vegetable was in season, those who had the time and the money made preserves for the whole year. Before my mother became incapacitated, she made jams. She and I would get up at five, bought the fruit in the market, and brought it home in a two-handled laundry basket. The jam would be cooked in a 10-litre pan, bottled, and steamed on top of the kitchen range in the cast iron pot no longer used for warming bathwater. People also made their own pickles, tomato ketchup and compote. Nanóka was known for her pickled cucumbers and candied quinces, Jancsi's mother for her mixed pickles (*csalamádé*), and Máli néni for her pickled plums (*ecetes szilva*). My mother's efforts were creditable, but Terka's apricot and morello cherry jams were memorable. Decades later she still sent me bottles of her fragrant jams to England.

LIVELIHOOD

Post-war Hungary had hyper-inflation, the worst in history. There is a bundle of inflation money on my shelf. I have no sample of the highest denomination: a banknote of 100 quintillion Pengő (in numbers, 100,000,000,000,000,000,000). Money was quite literally not worth the paper it was printed on. Here is a picture of a street cleaner sweeping up worthless banknotes. Salaried people rushed to buy anything in sight on their way home, because in a few hours their money would be worth nothing.

Hyperinflation banknotes, Hungary 1946.
Kaposi family collection / Photograph of Mafirt–István Mizerák,
Hungarian National Museum Historical Photo Department

People tried to avoid money altogether, demanding payment in kind. I had private language lessons – we almost starved, but my father's priorities were unchanged – and my mother paid my teacher the tuition fee in little packets of flour. The teacher did not have a good bargain: we only had some poor-quality French flour, perhaps mixed with chalk, obtained from some obscure source. Bread was almost never available, and those who could, baked their own. I was ashamed to fetch our homemade bread from the baker, because it was flat as a pancake, the laughing stock of the bakery and the street. Those who knew a source of better flour did not share their secret with us.

By the summer of 1945 we had a home, but we could not live for ever on someone else's soup; we had no clothes, and we had to pay the rent.

My father was still a weak skeleton, so once again the role of breadwinner fell to my mother. She found a job at the cotton works, the *Újpesti Pamutgyár*. She started on the same day as a little peasant girl half her age, and my mother was not the first to learn how to operate the weaving machines. The job made her frustrated and humiliated, and in any case she soon had to give up being a factory worker, because her spinal trouble started.

First the discomfort just restricted her movement, but it gradually built up to crippling pain. By the age of 36, she was a bedridden invalid. Hospitals were ill-equipped, and it took several years for hernia of a disc to be diagnosed. Doctors speculated that the condition might have been caused by injury sustained at Magdalenenhof.

In early 1946 my father was beginning to regain some of his strength, and rented a small shop in the centre of Újpest. He had not much option, but I will never understand his choice. The business traded in technical goods: driving belts for rotating machinery, ball bearings, machine tools, gear boxes, nuts and bolts. Although intelligent and vastly knowledgeable, my father knew nothing about technical merchandise. He might have learnt, and the business might have prospered, but factories were in ruins, transport was hopeless, there were no telephones, at first post was nonexistent and later it was unreliable. There were no banks, and inflation was raging. Crime was rife, holding stock was risky. My father was naively trusting, lacking commercial finesse, and was frequently cheated by customers and suppliers.

Inflation meant trading through bartering. This is how I got the most beautiful full-length sheepskin coat, elegantly tailored, exquisitely pale in colour, warm as an oven, light as a feather. The fur processing factory needed a garment for an exhibition to impress foreign customers. They took me as their model, their top craftsmen made the coat, and when the exhibition was over, the coat was given to my father in payment for goods supplied. That coat kept me warm through all the winters in Hungary; I wore it when we left the country in 1956, and I might be wearing it still, had it not been torn to pieces as I was climbing through the barbed wire at the border. That story will be told later.

The business employed a delivery boy who had a heavy goods bicycle with a big metal basket at the front and another at the rear. When the bicycle could be spared from the business, I was allowed to borrow it. It was so heavy that I was hardly able to ride it, but I loved it just the same. By then I had made a friend: Donáth Judit, daughter of one of Újpest's wealthy factory-owning Jewish families. Picture the pair of us: Judit, tall, sporty, smartly dressed, riding her silver racing bike, Don Quixote on her steed; and me on my father's heavy black goods bicycle, a squat scruffy Sancho Panza on a donkey. In 1948 Judit emigrated to England, married my friend Gábor, and became my daughter Esther's 'godmother'. She was my best friend until she died, aged 35.

By the winter of 1947/1948, all illusion of democracy disappeared. 1949 saw the first single-party election. The People's Republic was declared, the Iron Curtain was in place, the Cold War had begun. The People's Republic put an end to all private enterprise. At a stroke, factories, shops, and businesses were nationalised, as were all but the smallest, privately owned homes. My father's business was no more. He found a job in the civil service. I guess he was relieved that his business career was over.

There was no unemployment in the country: the right to work was enshrined in law, and those who did not work were regarded as pariahs. The economy was starved, wages were pitiful, families with both parents working had barely enough for food and rent, pensioners were starving, some dying of hypothermia. There was no notion of sex equality. Mothers of young children worked full time, but also did the shopping, ran the home, and cared for the children. They dragged their babies and toddlers to the nursery before starting their daily job, collected them at the end of the working day, and started their second shift of shopping, cooking, and doing the laundry. The income of distinguished professionals like my lawyer and doctor uncles were sometimes lower than those of unskilled workers, and their wives' earnings were needed to support their families. A doctor's certificate was required for missing work even for half a day of illness, and doctors were under heavy pressure to keep sickness statistics low.

HEALTH

Magdalenenhof never allowed us to forget it. Winter brought back frostbite. My hands were raw and painful, with lesions and swollen knuckles. In the severest weather I tried to stay indoors, but school was a must, a long walk each way. After being outside, thawing out my hands was difficult. Sudden temperature change caused bleeding. Lukewarm water relieved the pain, but it softened the skin. A wound would open up, and would not heal. The best solution was to bury my hands in my mother's armpits. Toes were also bad, but heels were even worse, and there were times when I was unable to wear shoes. The shoes in postwar Hungary were tough, without being hardwearing. After our marriage, my mother-in-law 'wore in' my shoes for me. Her feet were slightly larger than mine, and on the rare occasions when I had new shoes, she wore them for a few weeks, stretching them and making them a bit less unyielding. I am grateful to the Gulf Stream. Even in England's gentle climate, the knuckles of my fingers show traces of the frostbite acquired when picking sugarbeet 75 years ago.

Gradually the hernia of the disc in my mother's spine worsened, and by about 1950 she was in unbearable pain. She talked of not wanting to live. Surgery was recommended, but such spinal operations had not been performed in Hungary before; post-war hospital conditions and equipment were inadequate, and the procedure was said to be life-threatening. She opted for it without hesitation. The operation lasted seven hours, and afterwards she had to lie on her stomach for more than a week. Nursing care was poor, negligence of nurses caused the wound to open, and she almost bled to death. She was strong and determined, and in due course got almost well, but we lived in fear of the trouble recurring. True enough, in 1980 she had an accident, knocked down by a van on her way to a Covent Garden opera rehearsal. Her knee was bruised and her wrist broken, but she defied police and ambulance, insisted on going to the opera – she, too, had her priorities. The wrist soon healed, but the knee injury led to a limp, which in turn caused a recurrence of the hernia of the spine. The surgeon at the Royal Free Hospital operated on the spine and also attended to the knee six months later, each operation taking over four hours. Tough cookie that she was, my mother recovered well, and was fit in body, if not in mind, for the rest of her life.

KEEPING HOUSE

It was soon after my 16th birthday when my mother became bedridden. We could not afford help, and although willing, my father was inept, so I took charge. I am not complaining; I was willing and apt, and had coped with worse. School remained top priority. My school in Budapest was five miles away; the school day started at 8 am, tram transport covered about half the distance and was unreliable. Shopping was difficult: food supply was erratic, and there were no shops near our convent. I juggled school and domestic tasks.

History characterises post-war Hungary as being in a 'pre-industrial' state. Domestic appliances such as a fridge and a vacuum cleaner would have helped, and frozen or ready-cooked food would have been useful, but even if we had been able to afford them, none of these were available. Cleaning had to be done to the high standards of our family. I did not miss the vacuum cleaner: if you never had one, you did not miss it. Nanóka had taught us how to clean house, and I put her methods into practice. I almost enjoyed the process. Starting from the top of the furthest room and driving the dust and dirt room by room in front of one, the last bit to be cleaned was the floor of the entrance hall. I often recalled great-grandmother Eszter's crude but apt saying: 'when one finished, the house was so clean that the only place to spit on was the housewife'. When I finished, I heated water on the range and washed myself from top to toe in that big enamelled washing-up bowl. When even I was clean, there was nowhere to spit at all.

Meals had to be provided daily. I had no chance to cook and shop every day, but Nanóka had taught us what food kept well. These days I read the 'use-by' dates on food we buy. Some of them are sheer nonsense. Nanóka also taught us how to preserve food without ice. You made jams, compotes and candied fruit, and pickled various kinds of fruit and vegetables when in season. You dried mushrooms and made kefir and cottage cheese. You condensed and bottled tomatoes, hung smoked sausages, preserved cooked meat and liver in fat. You made pasta in bulk, and dried it. You re-boiled soups, and double-baked bread. I know many more methods of food preservation.

Sophisticated households such as the Kaposis', but unlike ours, had an *ice cupboard*. It was a sizeable metal box with cavity walls, double floor and double ceiling, insulated by rags stuffed into the gaps. The inside was divided by a perforated wall, one side for ice, the other for food. It had a drain with a bucket under to catch the melted ice water. After my marriage I lived in the Kaposi house, so I participated in the procedure of getting ice for the icebox. Every other day, all year round except in deep winter, a great carthorse dragged a cart along the street, piled high with a dripping load of yard-long blocks of ice. The horse's job was tough: many streets, including the Kaposis', were unpaved, so there were clouds of dust in the summer and deep mud in the spring and autumn. The iceman (*jeges*) whipped his horse fiercely, swore at it viciously, and announced his arrival by yelling loudly. At his call, people rushed out with great buckets into which the iceman threw lumps of ice, hacked off from his blocks with a pickaxe. My mother-in-law had her first electrical fridge in 1959, imported from Austria. We sent her the money for it from England.

SOCIAL / CULTURAL LIFE

My family had no religion; we were not in the habit of going to synagogue, but we knew nobody in Újpest and, perhaps out of curiosity, when Jewish New Year came, my parents and I walked along Attila utca to the synagogue. Újpest's synagogue had been built for a wealthy pre-Holocaust community.

The synagogue had been sacked in 1944, and was damaged during the war. In the autumn of 1945, it had not yet been restored. Services were held in a small side-building, large enough for Újpest's diminished Jewish community. Only about 70 people gathered. The rabbi conducted the service, and the cantor sang lustily, but out of tune.

Újpest's Neolog community was traditional. English Jews assume that the customs of Neolog Jews of Hungary are as relaxed as those of the Reform Jews of England. Not so. Neolog

Újpest synagogue on a postcard, early 20th century.
Photo: Bernát Schön. Hungarian Jewish Museum and Archives

ritual demanded separation of men and women. Synagogue services were conducted downstairs in the main hall *by* men, *for* men. Women were confined to the gallery, their view blocked by a screen; they could see nothing, and understood less. In Újpest's makeshift gathering, temporary shields were erected, separating men from women.

Soon after my mother and I arrived, a lady welcomed us newcomers. I knew her daughter already: Hartmann Panna was in the class below mine at school. Donáth Judit, the girl in the class above, was also there. Panna's mother was a friendly lady who invited us to their home in Árpád út, around the corner. Things were looking up. We three were the only Jewish girls at our school.

Before Communist times, religious education was still compulsory. Our teacher was a frail old lady whom we called *Citrom*, Lemon. She made only one demand on us: when the synagogue organised a Jewish festival, we had to participate.

The first such event was *Simkhat Torah*, the Festival of the Book, one of the few jolly Jewish holidays. Újpest's handsome synagogue had been built for a community of 20,000. It had been ransacked in the war, and the few survivors could easily be accommodated in a small side building. Adults and children combined efforts to mount a programme of music, drama and poetry. I performed a little monologue, playing the role of two people: a male journalist interviewing a woman. One of the musical offerings was Beethoven's Romance No.2 in F major, played on the violin by an almost grown up boy of 16. After the show he came over to me. His first words were: 'Do you like music?' He appeared impressed that in a previous life I had played the piano. I knew nothing about orchestral music, but he knew a lot, so he asked if he could show me some of his miniature symphony scores. I was shy

Student travel card of Kaposi János, the author's boyfriend and later husband, 1947.
Kaposi family collection

and surprised that such a mature personage noticed me, but as you see in the picture, he had almond-shaped eyes with curly lashes, so I took him to my mother who said yes, he could come along next Sunday afternoon. He was called János (Jancsi), and the date of that festival was the 23rd September 1945. I was still 12.

Week by week, month by month, disoriented lonely Jews drifted back to Újpest from the camps, skeletal and sick, many with numbers tattooed on their arm. Some found one or two members of their family, but most were alone, children without parents and siblings, mothers without husbands and children. There were as many sorrowful stories as people. We also heard of families that disappeared altogether. We newcomers had not known these lost families, but members of the Jewish community mourned their friends, and told us about them. Jancsi had been at the local Jewish primary school. Only two of his schoolmates survived. That's when I first came across survivors' guilt: the guilt of the innocent.

The synagogue became a community centre. Family fragments tried to mend themselves, some even formed new relationships. Here is an example. Once there had been two Jewish couples, friends. Their children grew up together. The son of one family became engaged to the daughter of the other, his childhood sweetheart. During the war all members of both families were murdered, except for the would-be groom and his fiancée's mother. He was younger than her lost sons, she was older than his lost mother. Trying to console themselves and each other, these two devastated people married. We knew them well. Theirs was a successful marriage.

In the summer of 1946, my entrepreneur father (joke) visited a large timber workshop in search of business. About a dozen people were working there. My father asked the freckled boy in the courtyard for the foreman. The boy shrugged his shoulders and said that there was no foreman. My father said he would see the owner then. The boy said he thought it might be him. My father brought him home to our convent, and my mother gave him a share of our yellow pea soup. Before the war his family had comprised five brothers, and each had several male children. It was a joke in the town that their women could only produce boys. The Schwartz were a wealthy clan, distantly related to Nanóka's brother-in-law. They had all been in the timber business: dealers, mill owners, carpenters. They all died. The sole survivor was 14-year-old Sanyi. I don't remember which hellhole he had been in, but he had a number tattoo. He returned to Újpest in the winter of 1945. He was stunned or in shock; he made no contact with anyone but his own workmen. Until my father discovered him in the summer of 1946, and for several years thereafter, Sanyi squatted in the entrance hall of his parents' elegant house, which the council had allocated to others. Sanyi himself was not entitled to an allocation because he was underage. When the Jewish community came to realise Sanyi's existence, the father of one of my friends, pillar of Újpest's Jewish community – let us call him Mr Smartguy – offered himself as Sanyi's guardian, and stripped him of all the family's assets. We learnt much later that Mr Smartguy had been the appointed recipient of food and closing aid provided by the *Joint* for needy members of the Jewish community, such as my parents and me. He told nobody about it. Instead, Mr Smartguy sold everything on the black market. It takes all sorts, even among Jews, even after the Holocaust.[96]

We started to build a life. The community began to organise cultural events. At first the congregation used the talents of its own members, but soon they invited celebrity performers. There were concerts, such as the one involving the tenor Vári-Weinstock who

---

96   The American Jewish Joint Distribution Committee, also known as the Joint or the JDC, is a Jewish relief organisation based in New York City.

later changed his name to Gafni and had a career in major opera houses of the world. Well-known actors performed plays and sketches. There were solo and chamber concerts, poetry recitals, curiosity shows, even a magician.

Most memorable were a series of lectures by Professor Scheiber Sándor, rabbi, philosopher, historian, philologist, and sage. He was a great man, an inspiring lecturer who held his audience spellbound. I recall a few of his topics: the history of writing, linguistic links of the Greek, Latin and Hebrew languages, relationships between mythology and religion, development of number systems, and of course Jewish philosophy. He became Rector of Budapest's Rabbinical Seminary, the most prestigious teaching institution of its kind in the Eastern Bloc. The institution still exists, as does the Jewish grammar school named after him.[97] While we were students at the Technical University, Jancsi and I often skipped our classes and attended his lectures instead. At the time of the discovery of the Dead Sea Scrolls, Professor Scheiber was one of those eminent scholars who received a collection of sheets to decipher. When lecturing about the discovery of the scrolls, he told us of his poor eyesight and his difficulty in reading the fragile faded documents. Jancsi asked if he might help him by use of photographic techniques. This is how they became friends, and I still have some of their correspondence. Like my father, Professor Scheiber had his priorities. He visited us in England soon after we arrived here in 1957. We lived in a small cold rented room and had nothing. He stepped in, looked around, and asked Jancsi accusingly: 'Where are the books!?' I have one of his beautiful illustrated popular books. The pictures are fascinating, and so is his (Hungarian) text.[98]

Friendships started up. Among my parents' card playing friends were the Brichtas. They had identical twin sons a few years younger than me. They survived Auschwitz, the boys having been experimented on by the notorious Dr Mengele.[99] They were good at all school subjects except mathematics, and Jancsi tutored them for years. Later the family emigrated to Israel and changed their surname to Alon. Both boys became civil servants, and one of them, Károly, served as Israel's ambassador to the United Nations and to several countries. Victims of the war, neither of them ever married.

---

97   About Sándor Scheiber, see: Enikő Bollobás, The Two Doors of Sándor Scheiber. In *Hungarian Review*, Vol. IV. (2013) no. 4. http://hungarianreview.com/article/the_two_doors_of_sandor_scheiber

98   Tamás Féner–Sándor Scheiber, *"... és beszéld el fiadnak." Zsidó hagyományok Magyarországon ["... narrate it to your son." Jewish traditions of Hungary]*. Budapest: Corvina, 1984.

99   Dr Josef Mengele, German physician and SS captain, SS garrison physician in Auschwitz-Birkenau. In that capacity, he was responsible for selection of those fit to work and those destined for gassing. He also carried out human experiments on camp inmates, especially on identical twins. See e.g. Robert Jay Lifton, *The Nazi Doctors: Medical Killing and the Psychology of Genocide*. New York: Basic Books, 1986.

Opera and theatre performances were heavily subsidised, and therefore affordable. My mother renewed her pre-war season ticket to the Opera. Jancsi, his mother and I joined her. We also started to go to concerts, something my family had not done before. The collection of adults of broken families began to settle down into some semblance of normal life. For a short while.

Stray Jewish teenagers from broken families also began to build a life for themselves. The oldest, Szentirmai Gyuri, was 17; he had escaped military labour service by being just a few days younger than the lowest age of conscription. The youngest was my schoolmate Panna, aged 11. There were about 30 of us, but numbers fluctuated: some of the lonely youngsters found a foothold elsewhere, while a few others drifted back from the camps years later. Exceptional circumstances brought together young people of dissimilar ages, contrasting economic status, diverse aspirations and different cultural backgrounds. Under normal circumstances most of us would not have met, let alone become friends, but we had something important in common: we only just survived the Holocaust. Not being very imaginative, we called our society 'Our Society'.

Our Society created a rich cultural and social life for its teenage members. We organised lectures, debates, quiz games, chamber music groups, visits to such museums as had reopened, poker games with beans as stakes, gin rummy parties, rambles in the Buda hills, rowing training on the Danube, swimming galas in the river and at the swimming pools of Újpest. One of our number, who became a journalist in the UK, composed poems about us and our activities, and regularly published Our Society's News Sheet. One of the mothers had been a dance teacher. By the time we knew her, she was three times the weight she should have been, but she was still graceful, and taught us the rudiments of ballroom dancing. One of the fathers played football with the boys. The Donáth family had a skiff: a two-seater rowing boat with space for two passengers. Judit's father taught us to row, and took us on trips to uninhabited islands of the Danube. We rowed across in shifts, built camp fires, improvised cauldrons of soups, played various games, such as volleyball without nets and number wars, a fun game of agility and ingenuity.

JANCSI

Jancsi and I had similar tastes. Here is a little story about an event that happened soon after we got to know each other.

It must have been 1947, and Jancsi, 3½ years my senior, was still at school. Our two schools organised compulsory afternoon trips to the local cinema to see film after boring Soviet film about a romance between a *Stakhanovist* boy working in a factory and his girl in the fields of the *Kolkhoz*, both over-fulfilling the production norms of the five-year plan. The films were not all the same, sometimes the girl was the Stakhanovist and the boy the

178

Kolkhoz member.[100] The usual arrangement was that the boys' school occupied the stalls of the cinema, and the girls the dress circle. Then one day there was a surprise: a Soviet film with an exciting story and fascinating music! At the end of the film my schoolmates shuffled out, but I stayed on to watch the same film again. I noticed that a boy stayed in his seat downstairs in the stalls. It was Jancsi, and the film was Eisenstein's *Alexander Nevsky*, with music by Prokofiev. A masterpiece, one of the greatest films of all time.

Our attitudes towards the political regime were also similar. The Communist dictatorship radicalised teenagers. Some flung themselves into Marxist ideology, embracing it wholeheartedly, and becoming committed. Others scorned the state-imposed ideology, but hypocritically mouthed its slogans and carried out its edicts, while harbouring fascist or religious sentiments. We did neither of these. Our approach to the destructive political storm was to resist it passively, distancing ourselves from it as far as possible. Our temperaments were different: Jancsi was calm but stubborn, while I was more volatile but more flexible, but since our values were the same, we never disagreed on any issue of importance.

Unlike Jancsi who was quietly confident, I was an awkward teenager, shy and self-conscious. Quite a few of the boys of Our Society took an interest in me. Their attention was a welcome boost to my confidence, but since everyone liked and admired my boyfriend, other boys soon got out of his way. Jancsi himself was strictly a one-girl boy. He was clever, handsome and polite, and his family was well respected in the town, so several mothers tried to capture him for their daughters. Some mothers went as far as admitting their disapproval of his devoted attachment to me, a stray, a newcomer of Újpest society.

A FRIEND

I had to grow up without a friend in Budapest, and without ever having a non-Jewish friend anywhere. Jancsi was more lucky. Zoli was his best friend. They grew up together – their parents had been neighbours even before their boys were born. Zoli's mother was a teacher, a pious and charitable Catholic always ready with a bible quote. His father was a fierce atheist, a formidable man, a noted classics scholar who ridiculed his wife's piety and approved of Jancsi, but for some reason disapproved of his own son. He called his boy 'Hitler' before the war, and 'Stalin' after. This sophisticated family agreed on nothing much, and had nothing in common with Feri's uncouth friend Gazda Bandi, except that they were all humane non-Jews who detested Nazism. If only there had been a few more like them.

---

100   Stakhanovism: a Soviet system designed to raise production by setting goals and offering incentives to workers. It was named after Alexey Stakhanov, a coal miner who first benefited under the system in 1935. Kolkhoz: A Soviet style collective farm.

Zoli was devoted to Jancsi. In early 1945, when Jancsi had typhus and was quarantined in his house for weeks, Zoli climbed a ladder to his friend's bedroom window, visiting him daily, and when Jancsi was no longer delirious, chatted to him through the glass. I will relate later how Zoli became our protector in the turbulent times of the 1956 Revolution. He and Jancsi remained friends all their lives. Zoli was kind and generous; he was gifted, honest and highly principled. He tried to live like a Mensch, and the Communist regime destroyed him. He was Chief Engineer of one of the country's major Pharmaceutical companies. His options were to go to prison for poisoning the population, having placed into a key position an incompetent selected by the Communist Party, or go to Siberia, having defied the Party. Instead, he resigned his post, and for the rest of his life earned a pittance stoking boilers. His fate under Communism resembled my father's in Nazi times.

Szetey Zoltán, family friend, Újpest 1950.
Kaposi family collection

THE LIFE OF ADULTS

Given their socialist past and their unwillingness (or inability) to compromise, my parents only just survived the Communist era, doing mundane jobs much below their capabilities. After her life-threatening spinal operation, my quick-witted, conscientious mother found a low-grade administrative job in a government office. Not being a good *cadre*, she was never promoted.

My father's was a complicated story. The onset of the People's Republic put an end to his business enterprise. It must have been his knowledge of mathematics and statistics that earned him a senior post in the Planning Office (*Tervhivatal*), a powerful body in the new political order. The Planning Office was responsible for developing a succession of Five-Year Plans which prescribed every aspects of life in our well-ordered society. The plans embraced all areas of the economy and culture: the output of industry and agriculture, the processes of public administration, the manpower and profile of all sectors, the style of art and writing, the structure and content of education. Planning was comprehensive, and plans were rigid, detailed and hierarchical, setting targets for complete sectors, their member enterprises, departments, segments and groups, right down to the level of individuals. Plans were enforced relentlessly, and those who failed to meet them were declared enemies of the people.

Plans were set out by the Party. The Planning Office was the civil service, the administrative body which codified and implemented Party policy. At first my father applauded the notion of planning, and was thrilled at the prospect of being a planner. It did not take long for him to be disillusioned. I will show how manpower planning influenced my whole life. Meanwhile here is just one of countless examples of how to fulfil the plan without achieving anything.

The country had a factory which made pots and pans. The papers proudly published the factory's production figures, its 'overfulfillment' of output goals and its 'overcompletion' (*túlteljesítés*) of planning targets. And yet, there were no pots or pans in the shops for housewives to cook in. The reason was simple. The plan specified the factory's output in terms of the total volume of pots and pans produced. Managers of the company soon figured that it was cheaper and easier to make one enormous 10-litre pot than ten pots of 1 litre each. So, the factory met its plan by exclusively making huge pots which nobody wanted, while people had no pots for their soup. This is not a joke. It is a true story.

There were many similar instances of ignorant politicians imposing stupid guidelines which the Planning Office had to implement without comment, let alone criticism. My father was a thinker and an idealist; he hated to see wasted resources and lost opportunities, so he could not resist suggesting modifications of guidelines handed down by political masters. I don't know the details of the case, but the pots-and-pans example implies the sort of modifications he might have proposed. The outcome was predictable. He was branded a traitor, an enemy of the people; he was dismissed from his job, and was briefly put in prison. It took all of Feri's influence with the judiciary to get him out. After this, he was once again on the blacklist. He became diagnosed with Parkinson's disease soon after, and retired on health grounds, in his mid-50s. Did his illness lead to retirement, or did his job bring about his illness?

Nanóka never recovered her home or her business. Her trusted erstwhile employees never gave her back her possessions. None of this broke her heart. Loss of family members did.

Pici was trying to come to terms with the loss of her husband Pista, victim of Military Labour Service. She and Nanóka rented a small flat in Debrecen. Their landlord Dr Schiff Ödön (Ödi) was a prominent medical specialist whose brothers, sisters, artist wife and eight-year-old son were all killed in Auschwitz. In due course Pici and Ödi married and, together with Nanóka, they left disloyal Debrecen without a backward glance. They settled in Budapest. Pici was 31, Ödi 31 years her senior. It was a typical Jewish marriage in those days. They had one child, the pianist Sir András Schiff.

After he married into our family, Ödi became guardian of the health of us all. He gave advice, attended to us himself, or guided us to appropriate specialists. He was the senior consultant at one of Budapest's major gynaecology clinics, and told me to drop by for advice at any time. – One day I arrived when his receptionist was at lunch. I knocked and entered. I can still visualise my white-haired uncle sitting at his desk, his head buried in his hands, a picture of dejection. I thought he was ill. He told me how his job was destroying him. One of his tasks was to review the clinical judgment of his juniors. Twice a week he had a clinic when a dozen or more patients paraded in front of him at 10-minute intervals, and it was his task to classify them as fit for work, or keep them on the sick register. The planners, in their wisdom, gave him a quota: in any session of consultation he could keep no more than three patients on the sick list. Case notes would have served as guide, but they were not available in advance; each patient carried her own. As patients presented themselves one by one, he had to *estimate* whether or not the one before him was likely to be one of the three sickest of the session. He was anxious not to exhaust the quota too early, otherwise he would have no place for a thoroughly ill woman arriving later. He was also afraid of keeping back a place on the sick list at the end of the morning, because then the planners were liable to reduce next week's quota from three to two. This dedicated doctor said to me: 'I used to love my profession. I hate it now.'

THINGS FALL APART

1949 marked political change, and a changed life for us all. 'Our Society' disintegrated, as did our parents' social life. My great friend Judit, and everyone who could, left the country. Religious organisations had no place in the Socialist People's Republic. Churches closed or operated in a clandestine manner, and soon our synagogue's cultural activities stopped. People became too frightened to talk to each other, let alone gather in groups. Soon correspondence with friends and family in the west stopped.

The country's borders were sealed, and passports were no longer obtainable. (Not until 1966 did I hold a passport. It was a British passport.) Some desperate young people tried to leave the country illegally, and were caught at the border. Two members of Our Society were among those imprisoned more than once before succeeding to leave for Israel. This was supposed to be post-Nazi peacetime, and yet the age of atrocities had returned, and those pursuing freedom were punished.[101]

Jews were not alone trying to flee the country. Cardinal Mindszenty inspired some hot-headed Catholic youths, among them several of Jancsi's erstwhile classmates, to form an armed conspiracy, to fight their way through the border.[102] The enterprise was doomed, and they were caught. One of the conspirators, 20-year-old Weingartner Béla, was executed. Another, our friend Jámbor Laci, was condemned to death. His girlfriend

---

101   Vera and Miki Dotan, *To Arise from the Inferno*. Raanana: Docostory Ltd, 2006.

102   József Mindszenty (1892-1975), Cardinal, Archbishop of Esztergom, head of the Catholic Church in Hungary between 1945 and 1973. He was arrested and tortured by the Communist secret police and sentenced for life in a show trial for "crimes against the republic". He was released in the days of the 1956 Revolution, and after the Soviet invasion found asylum in the Budapest Embassy of the United States. In 1971, he was allowed to emigrate. He became one of the symbols of anti-Communist political and church resistance in the Communist bloc.

Hubay Kati, Jancsi's next door neighbour and lifelong friend, was sentenced to 25 years for aiding and harbouring a traitor. Later Laci's sentence was commuted to life imprisonment, and after the 1956 Hungarian revolution both our friends escaped to Britain.

Political terror dominated our lives, and destroyed our youth.

SCHOOL

How did Hungarian schools cope with a Holocaust survivor?

When we arrived 'home' in the spring of 1945, I was 12½ years old. Our clothes were rags, we had no home, no food, no money. My school record book is here. It is an imposing hard-bound document, registering year by year, semester by semester, subject by subject, my progress through all the years of grammar school from age 10 to graduation at 18. It shows that for my Year 2 in grammar school in the 1944-45 academic year, I was admitted to the very school which had rejected me in 1943-44.

Why did we choose that particular school? Was it because that was the closest? Or because we were in no state to make any choices? Or because we were not a family to bear grudges? Or because we did not have a choice?

In rags, and my bald head in a headscarf; without books, pen, pencil, paper or school bag – and presumably without breakfast – I turned up at school the day after setting foot in Hungary. This was the Senior department of the school where I had spent four years as a junior. The teachers would have remembered me as the top student who as a junior had won prize after academic prize. Several of the girls had been my classmates. It was common knowledge why I had been barred from entry to the first year, and why I was away from most of the second year. What did I expect from my teachers and classmates on my sudden and very late return?

They received me with total indifference: as though I had not arrived, as though I did not exist. Almost like the treatment meted out to me by my fascist teacher in the last year of the Juniors. The subjects of the curriculum included 'Religious and Moral Studies' (*Hit és Erkölcstan*). They had a sense of humour.

The form mistress assigned my care to Luca, the top girl. She had a serious round face and light-brown pigtails, and lived near what used to be our Rózsi's home. She had a room of her own, with a small semi-circular balcony. Most days she and I went to her home after school, and we sat on that balcony, studying. She was conscientious, but not friendly. I doubt if her mother gave me any food. Either the school or Luca might have provided me with pencil and paper, but neither she nor the school gave me any books. I had about seven weeks to catch up with the material of the academic year.

It was child's play. Only one part of the syllabus caused me anxiety: skipping on a rope. The curriculum for Physical Education prescribed specific skipping skills. I spent hours practicing in the courtyard of Vilmos Császár út 58, fearful of Concierge Mrs Hajdu, but thankfully she ignored me. My tutor Luca must have done a good job, and I must have got the skipping sorted, because the school report shows that I had top marks in all subjects. Why was skipping so difficult? Was it because I was clumsy (I was not), or because I had

183

been starving for a year, and we still had almost nothing to eat? Skipping is a tough form of exercise. Might I not have been exempted from the Physical Education examination, or given something less exacting to do? Who might have petitioned this on my behalf? My parents had other things on their minds, and my teachers had no interest in my welfare.

We left Budapest in the summer of 1945, settling in Újpest, some five miles away. Come September, I was entering Year 3 in grammar school, enrolling in the school nearest to our new home. The story of my new school is a miserable tale. At that time Újpest had two grammar schools: one for boys, one for girls, on opposite sides of a square. They may as well have been on different planets. The boys' school was a respected cultural and social centre, one of the best schools in the country. In its time it had its fair share of fascists, but moderated this by scholarly and humanitarian values. Kanizsay Dorottya Girls Grammar School was physically and intellectually a dump. In 1945 the newly appointed Head was Dr Sipos Lajos; a linguist, a mild, intelligent, but ineffectual man. Improving the standards and atmosphere of that school was beyond him.

September 1945: first week at the new school. At break time in the dreary asphalt playground, two big girls joined me: jolly Gerti, who became a Physics professor; and gangly Éva, who later married Újpest's charismatic young rabbi Murányi Miklós. They were in the final year, but had heard that there was a new Jewish girl in Year 3. They introduced me to Panna in Year 2 and Judit in Year 4, the only other Jewish girls in the school. Gerti and Éva said we three should regard them as our big sisters; in case of trouble we must seek them out, even call them out of class. We asked why we should have trouble. They explained that the school atmosphere was hostile towards Jews; there were many fascist girls and teachers. They two would be leaving at end of the year. They advised that we should move to another school. I heard them, but could not take their advice: we had other problems at home.

The big girls soon proved right.

I can still picture the heavy body and featureless round face of Erzsébet, an undistinguished member of my class. I even dream about her from time to time. Who knows what raised her to the status of spokesman for the community? One day after maths, she planted herself in front of me, saying that I was a filthy Jew, that everyone thought that I had no place in the school, and people like me had no place in Hungary.

I should have expected this, and should have had a strategy. Instead, I just lost control; I went for her, pulling her straggly hair and beating her where I could. She retaliated, of course. Being bigger and stronger than me, she needed no support, yet a whole mob came to her aid. The matter did not escalate to teacher or Headmaster level, but the point was made once and for all, there was no need to mention the issue again. Erzsébet was right. I was an outsider; I did not belong in the school, did not belong in the country.

In Year 4 there was a girl, just one, who did not seem to mind that I was Jewish. Koltay Anikó, thin and wiry, was a devout Catholic from a poor home, and the only truly intelligent and imaginative classmate I had in 4½ years at this grim school. That year our form mistress was Dr Lineberger, a small prune of a rat-faced spinster whose signature is in my record book. She was a good teacher. She was also a liar. I omit details of how she deceived me, how she ruined my chance of making a friend of Anikó.

At first, I found it hard to settle into the regularity of school. I was new to Újpest, I was hungry, I missed the Csengeri Clan, and grieved for people I lost. In the first semester I did well enough, but not outstandingly so, but by the end of the year I easily became the top student of the class, except in Embroidery. Standards were low; my top position was no great achievement. Embroidery was not the most important subjects of the curriculum, and yet, it became a critical issue.

Our art teacher, the elegant Mrs Istvánffy, taught us 'Drawing and Art History' and 'Embroidery'. I could not draw, but I enjoyed art history, so that subject went well enough. Embroidery should not have been a problem either: I had learned to embroider at the knees of Nanóka, Giza mama and Terka, who specialised in the subject at art school. Instead, Mrs Istvánffy found fault with everything: my work, my clothing, my hair (growing by now!). The matter reached a crisis over the embroidery of a pillowcase, Transylvanian style.

Folk art is an important branch of Hungarian culture. Style, materials, motifs and colouring vary from region to region. Thanks to Nanóka's shop catering for country people, I knew more than most.

Even now, I cherish my rich collection of Hungarian folk embroidery. Transylvanian folk embroidery uses stitching in a single colour, red, white or black, on beige linen background. I no longer have the particular item of this story, but here is a pillowcase, Transylvanian style, stitched in white. Embroidering a pillowcase like this is a lot of work. I applied myself to the task with diligence because the object promised to be beautiful, and also because it was an examination piece. Passing in Embroidery was essential to progressing to the next year.

Mrs Istvánffy did not look at my work for some weeks, but when she did, she said the stitching was uneven; I must unpick it, start all over again. My work did not seem worse than that of most others, but I did as bid. – After her second rejection, only a couple of days were left before the piece had to be handed in for examination. The situation was desperate. My mother took charge. We appealed to Terka, who stayed up all night, and there it was: a skilfully embroidered pillowcase, Transylvanian style. It was cheating, but even my father

Embroidered cushion, Transylvanian style.
Photo: László Csősz, 2019

agreed that we had no other option: needs must. I took the piece to school – and Mrs Istvánffy rejected it. She said it was nicely stitched for once, but in certain parts, where motifs were meeting, the work was inconsistent with traditional Transylvanian style. She said I had failed.

Home I went in tears. We consulted Terka. An expert embroiderer, she said Mrs Istvánffy was talking rubbish. She showed us books and samples of Transylvanian embroidery. Of course, her work was correct. Carrying the pillowcase, my father went to see Headmaster Dr Sipos. Days later, Dr Sipos and Mrs Istvánffy appeared in our convent. Dr Sipos expressed his regret, and asked Mrs Istvánffy to apologise to my parents (why not to me?). She did apologise! – Jancsi's father told us later that Mrs Istvánffy's husband was the District Vet, and had been a prominent fascist.

I show you my end-of-year school report.

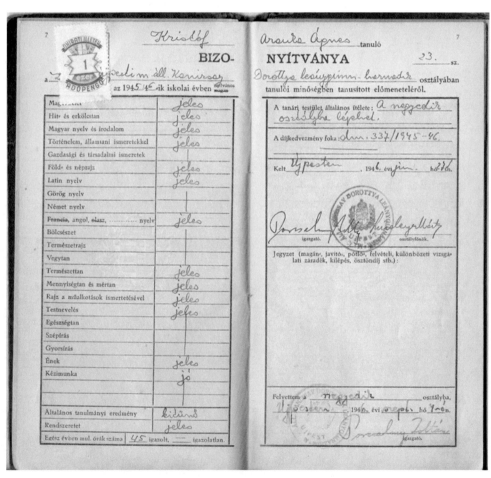

Author's school report, end of year 1946.
Kaposi family collection

The top grade is *jeles* (translates to 'notable'), and the second best is *jó* ('good'). *Kézimunka* means 'Embroidery'. 'Overall academic progress' (*Általános tanulmányi eredmény*) is the second line from the bottom. *Kitünő*, translates to 'excellent'. And yet, Embroidery was not my only problem at that school.

I never had the chance to engage in sport, but I am no clumsier than most, and could have done acceptably at PE. Instead, gym classes were a torment. When I fell off the equipment or dropped a ball, the whole class cheered. When the stars of the class selected team members for games, I was always left out, or left till last. I used any excuse to miss classes, which made matters even worse. Why did my classmates treat me in this way? They may have resented the only Jew being the top of the class academically, although I always helped others and regularly tutored my classmates. Perhaps they needed me to have an Achilles' heel.

Then a strange event occurred in Year 6. Volleyball was a new sport, introduced into Hungary's schools in 1948. Soviet athletes provided coaching for a couple of pupils selected from each class, and these had to teach the game to the others. Who knows how I came to be picked to be trained as one of the would-be tutors? The other selected was a good athlete, Erdélyi Pötyi, the queen of the class. Unexpectedly, volleyball training proved enjoyable. Even more surprisingly, Pötyi and I became friendly, in spite of her father having had an active fascist past. Many years later, Jancsi and I met Pötyi on one of our rare visits to Budapest. She told us that she had been ostracised by the girls at school, because she broke rank, befriending a Jew.

After a few training sessions with the Soviet athletes, it was our turn to teach the game to the rest of the class. I was not too bad as a volleyball coach and, having gained a bit of confidence, gym classes became enjoyable too, but by then it was too late. Kanizsay Dorottya Girls Grammar School gave up on me.

Two more episodes of my life while at woeful Kanizsay: my first job, and my musical education.

One summer I had a job. Not just some low grade casual vacation job for a schoolgirl, but a serious grownup employment at Tungstram, one of the country's foremost companies. I still have some paperwork about that job.

At that time in Hungary the school leaving age was 14. In the summer after Year 4, I would have been old enough to take up full-time work, but I was employed as a temporary in the Department of Wage Administration. I had a desk in an office for four, a big swivel chair and a small cupboard. I loved my beautiful pens and pencils. In those days there were no computers, each clerk had a hand-driven calculating machine. Payment was in cash, I had not even heard of bank accounts until my arrival in England.

It was a responsible job. I had to calculate employees' remunerations and tax deductions which varied with their number of dependents. Some were on monthly salaries, others on weekly wages, yet others were paid by the hour. Some had overtime payment or special bonuses, others were promoted or had a birthday part-way along a payment period which entitled them to statutory increases. Deductions for illness were different if someone was at home or stayed in hospital. I was in charge of ledgers, keeping people's personal details up to date. I had to oversee the work of typists who wrote out pay slips and typed people's name and employee code on special strong little brown envelopes with windows so that people could count their money without breaking the seal. I had to check that cashiers stuffed the correct amount of money into people's envelopes. Employees came to me with queries and demands. Aged 14, I had colleagues old enough to be my parents, but yet they accepted me as their equal. I was even promoted to the smartest kind of calculating machine. I had a wonderful time.

The best moment came at the very end. My boss knew that in September I was planning to return to school, but asked me whether I would consider staying on as permanent staff. He even offered me an increase. When I said I must leave, he said he and my colleagues were sorry to see me go, wished me well, and gave me a little present to remember them by. So back I went to join the Year 5 class at grim Kanizsay.

Now about music. I started piano lessons with Pici at the age of six, as was customary in the family, but then the camps imposed a gap in my education.

After the War, when we began to settle down in Újpest, Klári – a good pianist – and my parents teamed ups to buy an elderly upright piano, and I was enrolled in the *Erkel Zeneiskola,* Újpest's Conservatoire of Music. It was in the town centre, next door to my father's shop. This institution was meant to be similar to the Debreceni Zenede where my mother, Pici and Tamás Vásáry learned their music: it had similar size and academic/ cultural status, and its role was to prepare students for entry into the Liszt Ferenc Academy. In practice it was a mediocre establishment, lacking the atmosphere, traditions and quality of education that made the Debreceni Zenede outstanding. My teacher was competent but was uninspiring, and she was unduly impressed by my modest gifts. I was a woefully inadequate sight reader, a skill not considered important at the time. A pity: it would have made it easier for Jancsi and me to play chamber music together. However, I was quite musical, had a good ear, good rhythm, good memory, I learned fast, I even had some semblance of perfect pitch. My teacher was surprised how easily I understood theory, and she was amazed that I never confused complicated cross-rhythms. She mistook these secondary skills for musical talent. The poor soul might never have met anyone like my daughter Anna, not to mention my cousin András.

Music students were not meant to have the option or the initiative to choose the pieces they played. Even my monumentally gifted cousin András needed the external influence and encouragement of the famous London teacher Kabos Ilonka to break out of the straitjacket of Hungary's institutionalised musical education. As for me, I progressed dutifully through Czerny exercises, Bartók's Microcosmos, Bach's 2 and 3-part inventions, Haydn and Mozart sonatas, Chopin mazurkas, etc. – the standard repertoire for a young pupil. By the time I was 16, my teacher figured that I was the star of the Conservatoire, clearly heading for the Liszt Ferenc Academy. She thought that it was the role of the Director of the Conservatoire himself to prepare me for entry into that august institution.

If my teacher had been dull, the Director was worse: insensitive and lacking judgment. He insisted that I am destined to be a performing artist (?), and demanded that I practice eight hours a day. In preparation for the all-important entrance examination to the Academy, he gave me noisy showy pieces of Liszt and Grieg, which were not my taste. The last straw came when he even picked for me a unique Mozart composition in which I found no pleasure: the Fantasia in d minor, K397. Many love the piece, but I still think it amorphous, not the music for me.

Just then, I was changing school. In one bold move, I shook off the dust of both Újpest institutions: the Erkel Zeneiskola and Kanizsay Grammar School. This is how it happened.

Our mathematics teacher's name is lost from my memory, so let's call her Miss Maths. In the first Semester of Year 6, she invited my parents to school, and told them that this school was not for me. She said I should be prepared for reading mathematics or natural sciences at university, but these subjects were of little interest to others in my class, so she could not teach me to the level required for university entry. Compare the way this school treated me with my father's experience at Debrecen's Piarists.

NEW SCHOOL

My parents and I must have been remarkably unimaginative. Budapest had dozens of grammar schools for girls and yet, on the 31st January 1949, here I was again at Szemere utca, at the very school where I started as a Junior, where they rejected me in Year 1 as a Senior, and where I completed Year 2 on return from the camps.

Arriving mid-year in Year 6, I was a new girl yet again. Social links had been formed long before; the teachers knew the girls, the girls knew each other, and nobody knew me. As always, I was an outsider. There were two other new girls, but they came together, and were already friends. I was alone. For a while I even doubted that changing school had been a good idea.

A couple of days after my arrival, our Form Mistress Dr Czanik Zsófia decided to measure up the three newcomers, calibrating them against the rest. She taught us mathematics, and she set us a one-hour test. The test paper had half a dozen questions. She said to be fast and accurate. Should we finish before the hour was up, we must hand in our work, and ask for another test sheet. Should we finish even that, ask for yet another test sheet, etc.

I must have been inspired. I had nothing to lose, the questions were intelligent, I was fast and accurate as Dr Czanik told us to be, and while the rest were working on the initial paper, I walked up and down for new test sheets three or four times. Dr Czanik was surprised, checked my work, smiled more and more broadly, and finally she said, 'Welcome to the school'.

I was afraid of the backlash that would have been inevitable at Újpest. Here it did not happen. The girls took the event in their stride: So what's the big deal, if the new girl was a champion at maths? Láng Anna was a poet and a linguist, writing Latin verse in hexameters. Magyar Erzsi was a gifted physicist and musician and athlete, a member of the county volleyball team. Mari was composing hilarious stories worthy of publication, and was a member of the city's gymnastics team. There were many other talented people in the class. These girls were normal, interesting, and fun, not stupid, mean or vindictive. They took pleasure in our diverse abilities and characters. About a quarter were Jewish, and the Jews were among the brightest, but somehow here it did not matter. Horányi Györgyi was beautiful, non-Jewish, a brilliant draughtswoman who later became an architect. Many of the girls made notable careers in later life. For the first time, almost at the end of my school life, several of my classmates became my friends. Arató Anikó, an eminent structural engineer, is still my friend. Erzsi became one of the best friends of my whole life. She is dead now, but her daughter and granddaughter visited me a couple of years ago. I soon felt more at home at my new school than I ever had in all the years in Újpest. My classmates picked up on my fear of Physical Education, and two of them – the gymnast and the athlete – took me to their sports club for regular training. It was just as well.

Like the country, the education system was in continuous flux. They surprised us with ever more new regulations. The latest was MHK, *Munkára Harcra Kész*, 'Ready for Work and Combat'. This was Communists' planning. Rather than statistics characterising people, people had to fit into statistical straitjackets, such that the predetermined figures should come out right. The Planning Office's mania of statistical determinism was extended to the school population in the form of the MHK. In addition to meeting set academic criteria, each young person had to satisfy set requirements at a variety of sports: swimming, gymnastics, track and field. The necessary level of attainment advanced year by year, and if someone failed to meet the MHK targets for their year, they would be held back in a lower class where their performance was adequate and the statistics fitted. In principle at least, this meant that the athletically challenged had to repeat the year, perhaps even several times.

I was not keen to test how strictly they enforced this new system. Instead, several times a week before school I traipsed over to Margaret Island to the *Vasas* sports ground, the sports club of my new-found friends, subjecting myself to the encouraging shouts and corrective whistles of my classmates Erzsi and Mari, until they were satisfied that I could pass MHK. To my amazement, I did. It even turned out that I was fairly good at some field events.[103]

At Újpest, I had 'chosen' the 'Real' stream. Here there was no choice, and I was 1½ years behind in Latin among these linguists and other talented students. My father and Pici took me in hand. I enjoyed the logic of Latin grammar, the problem solving involved in

---

103   Vasas [Iron worker]: one of the country's major sports clubs and football teams, with socialist traditions.

unravelling the paragraph-long sentences of Tacitus, and making sense of poetry where the order of words had nothing to do with meaning, guided only by the rhythm of the meter. Our Latin mistress Kati néni was brilliant. She was young and beautiful, and had been a student at our school not so many years before. She *lived* the classics; her mother, father and husband were all classics professors. As my record book shows, at the end of the year I got top marks. In our last year we had to cover a large syllabus. Kati néni used bribery: if there was time after completing the set work, she gave us one of Catullus' unprintably erotic poems to read.

Whoever devised the national graduation syllabus for grammar schools must have been a sadist. Our English set texts were a slice of *Hamlet*, a Shakespeare sonnet, and a section each of Thomas More's *Utopia* and the *Canterbury Tales*. The modern language taught in school changed with the political wind. Ours was the last year doing a western language; thereafter, Russian was compulsory. Perhaps they had a better-devised curriculum.

Tempora mutantur. Not so long before, socialist and Jewish university professors taught in grammar schools, having been ousted from their chairs. Now the ousted were socialists, right-wingers and the clerically-minded. Our Physics master was a defrocked university lecturer, condemned to school teaching. He was a specialist in some obscure field, but had no idea about teaching, nor about school-level general physics. We pitied him.

Our Geography mistress Mária néni was in her 50s, with dyed red hair, too-skimpy skirts and too much makeup. I thought her a clown. Far from it. In Újpest, Geography was excruciatingly boring: memorising lengths of rivers, land areas of countries, depths of oceans. Here this beautiful subject came to life. We learned facts, but also concepts and connections. Climate, terrain and natural resources were linked logically to the development of communities and civilisations.

History, another subject I had previously thought boring, was superb. Our mistress used to good effect the intelligence of her pupils. She taught us dialectics and rhetoric. We had to study a section of the syllabus by ourselves, and one of us had to introduce it. The presentation was then discussed and analysed, our teacher assuming the role of a member of the class. She also set up mock parliamentary debates between political adversaries, such as Hungary's two 19th century giants Kossuth and Széchenyi. Her classes were full of excitement.

I never knew school could be like this. I admired my teachers, I loved my classmates, I made friends. But of course, there were dark sides. The political world penetrated the school environment. The political terror of those days is well documented; tourists should not miss visiting Budapest's controversial House of Terror museum. Whole sections of the population were banished from their homes and dumped in some remote village. The process was termed *Kitelepítés*, 'Relocation'. Before emigrating to England in the late 1950s, families of three of our close friends were among such exiles. Our friends were not harmed, but many others were. People could be taken away for trivial reasons, or for no reason at all. Some would return broken or injured, and some would never return. One of Jancsi's colleagues disappeared on his way out of the cinema, having said that the Soviet film which was compulsory to see was boring. It was commonplace for an official car to stop in front of a house in the dead of night to take away the inhabitants, who might never return. People were terrified of the sound of steps on the stairs. Julian Barnes writes beautifully about Stalin's Russia in his book about Shostakovich. Rákosi's Hungary was similar, on a smaller scale.[104]

There were widely publicised show trials for the politically prominent, some ending in execution of 'traitors', but many were condemned without trial. People might have been picked at random, or denounced by others. Why? Because someone disliked them, or their home was coveted by a member of the Party or an officer of the Communist secret police. We lived in fear. There were whispered jokes. Here is one, not very funny, but revealing:

> *Compulsory political seminar at 7am, before the 8am start of the working day. Leader encourages participants to engage in free discussion and ask any question.*
>
> *Comrade Smith: 'This is an agricultural country. So where is our milk?'*
>
> *Leader: 'Thank you Comrade Smith. We shall look into this, and report back at the next seminar.*
>
> *Next seminar. Same leader encourages participants to engage in discussion and ask any question.*
>
> *Comrade Smith: 'This is an agricultural country. So where is our bread?'*
>
> *Leader: 'Thank you Comrade Smith. We shall look into this, and report back on the matter.'*
>
> *Next seminar. Same leader encourages participants to ask any question.*
>
> *Comrade Brown: 'This is a free country. So where is Comrade Smith?'*

The system of overlapping spy rings was still being set up at my time at school; it only became fully operational when I got to university in 1951, but the signs were already there. We were starting to distrust each other. Vera, a beautiful copper-haired girl, was the only one who threw herself into the revelry of the Communist Youth World Congress, held in Budapest in 1949. She took part in political and cultural events, and stayed out for the Congress's overnight parties (!). The rest of us were frightened; we did not wish to be involved and kept away. I instinctively distrusted Vera. Decades later she visited us in London. By then she was over 70, still beautiful and engaging. Even Jancsi liked her. She

---

104   Julian Barnes, *The Noise of Time*, Vintage, 2016.

was honest; when I questioned her about our times at school, she confessed to having been an 'opportunist', listening to conversations, dropping a word about the rest of us 'in the right places': in other words, having been an informer.

However, some people were uncompromising. Compare Dr Lineberger, the deceitful form mistress at Újpest, with the form mistress at my new school.

At this school several girls in my class were no less clever than I was, but none of them had been trained as my father had trained me, so I soon emerged as the unchallenged top of the class. My once-famous memory was a victim of the Holocaust, perhaps because of starvation, so I had difficulty remembering long tracks of poetry, but I was still doing fairly well in Hungarian Language and Literature, taught by Mrs Aradi, a cold, distant older lady, Form Mistress in our final year.

School farewell ceremony (*ballagás*) of the author's cousin Sebes (Stern) Éva in Budapest, 1960.
Kaposi family collection

A few weeks before graduation, Mrs Aradi came to me with an expression of concern on her face, asking how I was. Surprised, I said fine. She insisted that I looked unwell, I should go home to bed at once. I protested, but had to do as I was told. An adamant Mrs Aradi sent me home again the next day, demanding that I should stay at home for at least a week. On my next appearance at school, she told me that now I looked a bit better, and could stay for a couple of hours each day, but not more. A week or so later she said how relieved she was that I was now all but recovered, and could rejoin the class full time, to prepare for the graduation examinations.

Quite soon afterwards newspapers published a list of the top graduating student of each grammar school in the country, selected on the basis of their academic record for the honour of studying in the Soviet Union for four years. Nobody was sent from our school. It would have been too dangerous for me to thank Mrs Aradi. We just smiled at each other. Mrs Aradi risked her freedom, or at least her career, for a pupil. Not because I was a Holocaust survivor – she may not have known that – and not because I was particularly excelling in her subject – I was not – but because she was a Mensch.

Grammar school graduation was a national examination. The Latin exam had several parts, including translating an unseen text from the Latin. One hoped for prose – poetry was much harder. This time we had a tough Ovid poem to translate. We commiserated with each other afterwards. Someone asked our star linguist Láng Anna if she found the exam hard. She said not particularly; she had studied this poem before, and had translated it into a metered verse. She knew her own poem by heart, so she just copied it out.

Our mistress Kati néni told us soon afterwards that a girl of our class had reported to the National Examination Board that candidate Láng had cheated: the paper was meant to be the translation of an *unseen* text, whereas Láng had not only *seen* the text before, but knew the translation by heart. Our teacher's views were sought by the Board. Kati néni scrutinised Anna's paper and found it a flawless translation and a beautiful poem. She advised the Board that the girl had been an exceptional student over the years and knew much of the Latin literature; her scholarship should be acknowledged by full marks, and she should be specially commended for the quality of her verse. We suspected that it was Vera the redhead who had raised the complaint. An incident of the times.

Having survived the hellish school in Újpest, this school taught me more than the subjects of the curriculum. It gave me a lesson in education, offered me some friends for life, and restored my respect for my elders. I loved this school, but my school time was over. I showed my father's graduation tableau before, and mine is overleaf.

It was a Hungarian tradition that, at the end of the graduation year, each school organised *Ballagás,* the 'Amble' ceremony. Wearing a navy skirt, white blouse, and carrying flowers, students formed a single file, holding each other's shoulders. I cannot resist showing a picture of the ballagás of my little cousin Éva, who died decades ago.

To the slow chant of traditional Latin songs, the amblers' snake glided along a through the town.

People lined the route, cheering, the celebration tinged with sadness. One of the songs is *Gaudeamus igitur,* enshrined in Brahms' *Academic Festival Overture.*

Author's grammar school graduation tableau, Budapest, 1950–1951. Top row of teachers: Latin mistress, Form mistress Mrs Arady, History mistress.

Kaposi family collection

A translation:

> *"Let's rejoice while we are still young. After a happy youth and tedious old age*
> *We shall all turn to dust."*

The other chant is less gruesome:

> *"Here we go ambling along,*
> *bidding goodbye to our friends.*
> *Our carefree schooldays are over,*
> *we are entering into adulthood".*

The farewell songs did not fit my experience. I had not had many carefree days since starting school at the age of six, and not many before that. I also thought that the end of school would not mean saying goodbye to the friends I made at this lovely school. I could not know that in just a few years we would have dispersed to all corners of the globe, most of us never to meet again.

HEADING FOR UNIVERSITY

My school graduation certificate is here on the shelf. It is studded with top marks. In fact, it has nothing *but* top marks. It did not do me much good.

In Hungary, and in countries of the Soviet Bloc, universities had no autonomy. They did not control their intake, they did not engage their staff, they did not appoint their professors, and did not award their own degrees. All academic matters were decided centrally by the Ministry of Education, guided by the Planning Office, commanded by the Communist Party.

I applied to university to study Physics, aiming to become a meteorologist. The distinguished Director of the Institute of Meteorology was Nanóka's neighbour. I had known him for many years. He took me to his Institute several times, introducing me to his staff who showed me their measuring instruments, their network of information collection and dissemination, and their mathematical methods. Before the age of computers, the mathematics was worked manually. The task was challenging, I was fascinated, and wanted to work with them. They advised me to study Physics, and specialise in Meteorology, the only route to their profession. What happened is another Communist story.

- I applied to the *Eötvös Loránd Tudományegyetem*, the University of Sciences, submitting my graduation certificate, and a supporting letter from the Institute of Meteorology.

- I was turned down, but was offered a place at the Electrical Engineering Faculty of the Technical University.

- I appealed to the Ministry of Education in writing, with a supporting letter from the school, and another from the Institute of Meteorology. I was turned down again, but there was an explanation: the Physics course was full.

- I re-appealed. The reply was that I must bring a fresh application to the Ministry, *personally*.

- Arriving at the Ministry, by chance I met my classmate Etelka who was there on the same errand, appealing against her university placement. She had also been told that the course she wanted was full. She wanted to study Electrical Engineering, and was given a place in Physics. This is not a joke. We had been sent the same letter by the same official in the same Ministry, both of us instructed to deliver, in person, the new appeal – to the same office.

- We went in together, asking for a straight swap. The official was kind; he did not call us troublemakers, and did not report us to higher authority. He just said we should go away quietly and do as we were told, or not go to university at all.

The official offered no explanation, but my father did. Social class was one of the parameters used when allocating university places. Etelka's father was a tram driver, mine an accountant. Different social categories. The swap would have messed up the planning statistics for the whole cohort. There was nothing we could do. There was nothing anyone could do.

In fact, I am grateful to those faceless Communist bureaucrats. Meteorology might have been fun, but so was Engineering. As my dear lost uncle Pista explained, engineers are problem solvers who use science and mathematics to construct useful and beautiful things. It is a challenging and rewarding profession, invaluable service to society. I am happy and proud to be an engineer.

HISTORIAN'S VOICE

Short History of Post-War Hungary

Between 1945 and 1948, Hungary was a multiparty parliamentary democracy. The first general and free election in Hungarian history was held in November 1945. The moderate right-wing Independent Smallholders' Party claimed victory, with 57% of the votes, with the leftist bloc, including the Communist and social democratic parties, scoring 41%. A grand coalition government was formed, in which the Hungarian Communist Party was gradually gaining control, backed by Soviet authorities. The Communists neutralised their opponents one by one, step by step, (the so-called 'salami tactics'), with increasingly drastic means. In 1947, they seized victory by a small margin, through fraud. This became known as the infamous 'blue-ballot' election, where the Communists used illegal methods, including multiple voting. By the end of the next year, the Communists had exclusive power over the country. Hungary became a Communist dictatorship and a Soviet satellite state.[105] After Stalin's death in 1953, the grip of the totalitarian regime eased somewhat. In 1956, following examples of other eastern bloc countries, an uprising broke out in Hungary against Soviet and Communist rule. The revolt claimed close to three thousand lives. After a few days of fierce street fighting, Soviet troops suppressed the revolt, and transferred power to a new Communist

---

105   For details about the so-called coalition years (1945-1948), and the emergence of the Communist dictatorship, see László Borhi, *Hungary in the Cold War, 1945–1956*. Budapest: Central European University Press, 2004, and László Kontler, *A History of Hungary*. New York: Palgrave Macmillan, 2002.

government. János Kádár adopted a slightly more moderate line. He gradually eased the political tone of the regime, and introduced some economic reforms, known as the 'Hungarian Thaw' or 'goulash Communism'. Finally, after 1989, the regime peacefully gave way to political transition.[106]

Jews and Non-Jews in the New Regime

After 1945, the 'Jewish question' reappeared on the political scene, albeit in different forms. After the Holocaust, many Hungarian Jews supported left-wing parties. For them, Communists and social democrats appeared to offer a guarantee that pre-war regimes would never return. It was more than a defensive reaction or sheer pragmatism: some believed that in a society without classes social tension and antisemitism would disappear. Many Jews were employed in law enforcement or attained key positions in the state apparatus. There were several Jews in the regime's higher echelons. The top leadership of the country between 1949 and 1953 consisted of four key functionaries of Jewish origin: Mátyás Rákosi, Ernő Gerő, Mihály Farkas and József Révai. Nevertheless, the Communist Party did not hesitate to pull the Jewish card to manipulate masses and incite hatred. Paradoxically, the role of Jews in the regime created the false impression in parts of society that the dictatorship was actually a Jewish plot, or even the Jews' revenge for the Holocaust, whereas, in fact, most Jews were hit hard by the Communist regime just as much as all other Hungarians were. Actually, as the middle class, the 'bourgeoisie' and intellectuals were the main targets of the Communists, Jews were over-represented among the victims of the regime.[107]

Post-War antisemitism

Significant efforts were made in the immediate post-war period for reconciliation and the rehabilitation of the Jews. The new Hungarian government revoked anti-Jewish legislation and restored legal equality of Jews. There were also attempts to aid and re-integrate survivors and combat antisemitism. Holocaust perpetrators were put on trial, some two hundred were executed, and thousands received long prison sentences.[108]

However, due to the economic crisis and the worsening political climate, the issue of large-scale economic rehabilitation and financial compensation was soon taken off the table. Anomalies of restitution soon led to serious social tension, adding an extra impetus to antisemitic sentiments.

---

106   For details, see: Stokes, Gale, *The Walls Came Tumbling Down: The Collapse of Communism in Eastern Europe*. New York: Oxford University Press, 1993.

107   Victor Karády, Szociológiai kísérlet a magyar zsidóság 1945 és 1956 közötti helyzetének elemzésére. In *Zsidóság az 1945 utáni Magyarországon*. Paris: Magyar Füzetek, 1984. 37-180; 110-153.

108   For the so-called people's court trials in a European perspective, see István Deák, Jan T. Gross, and Tony Judt, *The Politics of Retribution in Europe*. Princeton, NJ: Princeton University Press, 2000.

In 1946-1947, one of the largest waves of anti-Jewish atrocities swept through Hungary. Old prejudices, such as the blood libel, were intermingled with the effects of wartime propaganda, and new social and political conflicts.[109]

Returning survivors claimed back the assets that had been taken from them, but in most cases, non-Jewish neighbours were unwilling (or unable) to give up the apartments or valuables they had obtained in legal or illegal ways during the war. Economic crisis made bad times worse. The country was devastated, with barely functioning infrastructure and public supply, and chronic shortage of food and goods. Many people were starving, especially in urban areas. In 1946, Hungary experienced probably the largest-scale hyperinflation in world history. Money-based exchanges practically ceased. Just as in wartime, Jews served as perfect scapegoats for resentment against black marketeering and all other crisis-fuelled practices.[110]

---

109   In 1946-1947, only in the Debrecen region 19 people from several localities were put on trial for spreading rumours about ritual murder and cannibalism committed by Jews and for inciting violence against them based on those false allegations. See National Archives of Hungary, Hajdú-Bihar County Archives, XXV.1., Boxes 26-39. For details about Communist-era anti-Jewish attitudes and pogroms, see Éva Standeisky, *Antiszemitizmusok*. Budapest: Argumentum, 2007. 131-173.

110   At the end of July 1946, prices increased by 158.486% every day (!) on average. Ignác Romsics, *Magyarország története a XX. században*. Budapest: Osiris, 1999. 304-305.

8   UNIVERSITY IN STALINIST TIMES

1951 – 1956

When I was a newcomer to England, I was advised never to confess in any social gathering that I was an engineer, otherwise my friendly conversation partner would suddenly discover that she had to powder her nose, or urgently look for his lost car keys. I cannot heed this well-meant advice. The truth is that I am an engineer. It was not my choice.

The location of the University in Budapest is magnificent. It occupies a long stretch of the embankment of the Danube from the *Szabadság* (Freedom) Bridge southwards. Its northernmost point neighbours Gellért Hill, with its statue of Liberty and famous spa hotel. The area is scenic, contributing to Budapest being one of the most beautiful cities of Europe. The late 19th century University buildings are grandiose.

In my time, the Technical University of Budapest was the foremost technological institution of the whole region, with a student population of 10,000. Its staff and alumni include a splendid constellation of stars: Nobel laureates, famous engineers, and Olympic champions. It is the Alma Mater of several of my friends and members of my family. When I enrolled in September 1951, Engineering was the most sought-after of all subjects of study, far more in demand than Medicine or Law, and at this elite university the Electrical Engineering faculty was the most coveted. Yet, it was not a happy place.

New students entering university in Britain are overwhelmed with information: the history of the institution, the campus, the staff, the course, the student organisations, sports facilities, students' clubs and societies. Nothing like this happened to us. Information is power, and we had none. Did the authorities withhold information deliberately to keep us under control?

A terse letter told me to appear in a specific building of *Stoczek utca*, a short street named after the first rector of the university. It turned out to be the academic home of the Electrical/ Electronic Engineering Faculty. Everyone referred to the unloved and unlovable building as *The Stoczek*. There were no campus maps, so it took us a week to realise that The Stoczek was at the remote southernmost edge of the campus. This ugly, functionally inadequate building, unfortunate product of brutalist architecture, was part of the fountainhead of Hungary's architectural culture and civil engineering expertise.

I was one of a crowd of 350 would-be Electrical/Electronic Engineers. Until then, I had been educated in girls' schools, and had mostly been taught by women. Here the large majority of my fellow students and almost all the staff were men. I felt out of place, and the feeling never left me. I may have needed pastoral care, but the first time I came across the concept was a decade after graduation, when I became a Lecturer in British Higher Education.

On entry to a huge lecture theatre, we were handed a lengthy questionnaire. Some important person addressed us. He did not introduce himself. What he said was that, for engineers, political astuteness was prime. We needed no reminder. Radio broadcasts, loudhailers, newspapers and posters drummed into students, school children, toddlers, the working population, and the retired, how essential it was to be faithful disciples of Marx, Lenin, Father Stalin and Father Rákosi. Studying Communist doctrine did not stop when one left school or university. It was part of the life of every citizen at work and at leisure, from the cradle to the grave.[111]

Political subjects were the backbone of the undergraduate curriculum of all disciplines: the Sciences, the Humanities, Music, the Fine Arts, Engineering, all. Here is the list:

- Marxism/Leninism,

- Political Economy,

- Military theory and defence skills,

- Russian language.

These subjects ran through the entire curriculum. Instructors were not so much academics or tutors, more like political commissars. Our family and friends include several world-renowned musicians of Hungarian origin, among them Sir András Schiff, George Pauk (Professor at London's Royal Academy of Music), and Péter Frankl (Professor at Yale). They were brilliant students of Budapest's famous Liszt Ferenc Academy of Music, and in their last semester each gave a public concert to packed houses in the beautiful Art Nouveau concert hall of their Academy. None of them graduated, because they did not pass their examinations in some of the all-important political subjects. After the collapse of the Communist regime in 1989, all institutions faced a major challenge: what to do with teachers of the now-obsolete political subjects. Since these subjects were part of every curriculum, Political departments were by far the largest in every higher education institution. The staff of these departments had been all-powerful, feared by students and

---

111   See *HISTORIAN'S VOICE: Culture and Education in the Post-war Years*. See also Shostakovich's brilliant satirical cantata *Anti-Formalist Rayok* [Anti-Formalist Paradise]

staff. Then suddenly their world collapsed; they had no skill other than teaching their now-useless subjects, they had nowhere to go, each university, every organisation was trying to get rid of them.

By its traditions, the Technical University of Budapest was an Austro-Hungarian institution. This set the pattern of our strict, formal education, and our joyless, overloaded course. In some of Britain's foremost universities, attending lectures is voluntary. All our lectures and all academic activities were compulsory, although some were a waste of time. Lectures were complemented by tutorials, ran by junior staff or senior students. Tutorials were school-like: homework set and marked, discussions held, tests administered. Our cohort of 350 was divided into 12 tutorial groups. Tutorials and laboratory work were arranged on a half-and-half basis: while groups 1 to 6 were in labs, group 7 to 12 had tutorials, and vice versa. This meant that for two years we hardly knew half of our colleagues.

From the perspective of British higher education, it is unbelievable how crowded our timetable had been. In recent years I met some of my erstwhile colleagues who became professors of our University; one was even the Dean. I asked them whether I remembered rightly that we had 30 contact hours per week. They said no, our teaching week had never less than 36 contact hours; we had many hours of homework, and had to compose our laboratory reports besides. This is far in excess of any Engineering programme I ever came across at a British university. Was this Austro-Hungarian discipline, or did the authorities keep us busy deliberately, to give us no time to think? History shows, and my penultimate chapter will demonstrate that students are volatile, potentially dangerous individuals.

They told us nothing about the course, not even its duration. I thought I knew how long my course would be: Jancsi had graduated from the same course only months before I started. His had been an 8-semester, 4-year course. I was wrong. The whole country was in a state of flux, government policies were liable to change overnight, leading politicians fell out of favour from one day to the next. How could the education system be exempt from turmoil? Nobody told us, but it emerged that the course had been lengthened to 5½ years. This was not the only surprise.

If Political subjects were the most important, the rest had to be secondary. In first and second year we studied eight technical subjects:

- Mathematics,

- Physics,

- Chemistry,

- Projective geometry,

- Mechanics,

- Theory of machines,

- Material science,

- Engineering drawing

They did not tell us, but we gradually discovered that apart from ours, there were four other faculties: Civil, Mechanical, Chemical and Architectural Engineering. In the first two years most of the curriculum was common to all faculties. The shared curriculum allowed our professors to deliver mass lectures to huge mixed-faculty audiences. Here is an example.

The Chemistry building was at the furthest end of the campus. By the time the cohort of 350 Electricals had sprinted across from the Stoczek, the 1,000-strong Chemistry lecture theatre was filled to the rafters. Squeezed up against the back wall, most of us were standing. The lecturer was a tiny ant down a deep pit, his voice inaudible, his writing on the blackboard illegible, the whole subject incomprehensible.

How about standards?

My long professional life has included reviewing engineering education all over Britain and on four continents. In my experience, the mathematical, scientific and theoretical preparation of undergraduates in our university was second to none. However, our course was ill-designed, and our engineering creativity was never nurtured. And then, there was the sorry matter of laboratories and textbooks.

Laboratory and project work are essential elements in the formation of engineers. In our university, laboratories were poorly equipped and, in some cases, even unsafe; in new areas of technology laboratory support was almost nonexistent. Project work is costly. The country was poor. We had virtually no project work.

During my university years, electronics and communications – my own subjects – underwent revolutionary change. Transistors were then a recent invention, digital computers were a novelty, and the theory of computation was just emerging from World War II research. These developments originated in the US and Britain. Academics of our university were excellent theoreticians, aware of the trends and capable of following and even contributing to developments, but the iron curtain was firmly in place, and scientists and engineers were isolated. The country had no money, but in any case, up-to-date equipment would not have been accessible. Even textbooks were all but unavailable.

Of course, at the time we understood nothing of this. Textbooks of mathematics and 'classical' engineering were available in antiquarian bookshops, but lecturers of newer subjects had to provide typed booklets of printed notes which only those with money could buy. Access to the library was strictly controlled, a rare privilege. I shall relate how it happened that in my final year I came across a few western technical journals and conference proceedings. Most of my colleagues had never seen any such texts; they did not even know of their existence.

As in all universities, some subjects were poorly taught, but several of our professors were eminent scholars, and some were excellent lecturers. Foremost among these was Professor Simonyi Károly, a politically and humanly uncompromising genius. He taught us *Theoretical Electromagnetics*, the most demanding subject of our course, and perhaps in all Engineering. By magic, he presented the subject as beautiful and enjoyable. He was author of an elegantly written textbook, translated into many languages, and was also Deputy Director of the Central Physical Laboratory. When the regime dismissed him from both his university and research posts, he wrote a great and beautiful tome, narrating the history of Physics in the context of cultural developments in all fields of the arts and sciences. I cherish my copy.[112]

I met Professor Simonyi years after the change of regime. He admired the playing of my pianist cousin Schiff András, who sent him a dedicated boxed set of his performance of Bach's keyboard works. In return, Prof Simonyi sent András a dedicated copy of *The Cultural History of Physics*, in German. I acted as postman both ways. On my arrival at his home, I introduced myself as one of his many erstwhile students, saying that I was sure he would not remember me. He said he remembered me vividly, and while I had been his student, he had often asked himself whether it would be he, or me and my friends, whom the regime would imprison first. He died soon after our meeting. I will always revere him as scientist, teacher and human being. For inspiration, from time to time I return to his testimony and philosophy, summed up in a slim volume under the title: '*But what is the truth ...*'.[113]

Professor Simonyi Károly, Technical University, Budapest, about 1960.

Courtesy of photographer Tamás Szigeti, Hungarian Academy of Sciences.

Systems Theory, my lifelong interest, the subject of most of my research and my books,[114] was new even in the West, offered at our university for the first time. Dr Willoner Gedeon was

112   Károly Simonyi, *A fizika kultúrtörténete*. Budapest: Gondolat, 1986. In 1957, Prof. Simonyi was forced to leave the Central Physical Laboratory. In the early 1970s he was also dismissed as the head of the Department of Theoretical Electromagnetics, founded by him. After the political transition of 1989, Simonyi was rehabilitated, and granted the membership of the Hungarian Academy of Sciences in 1993.

113   Gyula Staas, *De mi az igazság ... Beszélgetések Simonyi Károllyal*. Budapest: Közlöny és Lapkiadó, 1996.

114   Among others: Agnes Kaposi–Margaret Myers, *Systems for All*. London: Imperial College Press, 2001; Agnes Kaposi–Margaret Myers, *Systems, Models and Measures*. Berlin: Springer Verlag, 1994.

an excellent young lecturer. Of course, there were no textbooks, nor even printed notes. Noticing me making notes at his lectures, a few weeks into the course he asked to see my notebook – *he* wanted to borrow *my* notes of his lectures, because he was writing a textbook. I felt honoured. We cooperated throughout the semester: he showed me drafts, I commented, he delivered lectures and invited my criticism of them. The subject was fascinating, our joint effort was thrilling, I was his star student, but at my examination I was not on form: my performance was good but not outstanding. I do recall his disappointment and mine. He left the country in 1956 and became professor at a Swedish university.

SOCIAL LIFE AND ENTERTAINMENT[115]
This could be the shortest section of this book. We had no social life. There was no sport. There were no cultural events. We had no youth.

There was no Student Union, but there was the DISz, the Democratic Youth Association, a political organisation. Membership was compulsory, but people like me did not know, and did not *want* to know, the location of the DISz office. One did not go there unless summoned, and being summoned spelled big trouble. The last chapter will show how DISz membership played a role in my obtaining British citizenship.

The Communist Party dominated university life, as it did the life of the country. I will soon relate how it happened that, in Year 2, I only just managed to avoid Party membership, but I had to pay *two* visits to the Party office in Year 3. However, the Party arranged some events for us all, and perhaps these could be classed as entertainment. Here are some examples.

THE VÁNCZA SHOW
Váncza István was a, quiet, unassuming colleague. I hardly knew him: he was in the other half of the tutorial group set, but his was literally a household name. Everybody knew the old jingle:

HALADJON ÖN IS A KORRAL, SÜSSÖN VÁNCZA SÜTŐPORRAL!
MOVE WITH THE TIMES, USE VÁNCZA BAKING POWDER!

One morning in second year, our classes were cancelled. Instead, the Party summoned the Faculty, some 1,300 of us, to the Aula, the very heart of the University, the central hall in the Central Building. The Aula was not exactly out of bounds, but one needed a reason for visiting it. It housed the Rector's Office and the University administration. This was the first time I entered it.

---

115   See *HISTORIAN'S VOICE: Years of Terror*

Enormous portraits of Comrades Stalin, Lenin, Marx and Rákosi hung on the huge pillars. There was a forest of red flags. Centre stage, under the portraits, stretched a long table, covered with red cloth. There sat our Party leader comrades and senior Party dignitaries.

The atmosphere was hushed. Then one of these important personages stood up. He was brief. 'The enemy has been active again, but we have been vigilant; the villain is about to be unmasked.' If possible, the hush deepened. After a dramatic pause, another grandee rose, and uttered nothing but a name: 'Váncza István'. Our colleague was visibly shocked, but he obediently separated himself from the rest. He was commanded to stand in front of the red-clothed table. Now came the full speech. Here was the enemy, a member of the hateful capitalist elite, *osztályellenség:* enemy of the working class. The speaker went on at length, while our colleague Váncza stood there, stunned, motionless. Anyone who had befriended this enemy, the speaker said, was an *osztályáruló:* traitor of the working class. Year 2 – our year – was shamed, the speaker continued, they tolerated the enemy, they hid him for more than a year, turned a blind eye to his destructive activities. We must be grateful to a member of the year (*who!?*) whose watchfulness enabled us to unmask this vicious foe who will now be expelled, and mercilessly punished. At that point spontaneous rhythmical clapping ensued.

Now the drama reached a new phase. Some ostensibly improvised, spontaneous contributions were offered from the floor, condemning the traitor, praising the comrade whose vigilance led to his downfall. The text of these miniature speeches had been handed out to trusted cadre prior to the meeting. The speakers should have memorised their text, but some failed in their task, and read it out from their crib sheet. Each such individual unsolicited contribution was received by enthusiastic cheers from the crowd, and those at the red table initiated rhythmical clapping and chanting of slogans, such as 'Stalin, Rákosi'.[116]

While all this unfolded, Váncza stood stiffly in front of that table. Then a couple of the luminaries stood up, grabbed the culprit by either arm, and frogmarched him off the scene.

None of us dared to ask what happened to our colleague.[117]

---

116 'Cadre' is an important term in a Communist regime. Used as a noun, it referred to someone trusted by the regime. It was also used as a verb: 'to cadre' (*káderezni*) meant to subject an individual to political scrutiny.

117 The legendary baking powder was invented by pharmacist József Váncza before World War I. It was made famous by his entrepreneur son, József Váncza Jr., in the 1920s, partly due to modern advertising methods. Theirs was among the first firms using neon signs in Budapest. In 1948, the company was nationalised, the family was dispossessed, and faced discrimination as being 'bourgeois'. József Váncza's grandson István might have been chosen for the university trial because of his well-known name. After a period of suspension, he had been readmitted to university. However, his sister was not allowed to enter university at all. A story of those times.

This was the time of show trials, in the style of Stalin's purges. As the Rákosi regime developed, dramatic events of public denunciation became formalised. The feudal institution of 'Courts of Honour' was revived. These 'courts' followed strict legal procedures: the accused was identified by the authorities or was denounced by some individual; the trial was public and publicised; judges, prosecutor and defence counsel were appointed. Compulsory volunteers were picked for viewing the trial. The press came. The usual charge was that of being an imperialist agent, a traitor, an enemy of the People's Republic and the working class. The accused would invariably plead guilty to the charges. Witnesses would come forward for the prosecution, never for the defence. The accused himself would act as main prosecution witness, confessing to the crime, adding to it, exercising 'constructive self-criticism', *építő önkritika*. Judgments were made, punishments announced. Groszmann Feri is a friend, a Mechanical Engineer. He tells me that at his provincial university, trials by 'Courts of Honour' were all but commonplace.

THE SPORT OF CATCHING MILITARY ENGINEERS

One of the prime subjects in our curriculum was *Military Theory and Defence Skills*. In addition to the award of a degree, the successful graduate would become a reservist officer, Lieutenant of the Army, Technical Division.

Some could go even further. After Year 2, people could volunteer to become full-time professional army officers. Many country people found this an attractive option: they were given clothing (a uniform), boots, heated barracks and reasonable food, instead of virtually starving and freezing in student hostels. When Jancsi was an undergraduate, some homeless orphaned Jews also signed up, becoming reluctant army officers. Two of these unlikely warriors were our close friends.

Near the end of our second year, there was a compulsory voluntary gathering in the Aula, bedecked with the usual decorations and garlands of flags, emblems and outsize portraits of the Greats. Dignitaries at the red table called for volunteers into the Army. Many of our cold and hungry colleagues signed up. Then one of the distinguished personages addressed the gathering, thanking the volunteers for their patriotism; but, he said, there was a colleague who should be the foremost Military Engineer, and yet his name was absent from the list. He said Comrade Csákány was admired by all as a peasant cadre who set an example with his competence and diligence. He must not be shy: he should join the military.

I did not know Csákány Antal (Tóni) – he belonged to the other tutorial set – but we had all heard of him, the most brilliant student of our year. He stood up. His voice was quiet but clear; not even those in the farthest corner of the Aula could miss what he said: 'My father died in the war as a conscripted soldier. One member of a family is enough. If it is a condition for me to study here that I join the army, then I will go home and work the fields.'

We were stunned. Nobody dared question an order, let alone contradict one. To our amazement, Tóni was still among us the next day, in civilian clothes. A plucky peasant cadre, he was already the intellectual king of our year. Only he could get away with such defiance of the Party's authority.

OUTDOOR FUN

The Party offered us some Sunday entertainment. In 1949, Comrade Rákosi's government embarked on a major industrialisation programme. The village of Dunapentele, 50 km south of Budapest, was chosen as the site of the country's newest, largest iron and steel works. The village was to be renamed as *Sztálinváros*, Stalin Town, and developed into a city. We keen undergraduates were compelled to volunteer to devote our free time (*what free time?*) to building the new city. We spent many happy rainy Sundays on the building site, enthusiastically singing Party songs while pushing wheelbarrows in the mud or carrying on our shoulders stacks of bricks and bags of cement.[118]

MUSICAL ENTERTAINMENT AND EXERCISE

Mindful of our physical and spiritual welfare, compulsory volunteers like me, who could sing in tune, had to run choir practice for the rest. These joyous daily events ran from 7am to 8, when classes started. Singing Party songs would have been uplifting in itself, but it was often supplementary to marching. If no marching date was imminent, then, beside singing, our morning gatherings were occupied by discussing current affairs, such as the latest political trials, and press reports on overfulfillment of agricultural and industrial quotas.

Our buildings were almost unheated, but one could get warm by practising marching in preparation for the celebration of one of our glorious political festivals. There were several of these annually: 15th March (anniversary of the 1848 revolution), 1st May (International Workers' Day), anniversary of the Great 1917 Soviet Revolution, Father Stalin's birthday on 21st December, Father Rákosi's birthday, to mention but a few. It was compulsory for school children, students, factory workers, office workers and all to volunteer to participate. Large groups gathered at designated locations throughout the city, each group forming itself into an orderly column. Like tributaries to a river, columns of marchers combined into a single mighty stream, parading along Heroes Square where Comrade Rákosi and our other Great Leaders surveyed the flow from their high stand, waving benevolently at the enthusiastically cheering and chanting multitude. Shostakovich's satirical ballet *Bolt* includes just such a scene.

---

118   See *HISTORIAN'S VOICE: Years of Terror*

To prepare for these auspicious events, everyone had to learn military-style marching. Weeks before the celebratory date, marchers had to assemble daily at their collection point before the start of the working day, and proceed to exercise grounds. Forming 16-wide rows, some marchers carried banners, some flags, all singing Party songs lustily, or chanting rousing slogans rhythmically.

1ˢᵗ May celebratory march on Heroes Square in Budapest, 1951. Photograph by the newspaper *Szabad Nép*.
Hungarian National Museum Historical Photo Department

Our university was favourably positioned: traffic was diverted from the Embankment, clearing it for students to exercise. Each row of 16 had to be perfectly aligned, so that a spectator on the side should see only the nearest of the 16. With practice this became manageable. It was much harder for the 16 to remain perfectly aligned while turning a corner. The concept was easy, especially for engineers: angular velocity had to be constant.

This translates into the one in the centre of the turn marching on the spot, the person furthest from the centre racing along at speed, all others doing something in-between. Sometimes one of the Party Luminaries commandeered the exercise, using an ear-splitting whistle to indicate displeasure at the straggly lines. It was easier on the eardrums when a Sergeant Major took charge, a real soldier. He did not need a whistle; he had a splendid pair of lungs on him, so that all thirteen hundred members of the Faculty on the march, and even students of other faculties in the buildings, could hear him uttering encouragements.

STUDENT INTAKE

Student intake was carefully planned. I was a living example.

The country needed good engineers, and the technological elite of the future had to be good cadres. These two considerations often conflicted. Our nation's Planners found a solution.

- The majority of the intake was made up of competent run-of-the-mill students who had graduated from grammar school with good enough grades to meet the university's exacting standards. Let's call them the **Bulk**.

- The **Eggheads** were the crème-de-la-crème, top products of grammar schools. They had all the advantages: they were clever, typically middle class, relatively well housed, reasonably well fed from home. However, they were politically suspicious, because they knew too much, thought too much. They were barely tolerated, they needed survival skills. I belonged to this group, but I soon found that some of my fellow Eggheads were brighter than I was, and most had much more inclination and talent for Engineering than me. I had to work hard to remain an Egghead, if only for my father's sake. He should have been a prime student at this university, but never had the chance.

- The third group were the **Cadre**, the desirables the Planners were looking for. They came from working class or peasant backgrounds, mostly from the provinces. At university most of them shivered and almost starved.

The Cadre further subdivided:

A small group of gifted and highly motivated students had managed to overcome their social, economic and educational disadvantages and made it to grammar school, or graduated from secondary education otherwise. These were the **Star Cadre**, admired by the undergraduate community. Two outstanding examples were Csákány Tóni and Zombor Nándi,[119] whose story is yet to come.

---

119 Not Nándi's real surname.

The majority of the Cadre had left school at 14, learnt a craft, or worked in fields, mines or factories. Some such young and not-quite-so-young people were plucked out from their environment, and were subjected to a short cramming course, leading to substandard graduation. They were then pressganged into university courses for doctors, lawyers, teachers and engineers. In our year there were many such reluctant and perplexed students. Let's call them the **Bemused**. One of these was Alexi Pityu, a key character of my undergraduate education.

And then there was fourth, the most important, most select, most powerful group.

• The **Politicals** were chosen from the ranks of all others. They were dedicated Communists or ruthless opportunists who became feared members of the university's Party organisation.

As always, there were whispered unfunny jokes. Here is one about the new type of Communist intellectual.

> *In Little Mudsville villagers are always quarrelling. Joe is the most reliable cadre; the Party Secretary selects him to learn how to deal with the feuds. Joe enrols in school, graduates, and goes to study law at Budapest's revered Eötvös Lóránt University of Sciences and Humanities. Gaining his degree, he returns home, and becomes the District Judge, settling all disputes.*
>
> *But in Little Mudsville crops are poor and cows are dying. The Party Secretary tries to send someone to the famous Gödöllő Agricultural College. Nobody wants to go. The consensus is that Joe should go – he is already an educated man. The Party sends Joe, he gets his degree, and returns home, adding 'District Agronomist' to his legal title.*
>
> *Now Little Mudsville is advancing in the world, and when talk of electrification starts, Joe is the obvious candidate. He enrols in the illustrious Technical University of Budapest, and on graduation he adds to his titles 'County Electrification Engineer'.*
>
> *Public health is the next issue at Little Mudsville. The Party Secretary turns to Joe automatically: he should go to Debrecen's renowned Medical School. Jo refuses adamantly. The Party Secretary demands to know the reason for Joe's stubborn dissent. Joe explains: as a doctor he would have to make out prescriptions, and that means that he would have to learn to read and write …*

The 'Study Partnership Scheme' was a new invention, introduced for the first time in our year. Those who find it hard to credit this should remember that I lack imagination, I tell only the truth.

The scheme was simple and ingenious. Each Bemused was paired with one of the Eggheads. The Egghead was responsible for the progress of his/her Bemused. If a Bemused dropped out, his/her Egghead was expelled. That's it.

Some of my fellow Eggheads had great trouble with their Bemused. I was lucky. My Bemused was Alexi Pityu, a charming tiny miner boy with an endearing regional accent. Straightforward and honest, Pityu was a *palóc*, from a region of northern Hungary famous for its folk art. Before the war, men in his family had been involved in the Trade Unions. When the Communists came, Pityu joined the Party, because he saw this as a chance to rise from grinding poverty. He had no talent for, and no interest in, studying, but when the Party required him to go to cramming school, he did his best. Graduation was difficult for him, but when his Party Secretary told him to join our University, he did. Cold and hungry at the hostel, he understood little of the lessons; he hated Budapest, and was homesick, and would have liked to go home.

I liked Pityu, and felt sorry for him. He liked me, and worked all hours, not for his own sake, but for mine. At first, we studied together from 7 to 8am, before classes started. This did not work, because on most mornings we had to attend compulsory voluntary Party activities; and in any case, Pityu needed more than an hour daily. He started to come home with me at the end of the day. This is how he became not just my Study Partner but a project for my whole family. My mother fed him, Jancsi helped him with engineering drawing, and my father taught him mathematics. This was when I learnt how much of the Engineering Mathematics syllabus my father knew. I tutored him in physics and chemistry, and helped him with homework and whatever else. Pityu failed at least one subject each semester, but thankfully he passed the resits every time.

Our Study Partnership lasted for four semesters, ending when Pityu volunteered as Military Engineer, and was told to choose Power Engineering. We parted as friends. He wanted to express his gratitude, and had nothing to offer but his loyalty. He decided to sponsor me for membership of his beloved Communist Party. He brought me an application form, already filled in. I just had to sign it. As sponsor, he had to write a testimonial, and I was touched by the beautiful things he wrote about me and my family. I let him down for the first time in our two-year partnership and friendship. It was he who had to submit the signed form, and I kept forgetting to return it to him. He kept asking. Then I lost the form. He filled in another. When I lost that too, he said with sincere sadness: 'I must have misjudged you. It seems you are not ready to become a member of the Party. I must withdraw my sponsorship of you.'

Over the years, Pityu and I met on campus from time to time, always pleased to see each other. I am almost sure that he managed to graduate.

PROGRESS

Students' progress was assessed on the basis of homework, scheduled assessments, and unscheduled written lightning tests called *zárthelyi*. These were tough, and could be sprung on us at any time, the main elements in deciding whether or not a student qualified for the end-of-semester written examination. The decision was binary: the student either qualified or not, but if one made the grade then the actual mark was not carried forward. The next hurdle was the written examination which qualified one for the oral examination. The actual end-of-semester mark was determined by the oral examination alone. The system was vicious.

Orals were public, anyone could attend. The mark obtained was entered into one's hard-bound *Index*, a record book registering progress of the student in every subject and in every semester through the course. The top mark was 5 (*jeles*, 'notable'), the bottom mark was 2, 'acceptable'. There were hundreds of us, so orals were carried out in several parallel streams. The name of the examiner was seldom specified, but location gave a clue. I have a photograph of my *Thermodynamics* exam, conducted by an Assistant Professor (*Tanársegéd*) in a mean little tutorial room. An exam scheduled for a large lecture theatre implied that the Professor himself would be the examiner. Being on the Professor's list was a doubtful privilege: it assured a large audience of students, junior staff, and stray people who fancied viewing the spectacle.

The oral itself was a cross between a lottery and haggling in a fleamarket. The lottery started with the candidate's pulling a card from a large stack, usually two questions per card, both to be attempted. One prepared the answers while the examiner was quizzing another examinee. The lottery continued when the candidate was called to the platform. As likely as not, the examiner would say: 'I am not interested in the subjects on your card, tell me instead about …'. He was the boss, one had to improvise.

Then haggling would start. The examiner would say: 'OK, you got yourself a 3' (mid-grade). The candidate might leave meekly or might plead: 'Please Sir (or was it Comrade?), I hoped for a better mark'. The examiner might consult the Index to see the candidate's past history, and refuse: 'You should count yourself lucky with a 3', or might graciously consent: 'OK, let's give it a try', and would nominate a new topic. The oral might take an hour or more, and having started from a mark of 3, the victim might end up with a mark of 4 or even 5, but might also fail, the examiner saying: 'You are remarkably ignorant about this important topic, come back after the summer for a re-examination'. The candidate might beg: 'But Sir, you offered me a 3 before, may I just have a 2 now?' Such pleading would never succeed. It was not unusual for a student to have been offered a mark of 4 at first, and then fail altogether while attempting to obtain a 5. Failing in just one subject would allow the candidate to be re-examined. Failing in two would usually be fatal, except of course for the Bemused.

Here is the story of one of the first oral examinations of my undergraduate life. I thought it was the last.

Civil and Mechanical Engineering were the Senior Service faculties, housed in the splendid 19-century edifices of the campus, while we Electricals slummed it in the Stoczek. Projective Geometry exams were held on the Mechanicals' premises, and my exam was scheduled in the magnificent formal dining room of the Central Building, lit in the winter gloom by a vast crystal chandelier. About a dozen examinees were sitting on high-backed carved chairs around the huge antique dining table, a further dozen perching on tall lab stools around the walls. I needed courage to totter in.

The examiner was Dr Strommer (soon *Professor* Strommer), our celebrity lecturer, even taller and more formidable close to than from a distance in the lecture theatre. I presented myself, Index in hand, and he gave me three things: a piece of paper not bigger than A5, a stub of a blunt pencil, and a small card with a single exam question. He stabbed a finger towards a stool by the wall, which was just being vacated by an ashen-faced student. I sat down (up?), expecting the whole crowd soon to adjourn to a drawing office with the tools necessary to tackle a task in projective geometry: A0-size drawing board, set squares (right-angled rulers), properly sharpened pencil and rubber. After a minute I became aware that others perching on stools were scribbling on their piece of paper. Dr Strommer loomed large in front of me and barked: 'Get on with it, Colleague!' (not Comrade). The task would realistically have needed space and tools, but there was nothing for it: I had to start scribbling freehand, using my Index in my lap as the only hard surface. Dr Strommer circulated like a simultaneous chess champion, occasionally grunting at what he saw; dismissing some, admitting others from the small crowd of prospective examinees at the door. He stopped in front of me now and again, glancing at my scribbles, but said nothing, and moved on. My paper looked like a spider's web. An inept draughtsman, I tried to draw thin straight lines freehand, because inaccuracy might have prevented me from accomplishing the task, or – worse – it might have led to the wrong result. At last, unable to go any further, I just sat there, petrified. Up soared Dr Strommer again. He addressed me loudly: 'You still here!?' He snatched away my piece of paper and my Index, and gestured to a newcomer at the door to take my place on the stool. I stood up. He scribbled furiously in my Index. Knees knocking, I left. Failed. Only when back in the corridor did I dare look at the Index. Please look for his signature on the Index page. It fits his personality and underlines my story. The brute gave me top mark.

SCHOLARSHIP

As students, we were constantly reminded of our privileged position in society. There was another side to the coin. University education was free, but one sacrificed potential earnings.

The hairdresser who cut my hair was a girl of my age. She started work when she was 14. She thought I was a big joke, still at school in my early 20s. She said my earnings would never catch up with hers. Had I stayed in Hungary, I am sure she would have been right.

In our first semester we heard rumours that good examination results might qualify one for a scholarship. I gathered enough daring to enquire. The ogre in the Dean's Office confirmed that we could apply for scholarship at the end of each semester, and the scholarship would be awarded on the basis of end-of-semester examination results. 'Come back with your Index, Comrade, when you have completed your exams', she said.

The author's university record book (index), 1951–1952, first semester.
Kaposi family collection

After this, I redoubled my efforts, hoping to show my hairdresser that I could earn a bit of money. My first-semester results prove it. Except for Marxism/Leninism, all my marks are *jeles*, top grade. My Degree Certificate is proof that I earned top marks in almost all the subjects throughout the course. I was not the brightest spark, but few equalled my results, and you could count on the fingers of one hand the number who did even slightly better. How come that I never got a single penny of scholarship?

Index in hand, and armed with my first-semester results, I sidled along to the Dean's office. There sat the now familiar ogre. I gingerly held out my Index. She glanced at it and talked to me like I was an idiot: 'Scholarships will only start at Semester 2, but in any case, don't you see, Comrade, you needn't apply, you will not qualify.' Why not? I asked, in the secure knowledge that I had one of the best results of my whole year of 350. She announced: 'Scholarship is not calculated on the basis of the *actual marks* you achieved, but on your *percentage improvement,* semester-by-semester'. Light began to dawn – or perhaps to dim. I asked her to confirm that, having scored near-top marks in the first semester, there would be no scope for improvement for the rest of the course. 'Precisely!' she said with a beaming smile. I apologised for disturbing her, and left her office with my tail between my legs. Did they plan the whole scheme just to trick Eggheads?

FRIENDS AND OTHERS

I met Jóska on our very first day at university. I remember his surname, but don't include it here. He sat next to me when we were first shunted into the Stoczek, burdened with an armful of questionnaires. He was friendly, and older than most. Trying to ask my help with a rubric, he leaned over, looking at my form. Friendliness was gone. He asked: 'You were born in Debrecen?' Yes, I said. 'And your mother's maiden name was Csengeri?' Yes, I replied. He said: 'I know your sort. My grandfather had been a serf (*urasági cseléd*) in the Csengeri estates.' Should I have tried to explain that the Csengeri family had a rich and a poor branch, that my great-grandmother Csengeri Eszter had been a widow who supported her six children by selling shoelaces house to house? My colleague would not have believed me, and my protestations would have made matters worse. I said nothing.

When the political leadership of the year was publicised, we learned that Jóska was the Party Secretary for our year. He would have been a nice enough chap, and he was a better than average student, but because of his political position, he was feared by most. He had a seat at the red table in the Aula on critical occasions.

An angular, thickset man, Pali was the oldest in the year, a weak student who somehow never failed. I know his surname. He was a prominent member of the Party, superior even to Jóska. He too had a seat booked at that ominous red table at the Aula. I only had dealings with him once, and that was once too often.

In our second year, the state issued 'Peace Bonds' (*Békekölcsön*), similar to the 'War Bonds' of a few years before. In effect, this was a form of taxation. People 'volunteered' to buy these Bonds. Somebody had the bright idea that volunteer undergraduates should persuade pensioners to buy Peace Bonds. Pensioners were on the brink of starvation.

Our University's Party organisation issued a list of pairs of students whose job it was to go house to house, visiting pensioners in their homes, 'requesting' them to register for voluntary purchase of Bonds. As a suspicious Egghead, I was paired with Pali, a thoroughly trustworthy Political. He was in charge of our Bond Sale Team of two, and commanded that I should be the one who talked the pensioners into buying the Bonds. His task was to observe me, and judge how keen and committed to the cause I was. It was wintertime. Many pensioners were not only malnourished, but also freezing in their homes. I could read the hatred in their faces. I had the impression that Pali enjoyed the exercise.

Dobi István was unremarkable, an indifferent student. I am not even sure that he graduated. His one distinction was that he was the son of the Head of State.

A congenial member of my Tutorial group was Nándi, a working-class boy, a Star Cadre. He had missed a good part of grammar school education, but he was clever; he often spotted problems we were too immature to see. We liked and respected him.

On a Monday afternoon, our Political Economy Professor's lecture addressed the country's Agriculture policy. The Professor explained that smallholdings had to be collectivised (nationalised), because they were outdated, incapable of expanding agricultural production (*bővített újratermelés*).

Tutorials in Political Economy were called Seminars. On the Tuesday morning, the Seminar Leader of our Tutorial Group asked Nándi to explain why smallholdings had to be collectivised. Nandi had understood our Professor's argument and gave an articulate and convincing account.

This was the time of show trials. Imperialist agents were lurking everywhere; they even infiltrated the government and the very leadership of the Party. One of the enemies turned out to be the Minister of Agriculture, who wanted deliberately to alienate the rural population, perpetrating the *false* doctrine that smallholdings had to be nationalised. The papers and the radio were full of reports of the fall from grace of this rogue politician.[120]

The following Tuesday, the Seminar Leader declared triumphantly that the Minister of Agriculture had been an enemy, now exposed. By mistake, or to be provocative, he called on Nándi to explain why smallholdings need not be nationalised, that they *were* capable of expanded agricultural production. There was the familiar hush. Nándi said: 'My mother is a poor overworked widow. She can hardly change my shirt every week. Don't expect me to change my political views weekly.' With this, he walked out of the seminar. I don't recall seeing him again.

Gyula (I remember his surname), a clever and inventive colleague, knew that I loved music, and tried to explain to me his idea of using light in sound recording. The method was not yet feasible, he was ahead of his time, but in due course he made a good career in Hungary.

I was already in Britain, but the iron curtain was still strictly in place, when his company mandated Gyula to visit the Digital Equipment Corporation of USA to steal their PDP8 minicomputer design. He succeeded. As I understand it, the machine was manufactured in Hungary, and used in process control throughout the COMECON.[121]

---

120 Ferenc Donáth, *Reform és forradalom. A magyar mezőgazdaság strukturális átalakulása 1945-1975*. Budapest: Akadémiai, 1977, 143.; Mihály Ivicz, *A magyar mezőgazdaság XX. századi helyzetének elemzése különös tekintettel a kisbirtokra*. Doctoral Thesis, Pázmány Péter Catholic University, 2004.

121 *COMECON*: Council for Mutual Economic Assistance. It was an economic organisation from 1949 to 1991 under the leadership of the Soviet Union that comprised the countries of the Eastern Block and some Communist states elsewhere in the world. It was disbanded in 1991 when free-market policies were adopted by its members.

And there was one more colleague, an informer who almost brought my engineering education to a premature end. His story is soon to come.

I had several colleagues who in another life might have become my friends, but in a dictatorship, friendship is a dangerous thing. Friendship is trust, and trust may be betrayed deliberately, or through carelessness.

Éva was multi-talented, an outstanding student whose existence was precarious, because once her family had been landowning gentry.

Sanyi, the most cultured of us all, was doomed, because his father was a Protestant cleric.

János was a gentle young man who shared my musical interests. He was a troubled soul, a devout Catholic.

Two other Eggheads, Somló Péter and Nádor Péter, were dangerously middle class. Their fathers, Jewish lawyers both, had been killed in munkaszolgálat.

I liked them all. What a shame the system deprived me of the chance to befriend them.

CONSPIRACY I

I was a good student, I mentored my Bemused, I passed all my exams, and mostly with top grades, I never missed a deadline, I sang and conducted party songs, I marched and carried flags; and yet, I was expelled from my university.

By third year, many of our original cohort of 350 had dropped out, and the Power Engineers and the soldiers split off. There remained about 100 Electronic Engineering students, me included, and we no longer warranted division into tutorial groups. We began to get to know each other better. That is when I found myself in the elite academic group, headed by Csákány Tóni. Others were Szarvas Feri and Sima István, son of an eminent engineer. The others were brighter than me, but I was my father's daughter, the hardest worker, and good at exams.[122]

Tóni was a first-rate bridge player. One bitter winter morning a three-hour lecture was cancelled, because our eminent professor was ill again. We regretted his failing health, but we were relieved: the freestanding Physics building was exposed to the elements and had no heating. Tóni suggested a bridge game. István, who lived nearby, said we should go to his house; his mum would give us lunch: a cheese sandwich and a cup of lemon tea. On our way, Szőnyi Tibor joined us. He was a good student, smart, always friendly, but somehow, we felt uneasy about him – we were acquiring instincts. This time we could not shake him off. He joined us and proved to be a creditable bridge player. We had warm hospitality from Mrs Sima, and after lunch we went back to college for afternoon lectures.[123]

---

122   Not their real name.
123   Not his real name.

Next morning a group of Party dignitaries were policing the entrance to our lecture theatre. They stopped Csákány, Szarvas, Sima and me, and led us to the university's central Party office. Szarvas speculated that we might have been summoned to receive some honour for being the best students of the year. We sat in the corridor for a long while under the gaze of one of the minor officials, and then were summoned, one by one. When it was my turn, I was seen by a great man: the university's Party Secretary himself, together with two of his aides. The Party Secretary told me that I had been suspicious since arrival, and now my true colours had been revealed: I was an imperialist agent. Having abused my talents and my position as one of the year's academic leaders, I was a member of a conspiracy, aiming to corrupt lesser students by spreading alien western culture: the decadent game of bridge. I had been expelled and should leave the university forthwith. One of the aides led me through a side door, guided me to the street, and pointed towards the nearest tram stop. I did not dare to say that I knew the way.

A week later a messenger came from the university, commanding me to report to the now familiar Party Office. Some lesser mortal informed me of my conditional reprieve. I was allowed to attend lectures and labs but must go straight home at the end of classes. While on university premises, I was to associate with nobody. At the next lecture I saw to my relief that Csákány, Sima and Szarvas were also there. So was Szőnyi.

We had Tóni to thank for our stay of execution. On that ominous day he had been the last to be interviewed. The Party Secretary told him that he – Tóni – was well rid of these three bridge-playing class enemies; they had been unmasked and expelled. Csákány replied that the Party Secretary had been mistaken; that *he* (Tóni) was the source of the corruption if there was one; it was he who had taught us bridge (not quite true, we had played before, but he certainly improved our game). Tóni also said it was he who had suggested the game that day (true). He said if we were to be expelled, he would leave too, go home to his village – he had enough of this place. The Party Secretary pleaded and threatened, but then remembered the Military Engineering incident. He asked Tóni what would induce him to stay. Tóni said he would stay if we stayed, not otherwise.

Decades later I returned to Hungary at my university's invitation, as a respected British academic. I lectured at the Stoczek about Computer Aided Design, my field of research at the time (an unnerving experience, lecturing from the platform from where my professors had instructed me years before). The Dean asked me to supervise the PhD of a senior researcher and advise on the Faculty's research strategy. This is how I learned that Szőnyi was a contributor to the Hungarian research effort, Visiting Professor at the Faculty. I met him. He tried to ingratiate himself and invited me to collaborate in his research programme. I declined. He got his eminent Research Director to invite me to lecture at their Institute. This I could not refuse. He, Professor Szőnyi, personally delivered a great bouquet of thank-you flowers to Pici's house where I was staying, arriving when I was not there. He introduced himself to Pici as my erstwhile colleague and close friend. Pici, poor thing, asked him in for coffee, and thought him charming. He sent me a substantial cheque as remuneration for my lecture at his Institute, which I forwarded in *his* name to the Engineers' Benevolent Fund. I wished him no harm, but he died a particularly horrible early death.

CONSPIRACY II

The 1956 Hungarian Revolution gave people the opportunity to get hold of their secret personal files. The Secret Police compiled such files on everybody. I have Jancsi's file here, which makes for almost amusing reading. It shows that he successfully walked a tightrope, managed to present himself as technically and culturally astute, but politically moronic. We had my file too, but it is now lost. It showed how close I came, again and again, to being unmasked and punished as an enemy of the people. Incriminating details included Jóska's report about the landowner Csengeri family, my virtual failure at persuading pensioners to part with their crust of bread, and my misdeed of being a subversive underground bridge player.

My personal file included an additional topic. Jancsi and I married at the end of my first university year. We shared his parents' house. As the bean soup story recorded, it was a corner house, with a low garden fence, easily overlooked from two streets. The Kaposi family lived upstairs on a high mezzanine, and there were three small semi-basement dwellings below.

My personal file showed that the Secret Police regularly questioned several families in the vicinity, and also the three families downstairs. Reports stated that the old and young Kaposis led a quiet life: a lot of classical music was heard, but there were no large gatherings or noisy parties. My parents, Zoli, and his wife were identified as repeated visitors. However, the observers reported very suspicious events taking place twice a year: for about two weeks, three or four young men would arrive and spend many hours in the house, and sometimes they would even stay overnight! The informers remarked how still the house was during these visits: outside listeners could not discern what was being said, even classical music was not played! After these noiseless two weeks all would go back to normal, but the suspicious events were repeated at roughly six-monthly intervals. A conspiracy was suspected, and all neighbours were asked to stay vigilant.

The observations were correct, the authorities were thorough, but not clever. I was at university, studying for exams with a few of my colleagues at the end of each semester. One of the study party was Tóni, the peasant cadre who lived in an unheated hostel. The Kaposi house was always warm.

OVERLAPPING SPY RINGS

One must not be too ready to condemn disloyal informers, like the redhead Vera in my school, my colleague Szőnyi at university, and the neighbours around the Kaposi house. In Stalinist times everyone was an informer, and everyone was informed upon. We knew that spy rings existed, covering everyone, and every sphere of life.

- The Party had a hierarchical network. Members were tasked to report on each other, on a list of non-members, and on anyone suspicious.

- Ministries, local authorities, the Army, the Police, youth organisations and trade associations had their own networks and reporting structures, as had industrial and agricultural enterprises, theatres, schools and academic institutions.

- There were compulsory voluntary 'cultural' networks, such as circles for reading newspapers and discussing current affairs. Organisers had to report on members.

- In some cultural groups, membership was by persuasion rather than compulsion. Members were reported on, as were abstainers, and people's response to the recruitment process itself was recorded.

- Some cultural/social groups – sports clubs, knitting circles, fans of theatre, concert, opera, etc – were truly voluntary and self-selective, but anyone belonging to them was reported on, and some for conspicuously *not* belonging, such as a chess master not participating in a chess club.

- There was a comprehensive network of caretakers of buildings spying on tenants, and neighbours spying on each other, as in case of the Kaposi house.

The list above is but a sample, there must have been many other networks threading through the society of our youth.

Fascism had worked through the enthusiastic support of the nation. Communism failed to capture the imagination of the people; instead, the regime was held in place by fear, manipulated by the system of spy rings.

GIRL STUDENTS

When Jancsi was a student at the same Faculty four years before me, his cohort had the handicap of attempting to become engineers without studying the vital subjects of Marxism, Political Economy, etc, and they had stumbled into university on their own initiative, without the wise guidance of the State Planners.

In Jancsi's year there were six women, and they were a sensation. In our year, women were all but commonplace, making up 20% of the intake. The percentage increased year by year, because women proved to be tenacious. Few made it to the very top, but I don't recall any women dropouts.

Our male colleagues accepted us with equanimity, but staff, particularly senior staff, did not hide the view that women degraded the noble profession of Engineering. Some, like the Head of Laboratories, Nagy Sándor, treated us toughly. Others challenged us to prove ourselves. Worst were those who patronised us, regarded us as a joke. The concept of 'sexism' had not yet been formulated. Even in sophisticated UK, the Sex Discrimination Act was decades away. Our only protection was our wit and dignity. Labs were a challenge, girls were not supposed to be able to cope with equipment, but the story of my *Television Technology* examination may be the best example of the sort of attitude we had to put up with.

Professor Barta, Dean of our Faculty, taught us a series of subjects, of which Television Technology was the last. He was a middle-aged, intellectually middleweight man, an average lecturer. He was pompous – the Big Boss – and did not let anyone forget it (unlike modest Professor Simonyi, a researcher, an intellectual giant). To mark his importance among the many professors on the scene, Dean Barta made everyone address him as 'Prof'. He must have distinguished himself somehow, because his statue stands on the grounds of the university.

Prof Barta was too grand a personage to examine students himself, so I never encountered him close-to until the very last semester, when he honoured a handful of students by putting them on his own examination schedule. Exams were public events, and there was a big audience. I was not nervous; the subject was related to my degree project, and I even had some insight beyond the syllabus.

When I appeared at the door, Prof interrupted the current examinee mid-flow, to greet me with a broad smile: 'Ah, the queen of the year, the new lady engineer soon to grace our profession!' My knees turned to jelly.

I knew both topics on my question card, so I began to re-gather my wits. When my turn came on the platform, I delivered my answers, scientific and practically important stuff. I also answered his supplementary questions, and when he kept nodding, I thought the exam was all done. Then he said he had a question on a new topic: scientific uses of oscilloscopes.

We first talked about general oscilloscopes, their design and uses in science, technology and medicine, and then about sampling scopes. I thought I was on secure ground. And then came a whole series of questions about the colour of oscilloscope screens, and why green oscilloscope screens were the most usual. I was ready with answers: cost, granularity, energy conversion properties, photoluminescence of coating materials, discriminatory sensitivity of the eye to frequency ranges of the visible spectrum. He was still not satisfied, persisting: 'What else?' Barely able to hold back tears, I admitted defeat; I could think of no more reasons for preferring green scope screens to other colours. Now came Prof's killer punchline: 'How about true-to-life displays of underwater scenes? And how about showing on the screen a pretty little green dress, like the one you are wearing right now?'

TELEVISION FOR THE COUNTRY

Wisely, our curriculum included industrial practice. There was no choice of course, but by luck I had an interesting placement: working on development of the country's first television transmitter.

In January 1953, the Government established the Hungarian Television Company. The transmitter tower was built on the top of Széchenyi Hill in Buda, and the electronics laboratory developing the equipment was at the foot of the tower. I joined the development team in the summer of 1955. Officially my industrial practice should have lasted two weeks, but my industrial supervisor Visontai Péter arranged for me to stay on for the whole summer.

Our work was frustrating and unproductive. We were to build transmitter circuitry from faint, often ambiguous circuit diagrams. Timing of the transmitter was to be controlled by magnetostrictive delay lines, devices whose technology was poorly understood. The devices were unreliable, causing haphazard timing. My supervisor was competent and helpful, I was keen and diligent, but the very design was against us. I was returning to University at the end of the summer, and still the circuitry was making no progress. We began to hear the following whispered rumour:

In 1953, the newly formed Hungarian Television Company had invited estimates from companies worldwide for installing a working transmitter, to be operational by the end of 1954. The contract was won by Pye UK. It was favourably priced, and included installation, quality guarantees, maintenance for a period of five years, and penalty clauses in case of any delay. Just before the contract was to be signed, the Hungarian government intervened. Instead of buying a working system from Pye, they decided to pay the *same sum* to a Soviet company for *drawings* of an untested design, to be implemented by Hungarian engineers, using Hungarian material and equipment. The government may not have understood the difference between the Pye offer and what they bought, or perhaps they understood it but our great Soviet friends gave them no choice. The total development cost, including material, equipment and labour, was estimated to be three times that of the Pye project. To top it all, the Soviet design (the one I and others worked on) proved to be utterly flawed.

It was dangerous even to *listen* to this story. A transmitter was built in due course, but it came on stream years late, and I doubt if it had anything to do with that Soviet design. There is another, better known and very similar legend about the Budapest underground transport system. It is bizarre and would be funny if it wasn't so sad. These stories illustrate the monumental stupidity and criminal wastefulness of an intellectually bankrupt and politically corrupt totalitarian regime.

When experimental broadcasts started, TV programmes ran for a couple of hours once or twice a week, except when there was a technical hitch. The Television Company was commanded to demonstrate television, the new phenomenon, to the country's most important people: Ministers of State, government officials, and Party functionaries. These events took place on the Pest side of the river, in some government office on the corner of Váci utca and Kossuth Lajos utca. No more than 20 people could be invited at one time, everyone crowding around a tiny black and white TV screen of size 14cm x 18cm. Half an hour before the transmission started, a young engineer from the TV company gave a brief lecture, explaining how television worked. Then some still pictures were shown, or – on a really good day – a few frames of a film were transmitted. A few times I was the (almost) engineer who gave the talk. This is how I met some of our Great Leaders. Doubtless they were politically astute, but they had great difficulty in comprehending that the film on the screen was not played from a reel inside the box but was sent down all the way from the mountain on the Buda side of the river. Why would one do that, they asked? Why not just play the film right here? Or go to the cinema? What's the point of this whole new-fangled idea of television? Why was the country wasting money on it?

DEGREE PROJECT – THE FINAL HURDLE

In an English university the engineering student chooses his or her project from a list compiled by the staff. In a progressive British university, extra marks are given for initiative if a student proposes their own project.

I say it again and again: in a totalitarian state people have no control over their lives; they have no choice. I was fantastically lucky to have been given a dream of a project: theoretically demanding, practically important, based in one of the country's leading research organisations. My external supervisor was Dr Julesz Béla, an expert with worldwide reputation. When he left the country in 1956, he became a leading light in the Artificial Intelligence research team of the Bell Laboratories in the USA.

Dr Julesz was a remote figure, helpful but not friendly, hugely knowledgeable and very demanding. I saw him rarely, and I had to *earn* each supervision by demonstrating adequate progress in writing. When, many years later, I supervised PhD students, I imposed the same discipline on them. Many PhD candidates linger for years over their project, and dropouts among PhDs is high. All my PhD students finished in time.

The subject of my project was nothing less than providing telephone and television services for the country as a whole. Here is the country's situation at the time.

- Television was only just starting up. There was occasional transmission of a single channel from Széchenyi Hill to central Budapest. There was no television in the rest of the country.

- Telephone services existed, but they were rudimentary, utterly inadequate even in the capital. Mobile phones did not exist yet, but Bell had invented the telephone more than 140 years before, and at university we had a course which taught us how telephones worked – in principle. In practice, telephones were virtually unavailable, and the few that existed seldom worked. We were told much later that this may have been deliberate: the regime considered it dangerous for people to be able to communicate. The country had two distinct telephone systems: a secret one for members of the regime, and rubbish for the rest.

It was all but impossible for an ordinary citizen to obtain a telephone. If, for historical reasons, there was a phone in the home or business of someone in the vicinity, then it was advisable to make friends with such a precious individual. We never knew of anyone having a telephone anywhere near my parents' convent home. The only phone in the Kaposis' neighbourhood had belonged to the owner of the restaurant next door, but soon the restaurant was nationalised, and turned into a state-owned grocery store. The phone went with it, and its use was lost to the Kaposi family.

How about public phones? The only reliable ones were at the Post Office, a mile away. Opening times were restricted, and long queues were constant. There were a few phone booths on the streets, but they were permanently vandalised, or used as public conveniences. How about phoning from one's place of work? There were a few telephones in offices or factories, but using them was usually forbidden. An outgoing line was all but unobtainable, so those wanting to call *out* tried to take advantage of calls coming *in*. Smart Alecs invented ways of inducing the incoming caller to hang up. Assume your child had some problem, and you had to ring the council's education department. Lucky you, you had access to a phone at work. More luck: you managed to get a line. Just then, the council officer at the other end wanted to call his girlfriend, unable to get an outgoing line. On receiving your call, he would say something like: 'This is the Female Cadaver department of the South Budapest Mortuary. Can I help you?' You, the bewildered caller, would hang up, and bingo, the officer had a line, could ring his girlfriend! I am not exaggerating: I speak from experience.

Dr Julesz' concept was simple: a 12-band 'hybrid' system, 11 bands supplying telephone services, one band carrying TV signal. The Main Transmitter was to sit on one of the Buda hills, like the sun of a solar system, surrounded by satellite repeaters, each with their own subsidiary repeaters in a multilevel hierarchy, until the 12-band signal was available everywhere in the country. Repeaters were also to act as centres for wire-carried telephone services for subscribers in their locality.

My task was to design this system in detail: characteristics of the signal beams sent from the main transmitter to its repeaters and from each repeater to its satellites, the location, height and structure of the transmitter and the repeaters, the characteristics of aerials and the beam they were to radiate. I had to take account of the curvature of the earth, the contours of the land, the atmospheric conditions, the wind which might press on the aerial and deflect the beam, and the nature of the terrain which would absorb or reflect some of the signal. As well as technical characteristics, I had to consider energy usage and cost minimisation over the whole project.

This would have been cutting-edge stuff everywhere and was entirely new to Hungary. I needed books, periodicals, reports on international conferences, including those in the UK and the US, current technical literature barely available in Hungary. Some of the material was in German, but most was in English. I lived in the university library, a silent, beautiful place; admission for students by special permission only.

The project report was to be similar in size and presentation to a Master's thesis in the UK. I had to produce a single hardbound copy, a couple of hundred typed pages with additional photographs and hand-drawn illustrations. The dissertation had to be delivered to the Dean's Office, scrutinised by the industrial supervisor and an external examiner, a member of the Board of Examiners. If approved, the candidate was allowed to progress to the oral examination. The oral was formal, called Defence (*Védés*). I happened to be ill at the time my project report was to be submitted, so Csákány Tóni offered to take it to the Dean's Office. I said thank you. Big mistake.

The Panel at my Defence was chaired by the Dean himself (Prof Barta of the green screen). Other than him and supervisor Dr Julesz, the Panel had three officially appointed members, all professors, and there was also a large unofficial audience: lecturers and industrial experts who had the right to ask questions of the candidate. There was also a second tier of audience, people who could observe, but were not allowed to participate.

I thought I was not very nervous. I had enjoyed my project, and trusted Dr Julesz's guidance. I was confident, but on entering the examination hall, I was completely undone. Examiners were handing my report from one to the other, and they were all laughing. By the time they managed to compose themselves, I was almost ready to turn tail and run away. Fortunately, they decided to start questioning me about my work; they evidently approved of my answers, so I was beginning to collect myself, but I kept wondering what they found so funny about my dissertation.

Then suddenly it was all over. Prof Barta stretched out his hand to congratulate me, 'a new member of our profession'. He reminded me of the obligations of engineers to society. He said he was 'proud' to have been my Professor and Dean; I had been an 'outstanding and stimulating' student. He assured me of his support and that of the University at any time in the future. My supervisor Dr Julesz complimented me, and the rest of the Panel shook me by the hand and muttered nice things. I was ready to go.

Prof Barta stopped me, saying: 'Quite the draftsman, aren't you?'

How did I feel? Had they discovered that I was a useless draftsman, and that in my first year Jancsi had done some of my drawings instead of me? Would they withhold my degree award?

And then Prof Barta put before me a sheet inserted before the first page of my project report. It was Tóni's witty cartoon of my project, set in darkest Africa: a hilly tropical land with palm trees, naked little black girls on top of each mound with bones in their hair, sending smoke signals from one hilltop to the other. I had to laugh too, and said I could not draw such a thing if my life depended on it; I had never seen it before – it must have been Comrade Csákány's idea of a joke. They were not surprised: they knew Tóni to be a brilliant student and a skilled cartoonist. Prof Barta said they would keep the drawing in the Faculty library, together with my project report. I should have looked for it in 1993 when, on behalf of Britain's Institution of Electrical Engineers, I chaired the Accreditation Panel that audited the university.

So, I made it, it was official: I was now an Engineer. Here is my Final Degree Certificate. It is a hard-covered **red** book, just less than A5 size, without any pages, but with a supplement, listing all the marks gained in all the years of my course. The book bears the emblem of the Hungarian People's Republic, and the word *Oklevél*, 'Final Degree Certificate'. The inside of the book states that the Degree with Distinction has been awarded to me on 4th May 1956. It gives the title of my course, and is signed by Prof Barta as Chairman of the State Examination Board, and by the Rector of the university. The colour of the cover is significant. 'Red Degrees' were rare, much less frequent than 1st Class Degrees in Britain. Degree certificates of lesser mortals were books just like this, but in **black**.

Neither my pretty Red Degree, nor Prof Barta's warm pledges of support, did me any good. Prof betrayed me within the year.

Following the 1956 Hungarian Revolution, I left the country illegally, together with some 200,000 others. Arriving in Britain without a change of underwear, let alone educational documents, I claimed to be a graduate of the illustrious Technical University of Budapest. My British employers and the Institution of Electrical Engineers (IEE) appealed to Prof Barta as Dean for details of my course, and for a testimony of my university record. Prof Barta declined, refusing to assist a 'traitor'. In due course my parents managed to get the Degree Certificate to me, but it was too late: by then I was making my own way; my employers no longer needed written confirmation that I had been educated as an engineer. I was not even asked to produce my Degree Certificate when registering for my PhD. Neither the IEE nor the Royal Academy of Engineering, nor even the Churchill Trust, asked for it when electing me as their Fellow. It is just a useless document, gathering dust on the shelf.

The author's Final Degree Certificate, 1956.

Kaposi family collection

HISTORIAN'S VOICE

Culture and Education in the Post-war Years

World War II had a devastating impact on Hungarian cultural life and education. Most school buildings were damaged or demolished, staffs decimated, libraries and technical equipment destroyed or pilfered. However, the Horthy regime was replaced by a new Western-style parliamentary system, and this brought about new hopes. The new government promptly introduced educational reforms, offering equal opportunity for all. Jews and previously disadvantaged social groups such as the poor peasantry and the working class suddenly gained access to higher education and high culture. The number of students significantly increased. In the 1946/47 academic year, twice as many young people enrolled in universities as ten years before. Social and gender diversity gradually increased. These changes represented progress, as well as new challenges: there was a shortage of classrooms, equipment and staff.

The newly organised public administration and economy required new leaders and functionaries to fill the gap caused by war losses, emigration and disqualification of the politically compromised former elite. To speed up the 'changing on the guard' and educate thousands of the working class and peasant youth, the new regime established new workers' schools, people's colleges and crash courses. Already in 1946, more than one thousand such young people made it to university, comprising 5% of the cohort. This meant that some real prodigies could make it to higher education, breaking social barriers; however, in general, many of the new recruits struggled to meet the standards. By the 1954/55 academic year the number of students tripled compared with 1937/38, and the proportion of worker and peasant cadres reached 50%. In accord with the economic and technological priorities of the regime, the number of students at the Technical University was dramatically increased, whereas law studies and various branches of humanities were neglected.

Meanwhile, with the Communist party gradually assuming absolute power, culture and education were pushed under strict political control. In 1948, all schools, including Christian and Jewish religious schools, were forcibly nationalised. The Academy of Sciences, the Universities and all institutions of higher education were deprived of autonomy. Professors, scholars and other intellectuals who did not conform were expelled, silenced or even sentenced in newly constructed legal procedures, the so-called show trials. Many top intellectuals fled the country, including Nobel laureate Albert Szent-Györgyi who left Hungary in 1948. Science and scholarship were steered by the Hungarian Scientific Council, which engulfed newly established institutions, including research institutes serving the needs of the planned economy. All pupils and students were subjected to strong ideological indoctrination, both in school and outside schools. The curriculum included courses in Marxist-Leninist ideology. Russian became the only second language, replacing Latin, German, French and English. Where new university textbooks were available, they were usually copies of Soviet publications. The role of deans and rectors became formal: real power was in the hands of university party committees.

Communists exerted total control over the media. Newspapers and radio were degraded to pure propaganda tools. In the name of the socialist cultural revolution, all spheres of culture were forcibly standardised. Genres and styles of art considered alien and deemed 'bourgeois' or 'decadent', were purged; instead, 'socialist realism' became dominant. For example, experimental pieces of the composer genius Bartók Béla were banned. Operas and other traditional genres of classical music were neglected, giving way to operettas and musicals. In brief, the Communist regime favourited mediocracy and low art that could entertain the masses, just like the Nazis did.[124]

Years of Terror

After 1945, many Hungarians expected that the system replacing the Horthy regime would give them a life worthy of humans. They proved to be tragically wrong. By 1949, Hungary became a Soviet-style dictatorship. The Communist party state brutally oppressed its citizens, Jews and non-Jews alike. As the bitter bon mot from the era notes: 'the Jewish laws were not revoked, they were instead extended to Christians as well'. Besides the total centralisation of power and the introduction of Stalinist personnel cult of the omnipotent head of state Mátyás Rákosi, the regime launched a merciless retaliation campaign against 'reactionaries', which meant getting rid of all political opposition (left-wing and right-wing alike), traditional elites and intellectuals who opposed the regime or did not comply servilely.

The infamous State Defence Authority (ÁVH), the secret police of the Communist Party, constructed a card file system on nearly one million citizens, that is, more than 10% of the adult population. The ÁVH employed some 40,000 spies, who regularly reported on hundreds of thousands of their compatriots. Between 1950 and 1953, no less than one million legal procedures were initiated against Hungarian citizens. Close to 400,000 people were convicted and imprisoned or deported to forced labour camps. Thousands of families of the former ruling classes were taken to designated places of residence. The victims of the regime included quite a few Jews, including intellectuals, businessmen and other people deemed 'bourgeois'.

The Soviet-style economic policy involved total state planning and nationalisation in all spheres. The utmost priority of the cold war arms race meant that heavy industry was forcibly enhanced, culminating in megalomaniac giga-projects, like the establishment of the utopian socialist super-city Stalin Town (Sztálinváros, Dunaújváros today). At the same time, other branches of the economy vital to the life of the population were neglected. Infrastructure and technology lagged behind, and the construction of new apartments could not keep up with population growth. Agriculture suffered greatly, due to forced collectivisation, and food shortage was not a rarity. Despite the economic boom (the Gross National Product skyrocketing by 30% between 1950 and 1953), living standards of the masses decreased compared to the pre-war standards. About 30% of families lived under the subsistence level. As a consequence, the regime was quickly losing mass support. Stalin's death in

---

124 Romsics, *Magyarország története*, Chapter IV/5. For an English summary, see: Ignác Romsics, *The Short History of Hungary*. Budapest: Osiris, 2016.

March 1953 marked a significant turn in Soviet foreign policy, which also brought about changes in Hungary. Rákosi was replaced by the more moderate Communist Imre Nagy, who introduced economic and social reforms. The hardest years of Stalinism and personnel cult ended.

9   MARRIAGE IN STALINIST TIMES

1951 – 1956

Having known each other since 1945, a couple of years after Jancsi's graduation we started to talk about marriage.

Both my mother and my prospective mother-in-law married at the age of 19, so they were in no position to object to me doing the same. I was only in the first year of my university course, but I was apparently coping. The man I was to marry was a graduate in a job assigned to him by the Hungarian People's Republic, so our circumstances could be considered stable, not to say rigid, until my graduation. All my family knew and liked my fiancé. My parents agreed. His father smiled. His mother said, vaguely, that her son was too young to marry. This might have been an objection, but we chose not to take it as such. There was only one strong dissenting voice. Before coming to that, here is the outline of the family into which I was to marry.

Jancsi's father Ernő had changed his surname from Klein to Kaposi, naively expecting this to help to avoid persecution. He took a name honouring the Kaposvári Regiment, a branch of the Austro-Hungarian Army, where he had distinguished himself in World War I. He was a perfect gentleman whose stern military posture contrasted endearingly with his gentle nature.

Jancsi had a treasure-trove: certificates, school reports, diplomas, commemorative plaques and medals, documenting Ernő's life from before birth to death. Such a comprehensive record of a person born more than 120 years ago might be unusual, and if that person was a Central European Jew then it might verge on the unique. I have recently donated it all to the Wiener Library.

Ernő was badly wounded in the Great War. A series of operations saved his left arm, but only just. The arm lost all muscle, the elbow and wrist were rigid, and his hand shrivelled into a little stump. In spite of his handicap, he was graceful and well-coordinated. In his youth he had been a gymnast.

Following the traditions of Újpest's Jewish founder Lövy and industrialist Aschner, after the World War I Ernő persuaded the government to establish two businesses which created a livelihood for war veterans, widows and orphans. One of these was a security service, an innovation for the time. His veterans provided guards for factories and public events.

The second business was ingenious, based on Ernő's skill as a textile technologist. He trained widows and orphans to make hand-knotted pure wool carpets. He bought from the Middle East cheap old oriental rugs in poor condition, and his ladies made precise copies of these. Their products became a successful line of export for many decades, known as *Magyar Perzsa*, 'Hungarian Persian' carpets. I have several examples, around 100 years old by now. The vegetable dyes resist fading even in the strongest sunlight, and the wool, soft to the touch, is of such high quality that the carpets still look as new. My favourite is a runner, copy of an antique which the Kaposi family used to own. Another of Ernő's company's products is in my bedroom. This was mistaken by Her Majesty's Keeper of Tapestries for an 18th century original. He valued it 30 years ago as worth in excess of £10,000. Ernő became one of Hungary's foremost carpet experts, and was the managing director of both companies.

This little story throws light on the character of both Ernő and my mother. As a wedding present, my mother bought my cousin Éva a hand-knotted carpet which needed repair. She was dissatisfied with the work of the repairer. To settle the civilised dispute, the repairer suggested calling in an expert. My mother agreed. The repairer suggested Kaposi Ernő. My fair-minded mother said he should find a different expert, because Kaposi Ernő's son was soon to marry her daughter. The repairer said Kaposi Ernő was not only a distinguished expert but also a man of integrity whose professional judgment would not be compromised by personal considerations. Ernő was called in; he found in favour of my mother, the repairer re-worked the carpet, and the matter was settled amicably.

Jancsi's mother Irén was the oldest of four daughters of a grocer, an orthodox Jew. In the family picture Grandmother Netti is wearing a *sheitl*, a traditional wig. The family tree sums up a typical wartime tragedy. Grandmother Netti was fortunate to die before deportation. Grandfather and Aranka died in Auschwitz; they were on one of the last trains of the mass deportations. Three of the men of the family died in munkaszolgálat, including Jancsi's 24-year-old brother and Sári's 17-year-old son. It took miracles for Jancsi's uncle Pál and two

Runner, made in the workshop of the author's father-in-law Kaposi Ernő, about 1920.
Photo: László Csősz, 2019.

234

aunts to survive the hellholes of Bor and Dachau. To this day, Jancsi's cousin Tamás retains his street urchin's charm, acquired on the streets of Budapest, surviving the 1944-45 winter alone as an eight-year-old.

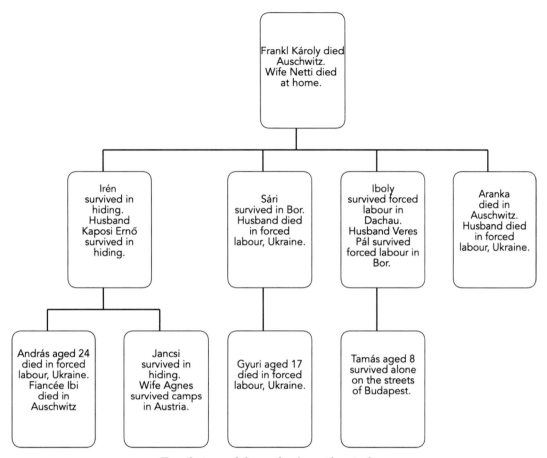

Family tree of the author's mother-in-law

Irén was a complex personality: intelligent, well read, a gracious hostess in good times, and generous provider of home and shelter for the needy in hard times. She had been a great beauty, and even in old age she acted accordingly, not simply entering a room, but *making an entrance*. She was full of contradictions in appearance and in character. She would look like a queen one day, but the next day would forget to comb her hair or even wash. She was a heavy smoker, with nicotine stains on her delicate long fingers, ash down her front, even holding a cigarette while cooking delicious meals. She was opinionated, erratic and undisciplined. Generous and charitable, she could be gentle and subtle, but could also be tactless and insensitive.

Family of the author's mother-in-law Irén. Frankl Károly, wife Netti, and daughters from the left: Irén, Aranka, Sári, and Iboly.

Kaposi family collection

Irén's mothering was another issue. Although Jancsi had been a sturdy well-built child, she accompanied him to and from school until he was a teenager and stopped him from doing sports in fear of injury. After the war she nursed him back to health bravely and single-handedly from life-threatening typhus, but never stopped telling him that he was a disappointment to her because she had wanted a daughter. In any case, the child she adored was not Jancsi, as she kept saying, but her older son András.

Irén was always kind to me and I admired her qualities, but I never liked her, because she was a snob. She was also unfair. She doted on my elder daughter Esther who resembled her in looks and in temperament, and she showed plainly that she favoured Esther over my younger daughter Anna. Miraculously, some of Irén's jewellery survived the war. With typical generosity, she gave me several pieces, including a Swiss gold watch, three gold bracelets and a diamond ring. She also gave a diamond ring to Esther for her 21st birthday, and promised one to Anna for *her* 21st, but she 'forgot' (? – she had a famously good memory). Anna was hurt. I gave Anna my own ring, but it did not help: it was not the ring Anna would have wanted.

I knew two of Jancsi's mother's sisters, Sári and Iboly. It was difficult to believe that the three were siblings. Iboly, survivor of Dachau, was a good sport. Her family's wartime story should be told. Her son Tamás was devoted to Jancsi and is like a brother to me now.

I recently found some pictures of Gyuri, Sári's son. He was less than a year older than Jancsi; they were on either side of the age divide for munkaszolgálat. Perhaps it was the wartime loss of the men in her family that made Sári the mean, bitter person we knew her to be; perhaps her very character was a victim of the Holocaust. I have a copy of Sári's will. It shows that she loved no living soul, least of all her sisters and their children. Of course, it was Sári who objected to our marriage. She told everyone, including both our families and all her friends (so ok, she *had* no friends, but she had acquaintances) that by marrying me, Jancsi was committing nothing less than social suicide. Jancsi was not deterred. Friends were surprised. Irén ignored her. Iboly laughed at her. My mother was hurt. My aunts cried.

Our wedding was planned for the summer of 1952, in the vacation after my first year at university. Incomes were not just meagre: they were inadequate, even if both members of a couple earned. I was to be a student for years to come; in financial terms I was a liability. We had nothing. Where were we to live?

Almost nobody owned their own home; people lived in rented flats, and allocations were controlled by the council. I longed for a home of our own, however modest – I had never even had a *room* of my own before – but we had no chance of an allocation even of a *szoba-konyhás*, one-room-and-kitchen flat.

National resources were scarce, and some were wasted on futile projects, so there was little left for easing the postwar housing shortage. The law stated that a couple or an unattached person was entitled to no more than one room (echo of the ghetto ruling of 4 m² of living space per person). If, as a couple, you lived in a dwelling with a living room and a bedroom, the council had the right – even the duty – to assign one of the rooms to the homeless on the waiting list. Disputes were commonplace, and at times even murders arose from overcrowding, or stressful sharing of homes.

This story would be amusing if it were not true.

Our friend Boskovitz Tibor (Tibi) was an engineer, and his wife Márta a doctor, a pathologist, sole survivor of her family. Tibi came from Újpest; all but one member of his family had been killed in Auschwitz. They lived in a three-roomed third floor flat in central Budapest. The other two rooms were occupied by two couples, one with a baby. The house was centrally heated, and hot water for the bathroom was available once a week, on Tuesdays, for six hours, from late afternoon onwards. Occupants of each room were entitled to two hours bath time per week, but Márta the compassionate doctor insisted that they allocate extra time for the baby, so it was agreed that each occupant, small or large, was allowed 6/7th of an hour of bathing time per week. Transport being unreliable, people would not always be home for the first slot, and usually hot water ran out before the end of the six hours, so the first and last slots carried a disadvantage. There was strict rotation. Our friends' room was only accessible through the bathroom. Nobody had a telephone of course. Every Tuesday, Márta and Tibi had to decide whether they wanted to be *in* their room or *out* of the flat for the 5 x 6/7 hours, the bathing time of the other inhabitants. To ease matters, they had a chamber pot in the corner. It was lucky that their room overlooked the street. No, they never emptied the chamber pot out of the window, but if they opted to be in and you wanted to tell them something which could not wait until Wednesday morning, you could holler three floors up from the street. Likewise, if they needed anything urgently on a Tuesday evening, they could yell down from their window, hoping that some passer-by might hear them and help. Their situation was bizarre, but not unusual. Tibi is dead, but until recently Márta lived in a large house in Sydney, Australia, with a big garden, two tennis courts, a triple garage and an Olympic-size swimming pool.

Back to marriage plans. Where were we to live? There were two options:

1. My parents could sink their resources into a little home for us. Jancsi would move out of his room in his parents' house. The council would allocate his room to a family. Jancsi's elderly parents would share their home with strangers. Ernő had a heart condition.

2. We would move into Jancsi's parents' house, losing the chance of a home of our own, perhaps for ever. Until my graduation, our income would have been far below our minimal needs, and it would have taken decades thereafter to save up for even the smallest of flats: not to *buy* the flat of course, just to secure the tenancy.

The Kaposis' handsome house had been architect-designed to Ernő's specifications. In 1922, when it was built, it must have been way ahead of its time. It was centrally heated from the boiler in the bathroom, had double-glazed windows, tightly sealing storm shutters, parquet flooring in the rooms, and ornamental floor tiles and wood-panelled walls to the roomy entrance hall, which also served as a living room. The doors, windows and woodwork had been made by the best furniture maker craftsman in town. The tall loft kept the house insulated from above. Three semi-basement dwellings, designed as servants' quarters or for providing rental income, shielded it from bellow. There were outhouses for washing and storage, and the spacious terrace overlooked a large garden laid with flowers, almond and walnut trees, mulberry trees and other fruit trees. When building such a house for his beautiful wife and young family, Ernő had thought of everything. He only failed to anticipate the anti-Jewish laws, the Holocaust, and the Communist regime.

Few had such generous and resourceful parents as we had. The four of them had a conference. The decision was that we move into the Kaposi house. My parents spent whatever savings they had on decorating our room and buying us a roomful of furniture. Those resources gone, the die was cast, virtually forever.

We could now start choosing the date, getting our rings, and planning our marriage ceremony.

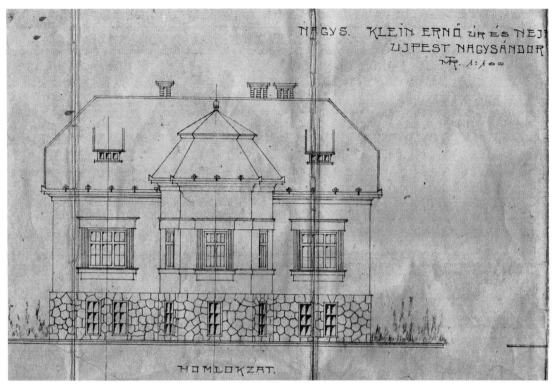

The Kaposi house in Újpest, 5 Nagysándor street, built about 1920.
Kaposi family collection

My first-year exams finished by the end of June 1952. We planned a late July wedding and a short honeymoon, leaving time to settle into married life before September, when university restarted. Easy, we thought.

We also thought that a marriage ceremony would involve exchange of rings. The Registry Office advised that gold was a controlled substance; only one shop in the country sold gold, and the only items on sale were 6-carat wedding rings. We were lucky, the shop was in Budapest. Provincial couples were less fortunate.

On the first Saturday of July, Jancsi and I went along to the gold shop, arm in arm, money in hand. We asked for a couple of rings. The man behind the counter smiled, congratulated us on our marriage, and asked for our marriage certificate. We said we were not married yet and we wanted the rings for the marriage ceremony. The man stopped smiling. He said gold was a controlled substance. We said we knew. He said people could only buy rings *on production of* their marriage certificate; the purchase would be recorded to prevent anyone buying two sets of rings, committing bigamy to profiteer with the gold. He told us to come back with our certificate after the wedding.

We managed to get married (only just), and in due course we obediently returned to the gold shop. Our troubles were not over. Rings came in two sizes: *his* and *hers*. Just then the man only had *his* in stock. We asked for two of *his*, and have the size adjusted for *her*. He talked to us as if we were two backward children: not possible, the weights differed. We bought *his* and returned for *hers* weeks later.

We both wore our 6-carat gold rings for decades. Mine was the wrong size, so I wore it on the wrong finger. Our daughter Esther was born in Nottingham, after seven years of marriage. The Matron of the Maternity Hospital discreetly enquired why I was not married to the nice man who visited us.

These were the darkest days of Stalin and Rákosi. Visiting the synagogue was almost a crime, but our straightlaced, traditionally minded families wanted us to be properly married from all points of view. Ignoring the risk, a three stage process was planned.

- Registry offices only worked on weekdays. We planned a civil ceremony to take place in Újpest's Town Hall on Thursday, 31st July, our parents, friends and family – whoever could get away from work – in attendance. There was to be a simple meal afterwards in a small restaurant.

- On Friday, 1st August, a quiet wedding ceremony was to be held in the synagogue.

- On Saturday, 2nd August, the closest family was to assemble for lunch at my parents' home.

The Registry Office allotted to us an 11 am slot. My fiancé booked his annual leave. Friends and family booked a day's holiday. And then, as usual, the roof fell in.

This was the summer break after my first year at university. I completed two semesters of Military Studies and had passed the examination. Then, on the 24th July, the authorities sprung one of their frequent surprises. All students of my year received a hand-delivered 'Notification of New Course Regulations'. Accordingly, we had to complement our 'theoretical' course of Military Studies with four weeks of annual summertime practical training. The Notification included call-up papers, specifying the military barracks and the date when to report, at 5am sharp. The call-up date was the 31st July. The date set for our civil wedding. I am telling the truth.

The wedding was off. Everyone cancelled their leave. Nanóka packed a rucksack with essentials, including knickers, bras, and smoked sausage. Terka baked *mágnás diós pite*, a delicious walnut pie that would keep for weeks. Jancsi said he would accompany me to the barracks – he knew the location, in Rákospalota, his grandparents' village. He said he could just get to work by 8 o'clock in Kőbánya, on the other edge of town.

On the supposed day of our wedding it was already warm at 5am. I wore a red-checked sleeveless shirt, shorts and hiking boots. My fiancé deposited me and my rucksack at the barracks, we bid affectionate goodbyes, and he went to work. The duty sergeant checked me in, and I joined a mixed crowd of students and conscripts. We stood for hours on the *Exezierplatz*, the exercise yard, with our sacks on our backs. It was getting hot. Karcsi, a bulky colleague, offered to swap his little rucksack for my great big one.

Then the Commanding Officer appeared at the door of his office and called my name. I thought I was hallucinating in the heat. The sergeant repeated my name, yelling so loud it would have woken the dead. The Commanding Officer said, 'You are excused.' No explanation. I asked what he meant. He said 'You are not required for military service. Go home.'

I staggered out to the street, starting to walk in the blazing sun through this unfamiliar village, in the general direction of Újpest. Suddenly I realised that I was still carrying Karcsi's rucksack. I wondered if he would enjoy Terka's pie, and what he would do with my bras and pink knickers. By the time I got back to the barracks, the novices had been formed into neat columns, preparing to march out. The Commanding Officer could not believe his eyes; he thought I came to plead for re-admittance. He almost smiled at my explanation, got a little soldier to root out poor Karcsi to exchange the sacks, and there I was once again, back on the dusty street, walking towards Újpest, carrying a full load.

What to do?

Everyone was at work in distant parts of town. I should phone someone. I zigzagged along the road from phone box to vandalised phone box, and finally found one that worked. Whom to ring? My mother's line was engaged. I tried Jancsi, and miraculously got through. I told him that I was somewhere in Rákospalota, having been dismissed from the army. He was calm as always and asked if I still wanted to get married. I said what did he think. He said I should make my way to the Registry Office, and he would do the same – we might still make it by 11 am.

We both arrived with minutes to spare. The Registrar said he had had notification that the marriage was off, but he was willing to ignore that; however, we needed two witnesses. My father's friend Erdős Feri (survivor of munkaszolgálat, with frostbitten and amputated toes) and our Auschwitz survivor friend Szekeres Marika worked in shops nearby. I fetched one, Jancsi the other. They asked no questions, downed tools, and came along. Marika had the presence of mind to buy a bunch of flowers from a booth on the corner. The flowers were a bit wilted in the heat, as we all were. A mucky street child became interested in the proceedings and followed us. Those present, in addition to the Registrar, were the groom and the witnesses in work clothes, and the bride in a sweaty sleeveless shirt, shorts, and hiking boots, carrying a rucksack and a bouquet of flowers. So much for the wedding dress especially made for me by Jancsi's cousin Bözsi. Also present was a barefooted child. I am telling the truth. We were late, so the ceremony had to be a bit more hurried than usual. The scruffy piece of paper here is our marriage certificate. Our names and occupations, and our witnesses' names, are clearly legible. The street child's name is not recorded.

The author's marriage certificate, Újpest, 31st July 1952.
Kaposi family collection

I never found out why I had been rejected by the army. Another miracle? I suspected that Feri, a senior army officer, had intervened on my behalf, but he staunchly denied this. It has just occurred to me that perhaps it was down to Form Mistress Mrs Aradi casting doubt about my fitness. Whatever the reason, I was the only graduate of my year deprived of the proud rank of Lieutenant of the Hungarian Army, Technical Division.

If our civil ceremony had been irregular, perhaps even unique, the rest of our wedding was commonplace. We were given a ketubah, a formal wedding certificate in Hebrew, incomprehensible for us, with a statement on the back in plain Hungarian, saying:

> *Kaposi János and Kristóf Ágnes have married today, in accord with the laws of the Jewish religion. 1st August, 1952. Rabbi's signature. Stamp of the Jewish community.*

At last I had occasion to wear my wedding dress: off-white raw silk, short skirt, simple design, such that the dress could be worn later when going to the opera. My mother made the wedding lunch, refusing all offers of help. Feri made a sweet little speech with tears in his eyes, and Ödi sang some lovely Yiddish songs which he had to translate for us, and some naughty Hungarian folksongs which needed no translation. That was it, we were married.

Times were hard, our relatives had difficulty meeting their own daily needs, let alone buying us wedding presents. Instead, they gave us some of their own cherished possessions. For example, my uncle Ödi's wedding present for us comprised parts of a

242

delicately flowered German porcelain coffee service that had been a favourite of his lost first family. 4 cups, 6 saucers and a sugar bowl without a lid: the only pieces left by the war. I use them constantly. There were no wedding photos, but someone took a picture of us at around that time.

Newlyweds
Kaposi family collection

One hears of lavish weddings, some leading to unhappy short marriages. The small sum of money spent on our wedding was no measure of the seriousness of our commitment to each other, nor of the quality of our 59 years of married life.

We lived in the Kaposi house, on the northern edge of Újpest, which itself was north of Budapest. I was going to university in the southwest, and Jancsi was working in Kőbánya in the far east of town. On a good day, travel on a crowded tram took us a couple of hours each way. Life was hard, but we managed.

Jancsi had no say in his place of employment. The nation's planners ordered him into a job at *Finommechanikai Vállalat*, 'Micro-Mechanics Company'. The organisation was new, huge, and top secret. It manufactured military communication systems. It was a frightening place, like an army camp in wartime, surrounded by a ditch with turrets, and guarded by soldiers with machine guns. Personnel had to wear regulation lab coats, stored in their offices. Movement was strictly controlled: a specific path to take at particular times of the working day, from front gate to place of work in the morning, from workplace to canteen at lunch, and then the reverse. There were no waste-paper baskets; every piece of paper had to be numbered and filed, and files were locked into steel cabinets overnight. People were searched on their way in and out. Jancsi's job was to build military radar.

Szabó Béla was one of Jancsi's colleagues, a gentle, musical engineer 10 years Jancsi's senior, sole survivor of a large Jewish family. One day, by mistake, Béla put a 15 cm length of solder into his trouser pocket instead of his lab coat pocket. The item had zero industrial or monetary value. The solder was found on him at the out-going body search. He was unmasked: a subversive. First the civilian police came, then the military police, and last of all the Secret Police. Béla was imprisoned and stood trial for industrial espionage and treason. He was lucky; the trial took account of his Party membership. He was acquitted, but not before being traumatised and publicly shamed.

That was the place where my peace-loving husband started his engineering career, where he earned our living. He was trapped. As custodian of military secrets, he could never have left this employment, and would never have been allowed to leave the country.

There is an ironic twist, another part of my story hard to believe. After the 1956 Hungarian Revolution, we arrived in the UK in 1957. We lived in the provinces, but given a chance, we visited London. Walking along Tottenham Court Road on one of our earliest visits, Jancsi stopped in front of a shabby Army Surplus store, his feet rooted to the ground. He examined some tatty old electrical equipment in the window and dragged me into the shop. His English was still shaky, so he made me translate his enquiry about the equipment and its documentation. He scrutinised circuit diagrams, construction diagrams and operating instructions. The item was an outdated but fully operational military radar, priced at about £100 in today's money. Jancsi was familiar with it: he had been working on details of its manufacture only a few months before. The Hungarians had stolen the documentation of this obsolete English radar and tried to reconstruct it in their top-secret military company. What was the state's tightly guarded secret? The design of that radar, or its pathetic obsolescence?

MARRIED LIFE

My parents bought us a roomful of second-hand furniture from some old people who needed the money. Craftsman-made, of pale cherry wood, it was beautiful, even ornate. There was a cupboard with a cut-glass mirror and arched doors, a small and a large chest of drawers with arched fronts, and a couple of small tables, all intricately inlaid. There were two armchairs and a sofa, covered in embossed gold brocade. The sofa was meant to open into a double bed, but it was too short lengthways and too narrow crosswise. The previous owners threw in a small brass chandelier which now hangs in my hall, and a brass table lamp which is in my sitting room. With one of Ernő's beautiful 'Hungarian Persian' carpet, our room was lavish.

Shopping for food was difficult. The restaurant next door was now a *Közért* (name of the dismal national chain of grocers). The shop stocked pulses, margarine, mustard, vinegar, shoe polish, kitchen soap and washing soda. Soggy white bread was usually available, as were some wilted vegetables. A neighbour would alert others if some item of food arrived at the Közért. Those within earshot would run to queue, hoping that something might still be left when their turn came. What one ate depended on chance.

Being an engineering undergraduate was a costly business. Notebooks and drawing stationery (poor quality paper!) knocked a big hole in our budget. Shoe repair was essential, and occasionally we even needed new shoes. Two months of hard saving would have been needed to buy Jancsi a shirt, and six months to buy me a jumper. Doing without new clothes saved time and aggravation. Service in the shops was slow, shop assistants rude, customers short tempered, and quarrels commonplace. The quality of textiles was miserable, materials were poor and did not take to dyes, dyes ran in the wash. When ready-made clothes started to appear, garments were badly cut, and yarns disintegrated; everything came apart at the seams, literally. There were no complaints procedures. Perhaps those memories stayed with me: I still hate shopping for clothes.

Some things were affordable. Travelling on trams was cheap. Buses would have been faster and more convenient, but they were much more expensive, so a bus journey was a luxury. I remember once treating myself to a bus ride after a particularly tiring oral examination. Fortunately, the type of entertainment we favoured was not costly. Season tickets for opera and concerts were heavily subsidised, available only for those at work. Jancsi had access to these, as he was his laboratory's Cultural Organiser. Theatre tickets might have been affordable too, but we decided to do without this brand of socialist realist culture.

We had a few good friends, young married couples in similar situations. Apart from Jancsi's great friend Zoli and his wife, our friends included a couple whom in normal circumstances we would never have met, let alone befriended. Bánffy Attila was of Transylvanian origin, a member of one of Hungary's ancient princely families. His wife, also Transylvanian, was almost as high-born. They had lost their castles and estates; it was a near miracle that they had not been deported to Siberia. We met them because one of Jancsi's tasks was to run an in-house course, converting useless Humanities graduates into much needed electronic technicians. These two young aristocrats were products of Jancsi's re-training programme. They were penniless like everyone, intelligent, unpretentious. Even my socialist parents grew fond of them, after overcoming their class prejudices.[125]

---

125   The 14th Century Bánffy Castle, situated near Cluj in Transylvania, is owned again these days by the family. It is on the World Monuments Watch List of 100 Most Endangered Sites and is under restoration by the World Monuments Fund.

The author and her husband at the Danube Bend near Budapest, 1953.
Kaposi family collection

In four years of married life in Hungary, we had two one-week holidays. How could we afford holidays? We couldn't, of course. One could not *buy* a holiday. The state owned everything, including holiday resorts, and the authorities disposed of holiday allocations as they saw fit. You applied to your employer; in the unlikely event that your application was not turned down right away, you might have been given a place anywhere and at any time, except where and when you wanted. I learned much later, when I no longer lived in Hungary, that not getting what you requested was not simply a matter of chance or ill fortune; a general principle was involved. Here is the philosophy:

- An effective way to subjugate people is to deprive them of choice.

- Frustrating the desires and ambitions of others is an effective way to demonstrate power.

- A good measure of power is the number of times you say 'NO'.

Here is a case. We applied for a holiday for the *summer* when university was not in session. We enjoyed mountain walking, so we asked for a resort in the foothills of the *Mátra mountains* (Trianon gave the mountains themselves to Czechoslovakia). Third time around, we had the great luck of being granted an allocation, but in the *autumn*, not the summer, and *by the river*, not in the mountains. Of course, one could decline the allocation, but this carried the danger of acquiring a black mark in one's file, and never getting an allocation again.

Once Jancsi's company surprised us by allowing two wives to join their husbands for a day, while the men were testing naval radar on Lake Balaton. Rumour had it that the other woman was employed by the Secret Police. It was not much of a holiday.

The dead hand of socialist realism killed art. Even music, our main interest, proceeded along cautious lines. We never heard of Gilbert and Sullivan, but creations of fifth-rate light music of soon-forgotten socialist composers was forever pumped out on the radio. Stalin had branded some contemporary music 'formalist', so 'modern' music was viewed with suspicion. Even the classics received the treatment. In the name of respecting the choice of the people, the same few masterpieces were performed again and again, ignoring other creations of the greatest composers. No more than half a dozen of Beethoven's 32 sonatas; Shostakovich's *Song of the forest* oratorio, but not the *Babi Yar* symphony, nor the string quartets, and most certainly not his controversial opera *Lady Macbeth of Mtensk*. Janacek's operas were not played until 1960. Sacred music was never heard at all.

FIRST JOB

My Red Degree Certificate testified that I was now an engineer. Finding a job was not my problem: I was instructed to report for work at the *Elektronikus Mérőmûszerek Gyára* (EMG): Electronic Measuring Instrument Company. It was located in Cinkota, a village some 10 miles out of Budapest. Getting to work involved two tram changes and a train journey, but EMG was worth it. It was the flagship of electronic instrument design in the whole of COMECON. It entertained a constant stream of visitors from the Communist bloc: observers, academics, students, industrial spies. Standards were high. I was impressed.

My boss was Boskovitz Tibor (Tibi), a balding young Jew, temperamental, rude, and very clever. I meet him for the first time at EMG, but he and his pathologist wife have featured in my story already: they were the couple trapped in their room every Tuesday bathtime. My job title was Junior Development Engineer, Assistant to Senior Designer Comrade Boskovitz; my salary a pittance, as befitted a novice. My colleague Nádor Péter also started his career at EMG, Assistant to Senior Designer Comrade Ilkovics. Arriving in May 1956, I spent a few eventful months at EMG, until the outbreak of the Hungarian Revolution in October of the same year.

For two years before my arrival, my boss Tibi had been designing the first sampling oscilloscope ever made in a COMECON country. Sampling scopes were sophisticated advanced instruments which we had learnt about at university. I was even examined on them by Prof Barta, but our university did not possess such a precious device. By the time I arrived, Tibi's design had reached the phase when a laboratory prototype was to be built. He involved me in his work immediately, giving me independent tasks and demanding full commitment. I was busy, happy, learning.

About six weeks into my job, Tibi told me that the sampling scope project was to be formally presented to EMG's Technical Committee, boosted by external experts. The Committee would evaluate his design. If approved, EMG would manufacture instruments for the market of the entire COMECON. The production line would require major investment, so in addition to an assessor of the Ministry of Technology, the Committee included a representative of the Ministry of Finance. Technical and financial experts were also to attend from several countries of the Soviet bloc, including the Soviet Union and East Germany. The project presentation was to be held in one month's time.

What follows is almost unbelievable, but I am telling the truth.

Preparing for the forthcoming presentation, we redoubled our efforts, worked over weekends, sometimes even overnight. The prototype progressed well. Then, about ten days before the date set for the presentation, Tibi dropped a bombshell: he was commanded to go to Turkey on urgent company business; he would be unavailable on the set date. I waited to be told the new date. Nothing. I asked what would happen. He said: 'You will do the presentation.' I thought he was joking, or had gone mad. He said he trusted me. I had been an engineer for a few months. This was real life, much more of a test than the Defence of my undergraduate project.

To start my presentation, I explained the general concept of the sampling scope, material learnt from textbooks at university. I then described Tibi's work: how he composed the specification, evaluated design options, justified the chosen design in concept and in detail. Next, the party moved to our lab, where I demonstrated our working prototype. Back in the Boardroom, I presented production requirements: space, instrumentation, staffing, training and financial considerations. The presentation took almost the whole working day. Their faces were inscrutable. I almost *hoped* that they would turn the project down. It would have served Tibi right, sending a boy (actually, a girl!) to do a man's job. – Tibi was in Turkey for another week. Having been feverishly busy before, I had nothing to do.

When at last Tibi reappeared, he had good news and bad. He was a hero: promoted, his sampling scope design was approved, and I was congratulated on my presentation. However, the COMECON had insufficient funds for production just then, but they were optimistic that manufacturing could start in the New Year (1957).

We were still waiting in late October, when Revolution broke out. Tibi and I left the country. Neither of us knew or cared whether his design and our joint effort ever became translated into a production line, but those months of intensive productive work, and Tibi's trust, gave me a tremendous start. This crazy, brilliant man was my friend for life. He died a few years ago.

While I sweated over Tibi's sampling scope, my colleague Nádor Péter was marking time. His boss Ilkovics was negotiating some future design project. Péter scouted around the factory aimlessly. He stumbled on a faded notice, inviting people to submit 'Proposals for Innovation' (*Újítási javaslatok*), to save money by rationalising the company's manufacturing processes. The notice stated that a percentage of the money saved would be paid to the proposer.

Péter was one of the original Eggheads of my year, holder of a Red Degree, at least as good a theoretician as I was, but also gadget-minded, the complete engineer. By the time my project presentation was over, Péter had some ideas about possible innovation proposals. I thought they had potential. We knew nothing about Production engineering; the subject had been squeezed out of our curriculum by Political subjects of prime importance, but having nothing else to do, we set to work, developing one of Péter's ideas into a proper submission, and a few days later we were notified that it had gained provisional approval. Being time-rich, we scanned the production department day after day, finding scope for innovations. We discussed the matter with our bosses Boskovitz and Ilkovics. They encouraged us, saying that the production department might never have employed engineers of our calibre before. We multiplied our efforts, learning about production technology and management. By October, when the Revolution stopped us in our tracks, a dozen of our fully-fledged proposals had gained approval.

Both Péter and I left Hungary illegally. Our employment with EMG ceased, as did our salaries. However, more than half a year later, when we were already working in England and Canada respectively, our parents still received monthly dividends from EMG's Production Department. The figures far exceeded our salaries.

I have been a misfit all my life. It takes one to know one. At EMG I met two.

We were used to the squalor of the university refectory. EMG's canteen was almost luxurious: clean and serving edible food. Sitting with Péter and Tibi, I became aware of a painfully slim young woman who always ate alone. I went to introduce myself. Her name was Ludmila. Through the fog of her shyness, I managed to grasp that she was Russian, spoke fluent Spanish but very little Hungarian, and no English, French or German. She seemed grateful for the company. She was an electronic engineer, a graduate of the University of Moscow, recently married to a Hungarian economist who had trained in the Soviet Union (as I would have done, but for Mrs Aradi's intervention). Ludmila had arrived at EMG a few weeks before. Her boss resented her because she was imposed on him, and nobody talked to her because they suspected her of being a spy. I think she was no spy, just a sad, lonely, homesick girl. Had it not been for the Revolution, we might have become friends.

The second to mention was a new graduate of the Eötvös Loránd University of Sciences, a quietly-spoken tall young man, a witty conversationalist, dark-haired, baby-faced. I forgot his name, but I recall us calling him *Vegyike*, a play on 'Chemist'. He was seriously gifted, an Egghead of the first order. As a schoolboy he won national prizes for science and mathematics. Not only had he a Red Degree, but also an award for being the outstanding graduate of the year. Nobody knew why he had been posted to EMG, least of all himself. The company had no need for a chemist, especially not a star chemist. He had no job title, no place of work. He was a pathetic figure, ambling around aimlessly, always in the way, looking in on Péter or me, or just sitting in a corner. A triumph of Communist manpower planning. I hope he managed to escape from the country after the Revolution, and found a position befitting his gifts.

A FAMILY OF OUR OWN?

When we left Hungary after the 1956 Revolution, my mother blamed herself and our other parents for deciding in favour of us sharing the Kaposi house. She was convinced that if we had had a home of our own, we would not have left the country. She was wrong. We had a much more compelling reason for leaving the country than just a desire for a home of our own.

We were young, married, well qualified, and we both had jobs. In a normal country it would have been natural for us to start a family, but this was not a normal country. Even if we had been able to set aside our memory of Hungary's fascist past, we would have considered it unthinkable to bring up a family in the oppressive atmosphere of fear and suspicion of the Communist regime which accused and convicted people of non-existent crimes, in a country where people could disappear without a trace. We knew of siblings and spouses spying on each other, children informing on their parents, parents disowning their children. The dilemma of my little cousin Ági was charming but had serious connotations. Aged six, she came home from school one day, distressed. It was the 21st December, Stalin's birthday, and they were told that they had to love Father Stalin more than anyone else in the world. She tried, she said, but could not obey: she loved her own father more. We were held captive in a country where we would never have children, and yet, we were not prepared to give up the hope of having a family.

We began to devise absurd schemes of escaping. There was no rational way, so we made plan after pathetic plan, each more naive and unrealistic than the last. Here is just one to demonstrate.

The iron curtain was not quite so stiff after Stalin's death, but one still had to register with the authorities any friend or relative in the West, even if one had no contact with them at all. My father collected yet another black mark, because he owned up to having a sister in Paris.

Economical with the truth, I did not confess that my best friend Donáth Judit was living abroad. We had not communicated for years, but I still trusted our friendship, and I somehow smuggled a note to her, asked her to buy us a motorbike, and send it to us as a present. That's all my note said, nothing else. The pipedream continued: given the motorbike, we would join some sports club, and enter a race abroad. Crazy. Neither of us had a driving licence, and we had no idea how to ride a motorbike, but we knew two men who could.

Pali, husband of Jancsi's aunt Iboly, was the manager of a garage. His knowledge of motorised vehicles was the key to his survival of the horror of the copper mines of Bor. He could drive, ride and mend anything with a motor, and trained his son Tamás as a motorcycle racing driver when a young teenager. Tamás himself was now a graduate automotive engineer. We thought Pali and Tamás would teach us roadcraft, and train us to ride a motorbike. But could they get us to the level where we could enter a race? A mixed race at that, a male driver and female passenger (or the reverse)?

One can immediately spot half a dozen flaws in this piteously naive plan. The fact that two sober young people like Jancsi and I concocted it at all, and on its basis committed the dangerous act of writing to a friend abroad, shows how desperate we were to escape. Our motivation to leave Hungary was not economic, not even political. We hoped to be free enough from oppression to have a family.

10   REVOLUTION

1956

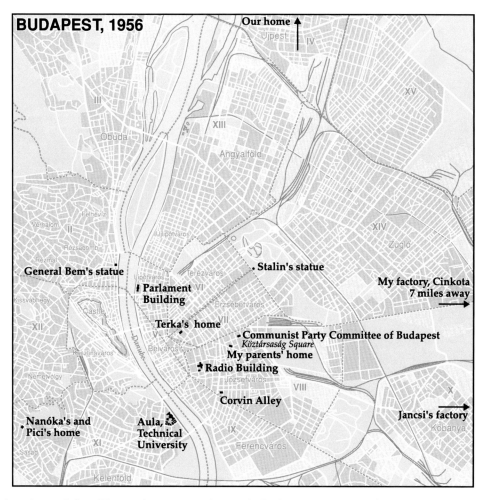

Key locations of the 1956 revolution, together with the home and place of work of the author and her husband, and homes of her family.

Hungary always mirrored a mighty neighbour on either side, turning fascist following Hitler, and Communist during the reign of Stalin. After Stalin's death in 1953, there was a political thaw in the Soviet Union, matched by a let-up of oppression in Hungary. In 1956 an idealistic revolution ensued, led by workers and students, poets and political dreamers, who wanted democratic elections and human rights for all. But this was Hungary. Within a week, the revolution turned vindictive, with fear of fascist connotations. Soviet troops soon put an end to this briefest attempt at democracy.

Although the revolution was lost, its influence reached the whole of Europe. Some historians even say that this revolution had global significance, sowing seeds for the eventual breakdown of the Soviet regime. Many books have been written about it, and yet, I must re-tell the story from my own viewpoint, and the map marks locations key to my story.

The revolution sought freedom from Soviet dominance and Communist oppression, calling for national independence and democracy. My husband and I sympathised with these aims. We were on the spot: the revolution started in the city where we lived, at our very university whose student I had been but a few months before. So, what did we do to promote the cause of that revolution?

Aula of the Technical University, Budapest, with commemorative plaque:
"This is the very place where the youth of the University held a meeting on 22nd October 1956 which had historical significance in starting the revolution"

254

We did nothing. We were not involved. There were practical considerations, as I am about to relate, but there was more to it than that. Had we taken part, had we fought for the noble aims of this revolution, we would soon have been told to keep away: this was none of our business, it was not our revolution, because it was not our country.[126]

The distance of over six decades allows me to identify four distinct phases of the turmoil and confusion of this revolution.

PHASE 1   PRE-REVOLUTIONARY PERIOD: FAINT HOPE 18TH MARCH – 21ST OCTOBER 1956

Stalin died in 1953, but for the next three years this had no effect on the life of the people of Hungary. A glimmer of hope arose on the 18th March 1956, when the radio broadcast Khrushchev's speech, denouncing Stalin. Optimists saw this as a sign of liberal reforms to come, but realists were sceptical, expecting a new hardline Soviet leader to emerge soon. In fact, Khrushchev's speech proved significant, because it undermined the position of Hungary's Stalinist leader Rákosi, weakened the authority of similar hardliners in other countries within the Soviet bloc, and created an environment where ideas of liberalisation could evolve. Rákosi's resignation in June 1956 enabled students, writers, and journalists to establish intellectual forums, and examine the problems facing Hungary.

PHASE 2   FIRST PERIOD OF REVOLUTION: IDEALISM 22ND – 23RD OCTOBER 1956

On Monday, 22nd October, students called a meeting in the Aula, the ceremonial central hall of my University. The Aula had been the location of state-sponsored political events, such as the 'Váncza show'. The place was the same, but the red garlands and giant posters of Lenin, Stalin and others were absent. The meeting formulated a *'16-Point Manifesto'*. Even from a distance of 60 years, it seems a sound document, not calling for hot-headed violence, but simply expressing the will to establish Hungary as an independent democratic state. The meeting learnt of the Hungarian Writers' Union's plan to show solidarity with pro-reform movement in Poland by laying a wreath at the statue of Polish-born General Bem, hero of the Hungarian Revolution of 1848. Students decided to organise a parallel demonstration, at which to distribute copies of their Manifesto.

Of course, the meeting in the Aula was not reported in the press, the radio or the television. Most of those taking part were students and others local to the University. The rest of the country had no inkling that anything unusual was happening. Participants at

---

126   See *HISTORIAN'S VOICE: Jews and 1956*

the meeting might not themselves have realised the significance of the event. Today the Aula is regarded as the 'cradle of the Revolution', and the memorial in the picture testifies to that.

On the morning of the 23rd October, students and writers gathered at General Bem's statue. Students distributed their Manifesto to passers-by. Soon a crowd of 20,000 assembled. They crossed the Danube to the Parliament Building, more and more people demonstrating support. By 6pm the multitude had swollen to 200,000. The demonstration was entirely peaceful, the mood was jubilant.

At 8pm, First Secretary Gerő, a Jew, a detested Stalinist hardliner, broadcast a speech, condemning demonstrators and the students' Manifesto.

Angered by Gerő's speech, an enraged section of the demonstrators marched to Stalin's 30-foot bronze statue and demolished it overnight. The rest of the crowd moved to the Radio building, attempting to broadcast the Manifesto. Failing to control the insurgents with tear gas, the uniformed Secret Police opened fire. Many demonstrators were injured, and 16 died.

Stalin Memorial in the City Park of Budapest, 1953.
Courtesy of FORTEPAN/Gyula Nagy

History assigns the origins of the revolution to the Buda side of the Danube, but by the end of the 23rd October the focus moved to Pest. At first, actions remained localised in the centre of the capital, spreading no further than the statue of Stalin, a mile away. All through the day, people remained oblivious, going about their normal business in other parts of the city, in the suburbs and in the rest of the country.

Jancsi and I were far from the action. Our home was in distant Újpest; he worked miles away in Kőbánya, and I in remote Cinkota. It was not until Gerő's broadcast that we, and the public at large, began to notice that something unusual was in the offing.

Some historians maintain that it was Gerő's speech that sparked the eruption of violence against Communist oppressors, against the Secret Police, and in some cases against the Jews. Those with a memory of pre-1945 events might have felt that it was inevitable that the crowd would turn against the Jews. Oppression under dictators such as Rákosi and Gerő would have made people feel that the hatred of Jews was justified. By the time Jancsi and I became aware of the wind of revolutionary change, the brief days of optimism and idealism were over, replaced by fear and anxiety.

Young people celebrating the destruction of the Stalin Memorial. City Park, Budapest, October 1956.

Photo by dr. Miklós Balás. Hungarian National Museum Historical Photo Department

PHASE 3   SECOND PERIOD OF REVOLUTION: ACTION AND REACTION, 24TH OCTOBER – 10TH NOVEMBER 1956

Nagy Imre, a 'moderate' Communist, became Prime Minister on the 24th October. The significance of the event was lost on most people.

All was quiet in the suburbs, and at the Kaposi house. Our day of 24th October started as usual. Public transport was failing, but it had failed frequently before. When I arrived at EMG, the factory was in a state of euphoric chaos. The usual armed security guards and Party functionaries were nowhere to be seen. A cheerful noisy group took charge of the hated Personnel Department – the home of the Commissariat, the centre of the web of spies. People broke open filing cabinets, read out names, and handed out personal files. My friends and I grabbed our papers and hung around for a while, but nothing was happening, so by midday we decided to head for home. Never before could one just walk out of the factory unchecked.

By then, there was no public transport at all. Someone flagged down a lorry travelling towards Budapest. The driver was surprised to be asked for a lift by a jolly white-collar crowd: he had come from the countryside where everything was normal. I soon realised that we were heading away from the direction of home, so I climbed down from the lorry, and continued on foot. Jancsi had a similar day. He arrived home in the early evening, carrying his personal papers. Along our route all was still. We had no clue what might be going on.

Meanwhile, in the centre of Budapest, drama was unfolding. Late that night Jancsi's friend Zoli appeared at our house. He reported on events and told us of his concern that the situation was volatile, and that the mood might turn against the Jews. He insisted that we barricade doors and admit nobody. He promised to bring us provisions and information about developments.

Only months afterwards did we learn the day-by-day sequence of events of the Revolution.[127]

- **25th October:** The Communist government collapsed.

- **26th October:** Armed protesters seized the Radio Building. A Hungarian army division joined the revolutionaries.

- **27th October:** Nagy Imre's radio broadcast announced, 'a broad democratic mass movement'. Nagy formed a government, including some non-Communist ministers.

---

127   See also Appendix.

- By **28th October**, the uprising spread to the whole country. Revolutionary militias were formed, fighting became widespread. In some places Revolutionary Councils took control of local government. Workers' Councils took charge of some factories and mines.

- **30th October:** Soviet leaders decided *not* to remove the new Hungarian government. On that day, armed protestors attacked Secret Police units guarding Party Headquarters on Köztársaság tér. Over 20 Secret Police officers were lynched by the mob. Decades later an excellent play recorded those events.[128]

- **31st October:** Soviet leaders *reversed* their decision, opting to crush the Hungarian revolution.

- **1st to 3rd November:** Khrushchev met leaders of Eastern Bloc countries, informing them of the Soviet decision.

- **4th November:** As in the war, Soviet forces entered Hungary from the east and north, moving towards Budapest in a pincer movement. One of their routes was through Újpest.

- Until **10th November**, sporadic street fighting continued, and Soviet tanks were shelling the buildings of the capital.

Throughout this time, chaos reigned.

- Remembering the war, some of the population took to their cellars.

- Prisons were opened, at first to free political prisoners, but soon *all* prisoners: thieves, murderers, all.

- Libraries were broken into, to burn Communist books.

- Buildings were damaged by shelling, and also by the angry crowd removing red stars and other Communist political symbols from façades. Some buildings were ransacked.

- Several Soviet war memorials were destroyed.

- National flags were hoisted on buildings, with the Communist hammer-and-sickle symbol cut out.

- Rampaging mobs were tracking down and murdering known Soviet sympathisers and Secret Police members.

---

128   János Térey-András Papp: *Kazamaták*. Katona József Színház, Budapest 2006.

Meanwhile armed resistance was weakening, and the revolution was gradually collapsing. A ceasefire was declared, but sporadic fighting continued.

Throughout this time, we were prisoners in our own home, guarded by Zoli. We argued that we were not in danger, since we had always distanced ourselves from the regime, but Zoli insisted that murderous mobs were not guided by fact or logic; Jews could be victimised, even if they had never taken part in political life.

PHASE 4   POST-REVOLUTION: END PLAY
11TH NOVEMBER – 18TH NOVEMBER 1956

By 11th November, the Revolution was all but lost, for better or for worse. Liberals regretted the missed opportunity for political freedom. Realists were resigned, almost vindicated: they had never believed that the revolution had a chance. Most were distressed about the restoration of the Communist regime, but felt a sense of relief that the shelling, shooting, chaos was coming to an end. The world might have learnt a lesson about toppling dictators without due preparation of a future regime.

Sporadic fighting continued for weeks to come, but Soviet and Hungarian troops were becoming dominant, stability was returning, and even Zoli agreed that his Jewish protégés might cautiously venture out – but at first only locally. We visited our friends next door. Jancsi's oldest friend Kati and her boyfriend Laci had been political prisoners; Laci had been a lifer. Both were freed during the revolution. We found them shattered, toothless, aged. In due course they settled in Oxford, obtained degrees at the University, and founded a family.

We were anxious about our family, although we did not realise the extent of the danger they had been in. The most vicious revolutionary violence had occurred at the Party Headquarter building in Köztársaság tér, just a few steps from my parents' and my cousin Klári's home. Their street Népszinház utca was a major thoroughfare, one of the routes the Soviet army took into the capital. Terka's family also lived in an exposed part of town, near the Parliament, near the Radio. Feri, a high-ranking Army officer and a Jew, was an obvious potential target. Only Nanóka's family seemed safe, in their distant leafy suburb.

19th November. We could wait no longer. We left the Kaposi house early in the morning, expecting to pay my parents a brief visit.

We found my mother beside herself. She had had no news from any of the family since the revolution started! Now my father had gone out to look for bread! This was the first time either of them had moved out of the building since the start of the mayhem. Klári and her family were well: luckily both their flats faced inwards towards the courtyard, and not towards the street with the rolling tanks. A Jewish neighbour had been taken away by an angry crowd, as was another, falsely accused of having been an informer.

Three photographs of the series taken between 23 October and 19 November 1956 by the author's husband Kaposi János and a friend in Budapest.

Top left: The damaged building of the Könyves Kálmán grammar school in Újpest. The woman with headscarf is the author.

Top right: Installation in front of the Party Headquarter building in Köztársaság tér. The script reads: "SOVIET-HUNGARIAN FRIENDSHIP "

Bottom: Street scene on Üllői Road, near the revolutionary headquarters at Corvin Alley

Kaposi family collection

261

Suddenly my father was back, surprisingly elated. Anticipating that we might arrive, he had bribed a lorry driver who was taking medical supplies to the border area and would hide Jancsi and me in his crates. The driver was coming in a couple of hours, just before 10pm. There were appalling risks, my father said: there was a curfew at 10, he had never met the driver before, he knew nothing about him nor where he was heading, but this was a chance, and there might not be another.

What to do? Should we breach the curfew, go with a complete stranger, without papers, to a region we did not know, and where we had no permission to be? Should we leave without preparation, without saying goodbye to Jancsi's parents? Or should we decline the one chance we had had in all these years to escape from this accursed country?

My father had no doubts. He was not just providing us with the opportunity, he was positively pushing us out. My mother was hysterical. She would never see her child, her children again – how could my father be so callous, so cruel?

I was always one for making quick decisions, and this time I had no decision to make. I would go, as long as Jancsi would come with me.

Street scene from the Hungarian Revolution, late October 1956.
Courtesy of FORTEPAN/Zoltán Marics

Jancsi was thoughtful and calm, as always. All his life he had distrusted snap decisions, taking time to make his mind up even over small matters. He remained the same for the rest of his life, exasperating his daughters and me by hesitating for long minutes over the most trivial decisions: which tie to wear, which soup to order in a restaurant. This time he had a life-changing decision to make, with every prospect of never seeing his aged parents again. The deadline could not be negotiated, and the decision was his alone.

Should we believe in luck, miracles, or coincidences? At that point another key character entered the stage: Pici had walked from her home, across the river, over a bridge guarded by Soviet tanks – a distance of about 8 km as the crow flies – amid sporadic shooting. She, Ödi and Nanóka had figured that we might be preparing to leave Hungary, but they thought we would come to see my parents first, so she set out for my parents' home as soon as the fighting had subsided somewhat. Ödi recalled a distant friend from medical school, a Dr Lebovics Izidor, known to his friends as Bubi, who lived and worked as a GP in Sopron, a beautiful ancient city near the Austrian border. Ödi and Bubi had lost contact decades before, but – just in case it would be of use – Ödi wrote a brief note to Bubi, saying that the bearer of this note was his precious niece Agnes and her husband Jancsi; would Bubi please help them in their aspirations?

All eyes were on Jancsi. The lorry driver was soon to appear: it was almost decision time. Jancsi needed solitude to gather his thoughts. He shut himself into my parents' bedroom, and we could hear him pacing up and down. When he reappeared, he was grey. He said we were going.

Now came feverish activity. My mother stuffed some of my father's and her own clothing into a small suitcase: pyjamas, a few pairs of socks, warm pullovers, and changes of underwear. They pooled most of the money they and Pici had and gave it to Jancsi. My mother offered to make supper for us, but there were no takers. There was nothing else to do. When the lorry driver knocked on the door, there were a few hugs. We did not even cry. My father gave the driver money. He told my father that we were going to Sopron. Remember Sopron, the hometown of Ödi's friend Bubi, to whom his note was addressed?

The lorry stood just around the corner, on notorious Köztársaság Tér. It had canvas sides and was packed with 1-cubic-metre cardboard boxes, all but two containing medicines and bandages. It was easy to fold ourselves into the two empty boxes, and the driver stashed our boxes somewhere amongst the others.

The 200 km journey was slow, with many interruptions: police asking for the lorry's and the driver's papers, Hungarian military checking the lorry's logbook, Soviet military scrutinising the cargo. At one point a Hungarian soldier told the driver to unload the whole cargo so that he could check the contents of each box against the manifest, but while they opened up the first few boxes, there was some shooting nearby and several impatient lorries pulled up behind us, so the soldier waved us on. The worst moment came when a Soviet soldier mounted the lorry and bayonetted through a few of the boxes. He missed ours. (Just a couple of small miracles?)

When we pulled up in Sopron, it must have been well past midnight. The next day had come.

20th November. The driver opened up the back of the lorry and freed us from our crates. We had no idea where to go, or what to do, but there was a curfew, and we had to get off the street at once. A policeman marched up to check on the late-arriving lorry. For once, Jancsi was smart and quick-witted – or just lucky? Before the policeman could demand our non-existent papers, Jancsi asked if he knew a Dr Lebovics. 'Of course,' he said, bursting into a beaming smile, 'He delivered all my wife's babies! He lives right here, in the house opposite! First floor, the door in front of you.' The enthusiastic policeman rang the bell for us and told the concierge to let us in: we were friends of Dr Lebovics. That was the last we saw of the lorry, the driver or the policeman. Still counting coincidences / miracles?

I have a clear mental picture of the small baroque building with carved stone arches, a staircase with ornamental cast iron railings, and stained glass windows. It might once have been a small palace but was now a smart block of flats. On the first floor, facing us, was a brass plaque: Dr Lebovics Izidor. We were cold and hungry, and after a frightening journey we felt a sense of relief: we had arrived. It was by now the small hours. We rang the bell over and over. The door cautiously opened for a gap, and a tentative voice asked if there was a medical emergency, and if not, what did we want at this hour? We introduced ourselves and offered up Ödi's note. The gap widened. An elderly gentleman in a dressing gown looked us up and down for a moment, and then shut the door decisively. Minutes passed. Scared and disappointed, we contemplated where to go, but decided there was no option but to stay in front of that door. We rang and rang the bell again. A small gap opened again, and a lengthy interrogation started. Where did Dr Schiff live? What was his wife's name? Had he any children? What kind of doctor was he, what

Dr Lebovics Izidor ('Bubi') and his wife
Bözsi, Sopron, 1960.
Kaposi family collection

was his specialisation? And more. We were puzzled but answered each question. The door shut again, there was whispered conversation on the other side. We waited – what else could we do? At last, the door opened wide. Two elderly people received us, in dressing gowns, and with open arms. They offered apologies and explanations. They thought that Jancsi looked like a *schegetz* (a Yiddish word for a typical Christian), and had surmised that we must have obtained Ödi's note by foul means, robbing or perhaps killing Ödi's niece and her husband. Eventually, the interrogation had convinced them that we were not fascist thugs – we were genuine. They offered us love and hospitality, fed us, prepared for us a hot bath and a soft bed with a big eiderdown, tucked us in and kissed us goodnight – what little was left of the night. They were guided by more than just Bubi's fondness for his old friend Ödi. They were devoutly religious, not in the sense of observing the minutiae

264

of ritual, but understanding the philosophy and morality of their religion. To these good people, being religious meant offering shelter and hospitality to strangers – Jew or gentile – protecting people in need, embracing them like members of their own family. They told us they regarded us as the children they never had. Bubi found us a guide who would take us safely across the border. Bözsi (Bubi's wife), a charming lady who suffered from a serious heart disease, surrounded us with infinite kindness and made us thoroughly at home.

In a normal country the good doctor would have picked up the phone and rang Ödi to confirm the credentials of a couple of suspicious strangers, but this was not a normal country. Neither of these two senior doctors had a telephone.

21ˢᵗ November. The guide Bubi found us was one of his patients, a farm worker whom he had treated beyond the call of duty in the past and who owed him favours. The man – let's call him Mr Bauer – knew the border area like the back of his hand. He was a Schwab: a German speaker, a citizen of Hungary, with half his family living in Austria. Mr Bauer said he was busy for the next couple of days, but would arrive without fail on Friday, 23ʳᵈ November, at 7.45pm, 'when it is dark and there is no traffic'. He asked for more money than we had, but Bubi was happy to top up our funds. He also asked for a bottle of rum for the journey: it was going to be cold; the three of us could share the rum to warm us along the way.

We could take our small suitcase with us, he said, and we would have just a short walk across the border; the whole trip would take no more than a couple of hours.

In spite of missing our family and being anxious about the future, we spent a pleasurable couple of days, being pampered by this delightful couple who played beautiful music for us from their huge record collection, fed us delicious food, and referred to themselves as our temporary parents.

23ʳᵈ November. Bad news: snow came down, making the terrain brighter, showing our footprints. Mr Bauer sent word that we would have to start an hour or so earlier; our trip would be along a slightly longer route than originally planned, as we had to put a wider distance between ourselves and the watchtowers of the border.

It was almost time for Mr Bauer to arrive when the doorbell rang urgently. In front of the door stood a family of four: a feeble young husband, his eight-months-pregnant wife, their two-year old son, and the husband's blind mother. They were friends of Dr and Mrs Lebovics. Let's call them the Family Nebbich, or 'N' for short.[129] They arrived with a large suitcase, stuffed with the toddler's nappies and belongings, and asked Bubi's help to escape across the border. Bözsi embraced us and asked us to help them. Bubi said all was going to be well: there was *broche* (blessing) on the toddler and on the unborn child. He gave an injection to the boy to make him sleep. Just then, our guide Mr Bauer appeared. He needed

---

129   Of course, the name is my invention for them. We may never have been told their real name.

some persuasion and plenty more money to agree to guide a party of six instead of the two young adults for whom he had originally contracted. He absolutely vetoed two suitcases, and since the child took priority, our little case had to stay behind. Hugs, kisses, tears. This farewell was much more emotional than the one in Budapest.

We were trying not to think about the ease with which anyone could follow our guilty footprints through the fresh snow. At first the father carried the boy, Jancsi took the suitcase, and I was guiding the blind granny, but soon the frail young father was wilting under his son's weight. We had to reorganise. Jancsi took the child, the man was now leading the blind granny, I was dragging the suitcase (wheely suitcases were in the distant future), and the pregnant wife was staggering along as best she could, all the while Mr Bauer urging us to make faster progress. There was plenty of shooting in the near distance.

Then two things happened at once. Mr Bauer warned us to walk as quietly as we could – we were nearing a watchtower. And, as if on cue, the little boy woke up suddenly; he started to scream, he felt sick. Mr Bauer was clearly on the point of panic. Forgetting about sharing the rum, he started to drink it himself in earnest, but not before saying that since the child would not shut up, we had to give an even wider berth to the watchtowers, taking a completely different route. This meant crossing a minefield, he said, but we should not be too concerned: *most* of the mines would have been exploded by the military a year or so ago. On the other hand, he said, we should mind the heavy barbed wire which had marked the border but had only been partially rolled up.

We stumbled along in the snow, sliding into some of the mine craters. Jancsi always had admirable balance; he managed to stay upright even with the boy on his shoulder, and so did the pregnant lady, thank goodness, but the blind granny and her son fell several times. Once they had to be pulled out from the bottom of a crater. I was not doing well either; I was the slowest of the party, hindered by the heavy suitcase. What would I have given for one of Nanóka's rucksacks! My balance had never been good; perhaps that is why I got tangled in the barbed wire. The rest of the party had gone ahead, I did not dare to call to them for help, and by the time I managed to break free, my beautiful sheepskin coat – the model coat made for me many years before – was torn halfway down the front. We had been walking for over four hours. It was way past midnight, so the 24th November had come. The rum bottle was empty, and Mr Bauer was the worse for wear. He had had enough. We were on top of a small hill when he pointed to a faint light far away, saying that's what we should be heading for – and with that he turned tail and left us.

Shooting continued all around. We staggered along. At one point I created panic: I thought that the large dark shape in our path was a Russian tank. It turned out to be a big bush. Jancsi teased me for years about being scared of bushes.

We were making hesitant progress on our own on that snowy hillside, guided only by a distant light. The boy was now peacefully asleep on Jancsi's shoulder. I was wondering what we would do if someone switched off that light, but nobody did. Exhausted, we arrived at a long, low building full of people. There was no welcome, but someone said we were now in Austria.

24ᵗʰ November. A fierce fire was burning in a small stove. A dour Austrian woman told us that this was the village of Klingenbach. She pointed to a table with a large samovar and a tray full of fresh bread and butter with cheese. We helped ourselves to sweet lemon tea, suddenly realising how hungry we were. The place was crowded with fugitives like ourselves, some asleep on the floor, some excitedly narrating the story of their passage through the border. We lay down on a straw mattress but were too tired to sleep. In any case there was constant commotion: people arriving in small groups, many in tears, reporting loss of some of their companions. The most dramatic was the case of a young man drenched in icy water, in a state of shock. He told us that he had started out as one of a party of six; they were discovered on the shore of Lake Fertő by the Hungarian border patrol, and had to conceal themselves in the shallow water among the reeds, but each time they tried to move out from their hiding place, they were shot at by the border guards. All his companions had been killed, one by one. He himself had escaped after hiding in the icy lake for long enough for the border guards to give him up for dead.

Dawn came. Looking around, we realised that we had been sheltering in the changing rooms of the village football ground, in the middle of the long side of the football pitch. On the opposite side of the pitch was the watchtower. How near had we been to Hungarian border guards in the night, walking towards that guiding light?

25ᵗʰ November. I don't think we had exchanged more than a dozen words with Mr N and his family since their arrival at the Lebovics' home in Sopron. Now Mr N came with the news that his uncle from Vienna was on his way to pick them up. Would we want to go with them? Of course, we would: anywhere, as long as it was further from the Hungarian border.

At about midday, Mr N the Elder arrived by car. He was no more friendly than his nephew. He was in a hurry, gave a brief hug to his blind sister-in-law, nodded to the rest of the N family, and signalled to his car, wanting to be on the way. There was rapid chatter between old and young Mr N. Old Mr N kept shaking his head, but ultimately he was persuaded to turn his attention to us. Young Mr N introduced us. Old Mr N asked if we had any money. We had to confess having nothing – we had given all we had to Mr Bauer, the guide. Old Mr N asked if we had friends or relatives in Vienna. We don't know a soul, we said. Old Mr N accepted the inevitable: we all crowded into his small car, sitting in each other's laps. Come gloomy early evening, we arrived at Old N's block of flats in Vienna. Young Mr N and family nodded goodbye to us and disappeared. We never saw any of them again. Old Mr N told us to wait in front of his block. He did not invite us in; he offered us nothing to eat or drink.

We waited on the street. Sleet was falling. At last Old Mr N reappeared, holding a map of central Vienna and a slip of paper with the address of a restaurant where his son was dining with friends. Vienna must have had working telephones.

Finding ourselves in a strange city was an eerie experience. To this day, I try to avoid arriving anywhere in the dark. Sleet still fell, we were cold, wet, hungry and apprehensive, but the map was good, and the restaurant was not far. It was Saturday night; the city was at peace with itself. Streets and shop windows were lit, brighter than we had seen since before the war, if ever. There were flashing neon lights advertising strange theatre shows, unfamiliar goods. Elegant gentlemen and stylish ladies were climbing in and out of cars and taxis, or sitting in warm restaurants at nicely laid tables. The restaurant we were looking for was large, full of diners visible through its windows. Jancsi volunteered me to go in to look for The Son. I don't recall the name or the address of the restaurant, but I could still draw a picture of the wide avenue, the forbidding façade, the swing doors with a crescent of heavy maroon curtains keeping out the draught, and the layout of the tables of diners. An intimidating waiter blocked my path, unsurprisingly reluctant to let me enter in my muddy boots and torn coat. I brought out the bit of rusty German I remembered from the camps, and tried to explain what I wanted. (Why was it me, why not Jancsi who had studied German for years, and had a reasonably respectable coat?) The waiter grudgingly led me to the table where The Son sat with several gentlemen in suits and ladies in their finery. They were at the main course stage of their dinner. All eyes followed me to their table. The Son was just like his cousin and his father: unsmiling, dour, a minimalist. Without greeting me or leaving his table, he thrust in my hand a few banknotes and a piece of paper with another address. He said this was a *Pension* – a kind of rooming house – where the money would pay for us to have a room for three nights. I tried to thank him, but by then he had turned his back and sat down to continue his meal. That was the last we heard of any of the Nebbich family. Perhaps it was not a handout, perhaps we earned those banknotes by services rendered.

The gloomy little Pension was minutes away. Our room was shabby and dimly lit, but it was almost warm. We had not eaten since that memorable tea and cheese in Klingenbach the night before. We were too tired to appreciate that our time under Nazi horror and Communist oppression was past, our revolution was over, we were no longer fleeing from the Communists, the Hungarian border guard or the Soviet army. We should have been happy, having arrived in the West. Instead, it took us two months of bewilderment and misery to reach Britain, our destination. Even so, never for a moment did we regret leaving Hungary.

My recall of this period is incomplete and fragmentary, but I can offer dates and vivid, clearly remembered anecdotes.

26th November. Our first full day in Vienna. Our funds were meagre, and we had no idea how long we had to stay in the city. First thing in the morning, I went shopping. I bought a banana and a *kifli:* a large bread roll shaped like a croissant. Food for the day.

It was well below zero, and snowing. How to find the British Embassy? The telephone book was no help. What was the country called? Britain? England? Anglia? We had never heard it called the 'United Kingdom', nor 'Great Britain'. When we located the place, we found a frighteningly long queue. Those in the queue said that they had been returning day after day and were told that it would take weeks – if not months – to be allowed entry into the country.

It was easy to find other embassies: they were all surrounded by long queues. People in front of the US, Australian, New Zealand, etc embassies were just as discouraging, and told the same story. The Israeli embassy seemed less popular: the queue was shorter and we even made it to the official at the door, trying to talk to him, but he too was discouraging, almost rude, and we were so tired and so cold that we gave up, and just started for 'home'.

27th **November.** Loudhailers started up in the streets. They were persistent, which was just as well, since Wienerisch German was hard to understand. We just managed to grasp the meaning:

> *'The city is dangerously overcrowded, food is scarce, water supply is failing, there is a danger of epidemic. It is the moral duty of all able-bodied refugees to go to the nearest railway station and take the first train out of Vienna.'*

It made sense. We were able-bodied and public-spirited. Rather than languishing in endless queues in the snowy city, and causing trouble to the Viennese, we blew the remains of our fortune on a loaf of bread and a hunk of cheese, and headed for the nearest railway station. In any case, we had no funds to pay for more nights in our Pension. There must have been aid agencies offering shelter and a home for those in need. It never occurred to us to look for them.

28th **November.** Early morning found us at the nearest railway station. None of the trains showed any designation of destination. Jancsi spotted a familiar couple waving at us; not friends, just acquaintances. I just remembered their surname: Segyó. They thought the train might go to Paris. Westwards from Hungary, Paris was as good a place as any. We boarded the train. We were on our way before midday.

The train had a French crew. It turned out that the Segyós were right: we were heading for Paris. Why was the train unheated? Why did the journey take three whole days? Wild rumours circulated among the cold, hungry passengers:

- The French resented us, thinking that it was our own fault to be refugees – we should have stayed in our own country.

- There were too many refugee trains; they paralysed the entire European rail network.

- Our train was stranded on the outskirts of Strasbourg for a whole day, because the citizens did not want a mob of barbarians entering their city.

- French Communist railway workers sabotaged our train, because they viewed us as traitors, leaving behind Hungary's Communist paradise.

1st December. We were still on the train when officials came to ask if anyone had any friends or relatives in France. We owned up to my aunt and uncle living in Paris. It took us weeks to realise that this meant giving up our refugee status, forfeiting its potential benefits.

NEW LIFE

Paris is a beautiful city for the rich, but we were penniless. We had the clothes we stood up in, and mine were torn dirty rags. We arrived in the depth of winter, and stayed in this unforgiving city for an unavoidable eight weeks. I admire Paris and have visited it many times since, but I would never learn to love the place.

On arrival, my aunt Margit and her husband Salamon were waiting for us. I had never met them before, but they were welcoming and loving. The officials in charge were pleased to be relieved of responsibility for us, and we were among the few released into the care of French citizens.

I have mentioned my father's sister and her husband before. They were kindhearted, hardworking people who had, by that time, lived in France for more than three decades, but they had never really settled in their adopted country. They had accumulated some resources, but afforded themselves no comfort, let alone any luxury. They had few friends, little knowledge of the French language, and no contact with French culture. They knew the Paris underground system but not the sights of the city, because the metro was cheaper than the bus. They could have served as an example of how *not* to be immigrants.

My father Imre and his sister Margit had shared a cruel childhood and were devoted to each other, but they had almost nothing in common. They had parted when Margit was 20 and Imre 19. Thereafter, they were separated by distance, political regime and way of life. After we had made a home in England, Margit and Salamon visited us often. Jancsi was devoted to Salamon, and we all loved to listen to his Yiddish stories and songs. We did not understand them, but he delivered them with charm and panache. He even taught us some steps of traditional Jewish dance. As I am writing this, I am wearing a beautiful shawl crocheted for me by my aunt Margit.

Arriving in Paris on that December day, we found that Margit and Salamon lived in a gloomy street, their home consisting of a small kitchen and two rooms. The toilet was a French-style hole in the floor on the half-landing, shared among several of the tenants. One of the two rooms was their bedroom/living room, and the other was their workroom. As a tailor, Salamon had a large cutting-table, several ironing boards, two sewing machines, and cupboards and chests filled with cloths, buttons, threads and other necessities of his trade. These kind good people were ready to put us up in their workroom for as long as we wanted to stay, but that meant suspending their work activities, and giving up their income. It was immediately clear to us that we should seek other accommodation, but how, and where? I had almost no French. Jancsi had none. We did not know Paris. However, we did have close relations besides my aunt and uncle: two families – let's call them the Browns and the Greens. They cared little for us and could not stand each other, but in their own way they both contributed to our survival in Paris.

The Browns were rich. Only much later did we discover just *how* rich. Mrs Brown simply ignored us, but Mr Brown's approach to his migrant relatives was constructive. Soon after our arrival, he gave us a banknote, value £5. It was a fortune to us, and we put it to good use: we spent most of it on postage stamps, as you will see.

The Browns invited us for dinner at their home near the Eiffel Tower. Once. The party was large, five or six elegant couples. We wore the only clothes we had. The guests were intrigued by our Hungarian origins. They knew about the operettas of Lehár and asked us to sing from the *Merry Widow*. When we said we would rather not, they asked – almost insisted – that I should dance a *csárdás* on the dinner table. When I declined even that, they were disappointed. The party broke up soon afterwards.[130]

As I will relate, our relative Mr Brown was tenacious. He did not give up on us. At least, not altogether.

My aunt and uncle were not complaining, but everyone realised that we were a problem for them. A few days after our arrival, the Greens offered to accommodate us in their spacious flat in a good part of Paris, near the Place de la Républic. I remember the address.

I don't know who resented us most: Mr Green, Mrs Green, or their 6-year old daughter. We were quiet, we tried to make ourselves invisible. Neither Jancsi nor I were big eaters, but we felt as though they counted the number of mouthfuls we ate at their table. The crunch came when, one night, I washed Jancsi's shirt – his *only* shirt – and, after everyone had gone to bed, I hung it on a coat hanger in the bathroom. Next morning, I found the wet shirt screwed up into a ball behind the toilet. These people may not have been deliberately unkind; they might just have been thoughtless, or afraid of us being leeches, planning to stay with them indefinitely.

We had some of Mr Brown's £5 left, so on that very morning I set out to find some cheap accommodation. Not knowing better, I chose the Pigalle area. I was bombarded with tomatoes from the windows by the ladies who worked there and thought I was trying to set up in competition. I could still find the street and the building.

By now we knew what the country of our dreams called itself, so we had no trouble finding the British Embassy. We need not have bothered. They were polite, but firm: Britain was busy helping the Viennese to empty their city of Hungarian refugees. We had lost our refugee status on entering France. The only chance we had of getting to Britain was to get a job with a British company. Our prospective employers would have to apply for work permits for us. Should the applications be granted, we could take up residence in the UK. We could not enter the country otherwise.

---

130 Csárdás: a traditional fast and jolly peasant dance, usually to Hungarian gypsy music.

We found the local library. They had a good collection of British technical journals. This was the advent of transistor radios, transistorised measuring instruments, colour television development, and early computer design. Journals were full of advertisements for electronic engineers. We were well-qualified and had the right expertise. I could even write English letters. We had £5, money for stamps. We wrote many letters and received many positive replies. A good half of the firms invited us for interview. In Britain. Catch 22.

Judit, my best friend in the world, lived in England. She was generous and resourceful, a mathematician with a good job as one of the early computer programmers, and her family was well-to-do. Calling from the UK, she made an appointment with the British Embassy in Paris. She jumped on an aeroplane and came over for a long weekend. We went to that Embassy again. We showed them our numerous interview invitations. Judit pledged to accommodate us in her home. To guarantee that we would not be a burden on the State, she offered to deposit a sum to be nominated by the Embassy officials. Polite as ever, they showed us the door. Only a work permit would do.

Judit went home to England in tears, but not before leaving most of the contents of her weekend case behind. She was a good six inches taller than me, her shoes at least four sizes bigger than mine. Her fine wool dressing gown was the only garment she left behind, but it was much too long for me; I recently gave it to my granddaughter Molly who is 5'10" tall.

Monsieur Roder was in his early 50s. In his young days he had been a professional footballer, with a wife, family and good income. He had had a severe sports injury, became disabled, and lost his income, his wife and his family. Having devoted his youth to football, he was not well educated, but he was a good man, a lapsed Catholic. He was doing some menial work for my relation Mr Brown; that's how we met. Monsieur Roder had no language other than French, so we could barely communicate, but he was kind and compassionate. Sensing that we were in trouble, he offered to share his home with us. His heart was big, but his income was minimal. He had a room in which he lived and slept, and a small kitchen which doubled as our bedroom. There was a tiny bathroom with a modern toilet and a device to be pulled up above the bath on which to hang shirts and underwear to dry. He also lent us money for food and stamps for more letters to potential employers in Britain. We stayed with him for six weeks, until we left for Britain. He even lent us the fare. I have often thought that there is hope for the human race while there are people like Monsieur Roder around.

At one point we thought that entry to Britain was a pipedream, so we tried the Israelis again. Not a success: just as in Vienna, they were abrupt and unhelpful. Perhaps we were oversensitive, hoping for a bit of warmth and consideration. However, our visit to that Embassy had an unexpected result.

Alan Snyder was another big-hearted man, a noisy, crazy, highly cultured American. Christmas was approaching, and he went to the *Israeli* Embassy to pick up a young professional refugee couple to entertain for a Christmas dinner. Why the Israeli Embassy, for a Christmas celebration? Because he was Alan – he never did what was predictable.

He was a historian, a civilian working for the US Military, in charge of general education and cultural development of army personnel. His wife Catherine was a poet and a superb cook. They had a toddler and a new baby and lived in a penthouse flat on the edge of the Bois de Boulogne. Alan thought that my English could do with improvement, and Jancsi's with basic development, so he gave us a tattered suitcase, jammed full of paperbacks: history, philosophy, literary theory, psychology. I sometimes still dip into them. When we were leaving for Britain, he drove us to the Calais ferry, and wrapped his own huge soft scarf around my neck because the crossing promised to be windy. A couple of years later he was posted to Britain, and they stayed here for several years. Our children grew up together. I still use many of the exquisite practical presents they gave us when we were needy new arrivals to the West: soft woollen blankets, crockery, cutlery, even a fish-shaped bottle opener which I still use for opening jam jars.

To continue with my story in Paris. Among his smart acquaintances in the Grande Synagogue de Paris, our relative Mr Brown spotted a Director of the Thomson-Houston Telecommunication company. Jancsi and I never met this great man – we did not even know his name, so we could not thank him when we learned that he had arranged interviews for us both with his company. Had we wanted to stay in Paris, this would have been a great career opportunity. We had almost no French and no papers to prove that we were engineers, but the technologists at Thomsons had heard of our university, and gave us the benefit of the doubt. They offered jobs to us both. We explained to our prospective employers that we had not given up the hope of gaining admission to the UK.

As potential employees, we had to undergo a thorough medical check-up. The tests brought to light that Jancsi was diabetic. This was a shock for us, and for them. The tests were repeated; severe diabetes was confirmed. Nevertheless, they decided to take us on. Doctors advised a strict diet, and the need for frequent check-ups.

We started work on the 9th January 1957, Jancsi developing radar circuitry and I devising instrumentation equipment. We did our best, and received our first and only payment on the 22nd January. I have both our contracts and our salary slips on file.[131]

My aunt, uncle and the rest of my French family were impressed, and tried to persuade us to stay in France rather than move to Britain. My aunt even found a room for rent in their own building in Rue des Jeuneurs. It was all too late; in a few days we would be leaving for the United Kingdom.

This is how it happened.

---

131   Jancsi's one-time net remuneration for two week's work was 18,380 FF, and mine 11,739. The historical exchange rate puts the FF to £ conversion at 0.001, which means that Jancsi's monthly pay would have been around £40, and mine £25. His annual net income would have been £480, and mine £300. By comparison, our earnings in our first British jobs were £750 and £500 gross, respectively.

Searching for a job in Britain, we wrote over 150 letters. We were only scanning the replies; there was no point to reading them, they were so alike. Companies were eagerly inviting us for interview, in Rochester and Portsmouth, Birmingham and Glasgow. We almost missed the one that asked us for an interview in Paris. It arrived a day or two after we started work at Thomsons.

Cyril Hall was not an engineer. He was a physicist, working on transistor design. On behalf of Pye Ltd Cambridge, he was visiting a semiconductor laboratory in Paris. His Personnel Department asked him, while there, to chase up a pair of unlikely job applicants. Mr Hall invited us for dinner at Le Thermomètre, a restaurant near his hotel on the Place de la République. He waited for us in the vestibule of the restaurant. We waited for him outside in the rain. At length we found each other. He said, to recognise him, he would hold a copy of the IEE Journal. Instead, it was he who recognised *us*: my coat left him in no doubt who we were. He said we should combine the interview with dinner, and led us to a round table, covered with a stiff white cloth, reserved for us.

I will never forget the pain and embarrassment of that dinner-cum-interview.

He asked what language we could use. I said Jancsi had good German, I too had some German, neither of us spoke French, and Jancsi had no English. Mr Hall said he had no language other than his own, except for just enough French to order a meal. Throughout the evening, Jancsi did not say a word.

Mr Hall gave us the menu. It was in French. We could not understand it, so I said we would leave it to him to order. We must have looked starved, so he ordered a huge meal. We were so nervous we could hardly swallow a bite.

Other than my eccentric teacher in Budapest and the monosyllabic officials at the Embassy, Mr Hall was the first Englishman we had ever met. Trying to be helpful, he talked painfully slowly, which was no help to Jancsi, and embarrassing for me. He declared right at the start that he knew little about electronics and could not

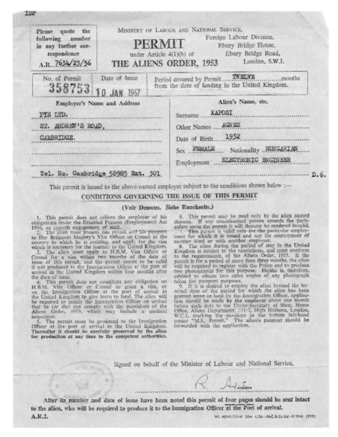

The author's labour permit, Pye Ltd, Cambridge, 1957.
Kaposi family collection

ask us technical questions, but was too English to ask personal questions, so he asked no questions at all, but told us of the London smog, and punting on the Cam. I had no idea what smog was, nor what 'punting' meant. He held the fork the other way around from the way we used it, and we tried to imitate this, without much success.

At last, the agonising interview was over. We were convinced that we had failed; how could we not have? However, Mr Hall assured us that he would recommend to Pye to employ us both; he shook us by the hand, and we never heard from him again. But sure enough, soon our work permits arrived through the post. The letter came on the 16th January, a week after we started work at Thomsons. We handed in our notices, worked until the 23rd, and sailed to Britain, arriving on the 27th January 1957.

My aunt and uncle did not need lessons on hardship. Having lost her mother at the age of six, Margit had known cruelty as a child. As a young shtetl Jew, Salamon had been maltreated in the Polish army. Even in peacetime, the two of them lived like fugitives. They did not understand their own life, so they could not help us to build ours. They gave us all they could: their love and kindness.

Our relatives the Browns and the Greens had survived persecution during the war years. I doubt if they learnt anything from their experience. They offered us help, but no family feeling. They seemed to have lacked warmth even within their own families. I thought it best not to speculate how they would have made out in the camps. After we settled in England, we stayed in touch with them dutifully; after all, they were family. In due course we even tried to build bridges, but there was no trust, so there could be no real closeness. Maybe the next generation would do better.

I am asked sometimes: what was it like, being refugees?[132]

When we left Hungary after the 1956 revolution, so did some 200,000 others. Most endured homelessness, cold and hunger, as we did. In addition, most suffered from homesickness. We did not share their pain. We spoke Hungary's language, knew its poetry, loved its music, admired its folk art, but, for all that, it had always been a hostile alien land. The country we left behind had great cultural traditions and we wished it well, but it was never our country. This was drummed into us when we were children, and we learnt our lesson. We left without a backward glance.

We were fearful that a vindictive Communist regime might punish our families for our crime of leaving illegally, but most emigrants left their loved ones behind just as we had done, and we hoped that our families' case might be lost in the multitude.

We abandoned our home, we came away with nothing, but I can honestly say that we never gave a thought to our lost possessions.

---

132   See *HISTORIAN'S VOICE: Refugees and Emigrants*

We both suffered physical reactions to our experiences. The worst was Jancsi's case of diabetes. We were also among those who endured nightmares for decades: vivid and painful dreams of being back in Hungary, struggling to escape, and failing.

What caused us the most pain was the fear that we would never see our family and friends again. The bond that tied my family together is at the very heart of this story. It was the key to our survival of the Holocaust, and gave us strength in times of cruel Communist oppression. Being parted from our loved ones was like a bereavement. We missed our parents, my grandmother, my little cousins, each member of our family, and our few hard-gained cherished and trusted friends. We had each other, but nobody else. We were alone in the world. Our youth was over.

CONCLUDING REMARKS:
POST-WAR ANTISEMITISM AND HUNGARY TODAY[133]

Újpest football ground with Rákosi's decorative photograph, 1949. Dignitaries in ceremonial box include Dobi István (Head of State), Gerő Ernő, Szakasits Árpád, Kádár János, and Péter Gábor.

Courtesy of FORTEPAN/ Márton Ernő Kovács

---

133   See also *HISTORIAN'S VOICE: Hungary since 1956: Antisemitism, Holocaust Remembrance and Populism*

After World War II, antisemitism appeared to be dormant for a while. In a Stalinist dictatorship there could be no voice other than that of the Communist Party, so there could be no antisemitic voice, but that did not mean that there was no antisemitism. It did not help the Jews of Hungary that the hated Stalinist Rákosi and several dominant figures of his regime had Jewish origins.

Government-funded Monument of German Occupation and the private Living Memorial, Budapest.

Photo: Szilas, 2014 (Wikimedia Commons; FoP-Hungary)

Leaders of present-day Hungary try to make political capital out of the errors and sins of Stalinists. To whitewash their country's role in the Holocaust, they equate Nazi terror with the outrages of the post-war Communist era. The House of Terror Museum of Budapest seeks to propagate, and even exaggerates, this false notion of historical balance. Data on victims of Stalinist Hungary are hard to come by, but every indication is that the number of victims of the Communist regime, however odious it was, amounted to a fraction of the number of victims of the Hungarian Holocaust. Even more glaring is the hypocrisy and blatant history-falsification of the recently erected monument on Budapest's Szabadság Tér, a square at the very heart of Budapest. The monument portrays Hungary as a victim of German Nazism, rather than Germany's ally and perpetrator of fascist outrage against

277

Jews, gypsies and others. Demonstrating their anger and repudiation of the shameless lie of the graceless monument, the good burghers of the city compiled their own monument in front of it: evidence of their broken homes, broken families, survivors' broken lives. A little suitcase returned from the camps. Photographs of those loved and lost. Letters from victims of labour service. Documents evidencing Hungary's murderous acts against women and children. Banners bearing messages like 'History falsification', 'Intellectual poisoning', 'A monument to whitewash Hungary's guilt'.

Hope is being lost and liberal democracy is being eroded systematically by today's democratically elected populist government. These days Hungary is among the countries of Europe noted for the upsurge of nationalism and populism.

APPENDIX: CHRONOLOGY OF EMIGRATION

Monday 19 November 1956	Leave Budapest at 10pm in the back of a lorry
Tuesday 20 November 1956	Arrive in Sopron in the small hours
Friday 23 November 1956	Walk across the border
Saturday 24 November 1956	Arrive in Klingenbach in the small hours
Sunday 25 November 1956	Arrive in Vienna in the early evening
Wednesday 28 November 1956	By train via Strasbourg
Saturday 1 December 1956	Arrive in Paris
Sunday 27 January 1957	By ferry to Folkestone and by train to London
Monday 28 January 1957	By train to Cambridge, our first UK place of employment

HISTORIAN'S VOICE

Jews and 1956

The country had strong antisemitic traditions, and the popular opinion was that the Stalinist dictatorship amounted to a Jewish rule. Even so, antisemitism was not an integral part of the 1956 anti-Communist and anti-Soviet revolution. Quite a few young Jews joined the revolutionaries, and some sacrificed their lives for Hungary's freedom. Nevertheless, there were several anti-Jewish atrocities during the revolution, ranging from verbal insults to pogroms. Most incidents took place in the provinces, during the initial phase of the revolution. The new revolutionary authorities tried to stop these outbursts. It is difficult to tease apart the web of motivation behind these events, because anti-Communism and antisemitism had become thoroughly intertwined. However, most testimonies and scholarly publications agree that, all in all, antisemitism was a marginal phenomenon in 1956. Of course, this is a retrospective view and those who witnessed or participated in the events could often have different perspectives. Many Jews were frightened by any kind of armed violence, and anticipated anti-Jewish pogroms. In addition to economic and political considerations, the grounded fear of antisemitic attacks also motivated Hungarian Jews to leave the county after 1956.[134]

Refugees and Emigrants

Spontaneous and forced migration and population movement characterised the modern history of several European countries. Hungary was no exception. Hungarian Jews were heavily represented in all major waves of migration in the 19th and 20th centuries.

One of the largest population movements of the Austro-Hungarian empire started in 1867, in parallel with great economic boom and social modernisation. This was the 'golden era' for Hungarian Jews, the peak of emancipation and integration. However, these great cultural and economic achievements concealed serious social conflicts, and hid the misfortunes of many, Jews and non-Jews alike. Population growth, changes in land distribution, and rapid industrialisation prompted entrepreneurs, adventurers and losers of the capitalist transformation to move to urban centres, or even leave the country altogether.

By the 1880s, an annual average of ten to fifteen thousand people left Hungary, mostly for the United States. This wave of emigration peaked in the early 20th century. Between 1905 and 1913, more than one million citizens – some 5% of the total population – left the country.[135] In 1907, for example, every fifth person arriving in Ellis Island, New York, was a former Hungarian citizen.[136] These emigrants reflected the multi-ethnic character of the Kingdom of Hungary. Their ranks

---

134   Vági–Csősz–Kádár, *Evolution of a Genocide*, 355-358.

135   *A Magyar Szent Korona országainak kivándorlása és visszavándorlása 1899-1913.* Budapest: Statisztikai Közlemények, Új Sorozat, Vol. 67.

136   For figures and data on the emigration to the US, see: https://www.libertyellisfoundation.org/

included lower class Jews, Magyars, Slavs, and Romanians, most of them landless peasants, miners and poor artisans. In his famous poem 'My homeland', the great Hungarian poet Attila József writes of the tragedy of this mass emigration:

> "Our masters were neither dumb nor slow
> to shield their estates from us,
> so a million and a half of our people
> staggered blindly to America."[137]

Before World War I, the motivation of emigrants from Hungary and from most European countries was chiefly economic, a personal strategic decision, although there were exceptions, such as Russian Jews escaping pogroms. In the early 1880s, Hungary's Jews also experienced violence, but here the liberal state protected its Jewish citizens.

After World War I, domestic conflicts and dramatic border changes prompted a new wave of population movement from Hungary to Europe and overseas. Some 20,000 Jews left the country between 1919 and 1921, most fleeing from antisemitic violence and radicalisation of the political climate. In 1920, the law of Numerus Clausus (closed number) dramatically reduced the number and proportion of Jewish students in universities, causing many talented young people to study abroad and eventually to emigrate. The country lost thousands of prolific minds, including future Nobel Laureates.

By the 1920s, the process of migration became more and more difficult. Contrary to the pre-war liberal era, many countries introduced strict immigration laws and alien control. The US also closed its doors to the 'unwanted' masses of Eastern and Central Europe. The western world became unwilling to accept large numbers of refugees trying to leave increasingly Nazi-dominated Europe. In the inter-war years, about 10,000 Jews made it to western European countries. From the early 1930s, the number of emigrants from Hungary gradually decreased, but the number of Jews leaving the country remained at the same level, and by the outbreak of the World War II, the majority of the people leaving Hungary were Jews. Their ranks included an increasing number of intellectuals, middle class people and the older generation.[138]

In spite of increasingly unfavourable conditions, for the majority of Hungarian Jews migration was still not a widely preferred option. Many had well-established livelihoods, personal relationships and family ties, and there was also the issue of national identity. A significant proportion of Hungarian Jews, particularly the secularised and Neolog, responded to persecution by stressing their patriotic loyalty and their achievements in the life of the nation. They were not ready to reassess

---

137   Attila József, *Hazám* (1937). Translation of the author.

138   Tivadar Szél, A külső vándormozgalom újabb alakulása. In *Magyar Statisztikai Szemle* XXI (1943), 83-102.

the integration strategies they had followed for several generations. A shared fate, a shared mother tongue and common cultural values were important components of a Jewish-Hungarian subculture. Severing such links would have caused severe conflict.[139]

By contrast, the Hungarian political elite had a very different view about Jews and their national identity. Forced emigration of the Jews was already on the agenda of the Hungarian government in the late 1930s, although it was soon swept away by the outbreak of the war. In addition to imposing more and more restrictions on the employment options and civil rights of Jews, the 1939 Second Jewish Law was a major step towards the gradual expulsion of the Jewish population. To carry this out, the government planned a new commissioner's office, and Article 22 of the law intended to speed up its operation. Regarding this matter, negotiations with Jewish leaders were in progress. It was the start of the war that thwarted the execution of the plan.[140]

During the war years, some 15,000 Hungarian Jews left the country, but as Nazi Germany invaded Western European countries one-by-one, most were eventually trapped. The Hungarian government abandoned its Jewish citizens, refusing them re-entry into Hungary as the war progressed, although they negotiated with the Germans to 'regain' the assets of Hungarian Jews living in Nazi-occupied areas. Together with other refugees in Belgium, the Netherlands, and France, many Hungarian Jews were arrested by the Gestapo and local collaborators, and were then deported to Nazi camps.

There was another movement of mass migration. Some forty to fifty thousand Jewish refugees fled to Hungary from persecution in neighbouring countries, many of them falling victim to mass deportations from Hungary in 1941 and 1944.

Between 1945 and 1948, some 25,000 Hungarian Holocaust survivors (from within the 1937 borders) were registered in camps for 'displaced persons' throughout Europe. Many survivors chose not to return to their homeland that had betrayed them; others returned, but left their country of origin soon. Bitter experience moved some to become Zionists, leaving for Palestine (from 1948, Israel). Others found a new home in the US, Canada, Australia, Great Britain, and other Western European countries. As the Soviet-style regime strengthened its grip on Hungary, the possibilities for legal emigration were decreasing, and completely ceased by 1949. Afterwards, special bilateral agreements allowed some 5000 Jews to leave Hungary for Israel, hundreds of others attempting illegal emigration. In total, an estimated thirty to fifty thousand Jews left Hungary between 1945 and 1956. This was proportionately much less than Jewish emigration from other Central

---

139   Victor Karády, Identity Strategies under Duress before and after the Shoah In Randolph L. Braham–Attila Pók, eds. *The Holocaust in Hungary: Fifty Years Later.* New York: Columbia University Press, 1997. 156–58.

140   At his meeting with the Jewish leaders, Béla Imrédy designated a target number of 100,000 emigrants over five years. Memoirs of Samu Stern, see: A Race with Time: A Statement. In Randolph L. Braham, ed. *Hungarian Jewish Studies 3.* New York: World Federation of Hungarian Jews, 1973. 1-48.

and Eastern European countries, perhaps because most survivors were from Budapest, where the integrated/acculturated Neolog tradition was always strong, and the relatively large community offered protection and a hope for a new beginning.[141]

Jews constituted at least 10% of the 200,000 or so Hungarian refugees after the 1956 revolution. With this wave of emigration, the Hungarian Jewish community lost about one fifth of its members, mostly the young, middle class, economic and intellectual elite. This was a devastating blow not only for Jewish future in Hungary, but for also for Hungarian society in general.[142]

Hungary since 1956: Antisemitism, Holocaust Remembrance and Populism

In the Stalinist era of the Communist dictatorship in Hungary (1949-1956), memories of the Holocaust and the 'Jewish question' were pushed into oblivion. Even the word 'Jew' was expelled from official speech. Continuously weakening Jewish communities held memorial ceremonies, but these were enclosed in synagogues and Jewish cemeteries. During the Kádár era of Communist dictatorship (1957-1989), the situation slightly and gradually improved: some memoirs, literary pieces and even a few scholarly works were selectively published about the Holocaust, but public discourse was still strictly under control. Antisemitic voices and Jewish identities were equally suppressed. Drawing conclusions from the 1956 revolution, Kádár's policy was to keep the social peace by any means. He believed that talking and writing about the Holocaust and the 'Jewish question' was to be avoided because it could stir up emotions.

The collapse of Communism in 1989-1990 brought about freedom of speech. The traumatic events of the 20th century came into the focus of both scholarly and public interest. In the two decades after the system change, the Hungarian political elite was consistent in condemning the genocide of Jews during the Holocaust. Consecutive (right and left) governments decided at last to launch a National Holocaust Memorial Day (April 16), and in 2004 a permanent exhibition opened in Budapest's Holocaust Memorial Centre, offering a very critical view on Hungarian complicity in the Holocaust. The 60th anniversary of the Hungarian Holocaust (April 2004) was the peak of Holocaust commemoration, and was a moment of grace. Sociological research showed that commemorations, articles, books, TV shows dealing with the history of the Holocaust did reach large groups of society, and knowledge about the events grew significantly. Antisemitic phenomena remained on the margins of political and public life.

However, this positive atmosphere quickly diminished. Political turmoil starting in 2006 and the economic crisis of 2008 brought about shocking changes. There was a cultural paradigm shift. The extreme right, which had been isolated and looked down upon only a few years previously, broke out of its lowly status, and became a mainstream trend, providing a new cultural identity to

---

141   Victor Karády, Szociológiai kísérlet a magyar zsidóság 1945 és 1956 közötti helyzetének elemzésére. In *Zsidóság az 1945 utáni Magyarországon*. Paris: Magyar Füzetek, 1984. 37-180.; 63 and 104.

142   György Haraszti, Zsidók és antiszemiták az 1956-os forradalomban. In *Egység*, Vol. XXVII. (December 2016), 10-12.

many. As elsewhere, the internet became the most vibrant forum for these ideas. Main features of this far-right culture include anti-capitalist economic ideas, xenophobia, ideas of white supremacy, homophobia, an anti-urban and anti-West ethos, and anti-democratic, autocratic political attitudes. Central elements are also fierce antisemitism, anti-Israeli sentiments and open Holocaust denial.[143]

The existence of these dangerous developments is discernible in the media and general ambience, and is convincingly reflected in data of sociological research. According to empirical research by the sociologist Kovács András, between 2003 and 2011 the proportion of radical antisemites in the Hungarian population grew from 9 to 20%, peaking in 2010 at 22%.[144] At the same time, the percentage of those who refused to respond to the survey radically decreased (17 to 3%). The number of radical antisemites may not have doubled, but far more people dared to express their antisemitic feelings. Kovács calls this the 'Jobbik effect', referring to the extreme right political party that made significant gains of parliamentary seats in 2010 campaigning with openly antisemitic and anti-Roma messages. Antisemitic public speech by the mainstream is becoming acceptable.

Kovács's research shows that in 2011, 20% believed in a Jewish conspiracy controlling Hungarian economy and politics. 12% would discriminate against the Jews legally, including their forced emigration. The data also show that in the election years, the combined number of both radical and 'moderate' antisemites increased, peaking in 2010 with a striking 44%, showing that manipulating anti-Jewish sentiments is still an effective method in the political arena. Data relevant to the memory of the Holocaust indicate that between 2003 and 2011 the number of those advocating the 'topic of the persecution of the Jews being taken off the agenda' had grown from 42 to 58%. In 2003, 4% said that Nazi Germany did not operate gas chambers; in 2011 this figure was 7%. Those who believed that the 'Jews' wished to benefit financially from their sufferings was 35% in 2003, and 45% in 2011.[145]

Hungarian Jewry has been spared domestic physical violence since 1956, but recent political and social developments are causing general disquiet in the Jewish community. The most recent sociological surveys conducted by András Kovács and his associates in 1999 and 2017, respectively, showed significant changes in the experiences of Jews in Hungary of antisemitic phenomena and their attitudes about it. Both surveys were based on interviews with nearly two thousand people. Generally, the actual experiences of antisemitic acts was less frequent than two decades before. For example, about half of the respondents recalled antisemitic statements in public sphere, compared to the three quarters of the respondents in 1999. In 2017 twice as many Hungarian Jews reported no experience of antisemitism whatsoever in the workplace, at state institutions or in their neighbourhood (42% vs 21%). Out of the respondents of the survey in 2017, one fifth had experienced verbal insults or harassment because of being Jewish in the previous one year, whereas 1% had fallen victim to physical violence, and 3% had been witnesses to such attacks.

---

143   Vági–Csősz–Kádár, *Evolution of a Genocide*, 358-362.

144   Kovács defines *radical antisemite* as a person who adopts several strong anti-Jewish stereotypes, connects very strong emotions to these views, and is ready to discriminate against Jews.

145   For further details, see: András Kovács, *The Stranger at Hand. Antisemitic Prejudices in Post-Communist Hungary*. Leiden: Brill, 2011.

However, the perceptions and interpretations of antisemitic phenomena considerably changed during this period. Despite the actual decrease of private experiences of antisemitic incidents, the respondents in 2017 tended to consider the situation worse, than they had nearly two decades before. Two-thirds of them expressed great concern about the extent of antisemitism in Hungary, and only one-fifth estimated it low or negligible. It is also telling that the respondents generally overestimated the proportion of antisemites in Hungarian society. According to the most recent survey, some one-third of the population hold antisemitic views, including radical antisemites who made up about one-fifth of the population. However, the average of the Jewish estimates was 38%, and nearly one-quarter of the respondents thought that at least every other of their compatriots or even more were antisemites. Only one in six of respondents shared the opinion that it was entirely impossible that the Jews would be persecuted in the following ten years in Hungary, and half of them found this possibility unlikely. However, 28% were afraid that persecution of Jews might happen, and 5% saw a serious chance of it.

It is also striking that there were no significant differences in age among those who proved pessimistic and optimistic about the future of the Jews in Hungary. Of course, those respondents who personally experienced some form of antisemitic phenomena tended to regard the situation as much worse. However, many of those who had not experienced any incidents, also viewed the situation as deteriorating.[146]

Despite the negative developments described above, the birth of a pluralist, democratic state after 1989 brought about positive phenomena, which prevail. Hungary, the homeland of the largest Jewish community in Central Europe today, has witnessed a vivid Jewish revival in the period following the fall of the Communist regime. The complex network of Jewish cultural, educational and religious institutions has been strengthened and extended. Several non-governmental organisations have been established for strengthening Jewish community life and identity, including those dedicated to Holocaust remembrance and education. Jewish history and culture have become popular and frequent topics of research, art and public discourse. Scholarly publications, memoirs and literary works published about modern Jewish history and the Holocaust in the last two decades would fill a small library. Concerts, films, plays and other artistic performances related to Jewish tradition and culture take place every year. These events attract many non-Jewish spectators. The Jewish Summer Festival is one of the largest and most fashionable cultural events of Budapest. Clubs, pubs, workshops, hummus bars and kosher shops are witnessing the presence of vigorous cultural traditions, an assertive and open-minded urban intelligentsia and youth strongly committed to preserving the culturally diverse character of society.[147]

---

146 András Kovács–Ildikó Barna, eds. *Zsidók és zsidóság Magyarországon 2017-ben. Egy szociológiai kutatás eredményei.* [*Jews and Jewry in Hungary in 2017. The Results of a Sociological Survey*] Budapest: Szombat, 2018.

147 Vági–Csősz–Kádár, *Evolution of a Genocide*, 363–364.

11 NEW LIFE

1957 and after

We landed in Folkstone on the 27ᵗʰ January 1957, in rags, but not as refugees. We were employees with labour permits, taxpayers from the moment we set foot in this country. I am a pensioner now, but I am still a taxpayer.

Life was full of surprise, full of contradiction. It took us years to begin to understand the ways of our new country, the ways of the world. I am still learning.

Our employer Pye did not pay our fare from Paris. It was not their fault; they were not mean, it just never occurred to us to ask.

How lucky we were. Of all the beautiful places in Britain, our first jobs were in Cambridge, a city of youth, scholarship and gothic architecture. The place was a sight for sore eyes and a cure for wounded spirits.

Early morning of the day after our arrival found us on the doorstep of the police station, intending to register. The fatherly duty sergeant was baffled. Why were we there? The paperwork would be sent to us by post. We said we had no identity documents. The policeman just repeated, with mild irritation: we should go home and *relax*. There is no such word in the Hungarian language. New country, new life, new word.

My next task was to register us with a doctor. I took along my husband's medical report, provided in Paris by the doctors of Thomsons. The GP was alarmed, and saw Jancsi that same day. Tests were taken, a specialist was consulted. No trace was found of diabetes. The conclusion: the condition must have been temporary, brought on by acute anxiety. We were warned to be vigilant: sustained stress could lead to full-blown disease. A quiet life was prescribed. Jancsi lived for 54 more years, and no trace of diabetes had ever been found. Yet another reason for being grateful to our new country.

Colour television was still a novelty. Jancsi was designing TV circuits for the domestic market. I too was busy: my undergraduate project might have become the foundation of our life in the West.

Just weeks before our arrival, Pye had won a huge contract: to build a commercial television network for the whole continent of Australia. The project was led by Dr Weighton, Pye's Chief Scientist. He was surprised and pleased to discover that one of the company's newly recruited stray engineers from a country behind the iron curtain had recent and relevant knowledge of multichannel TV networks. This elderly, eminent English engineer was immeasurably more experienced than I was, and yet I was better informed then he about key details of this particular task. My undergraduate project had familiarised me with wave propagation over surfaces in continental Europe and boundary disturbances at the meeting of different terrains, but neither Dr Weighton nor I knew how broadband signals behaved over desert. Searches in Cambridge University library offered no clue, so I suggested, and he agreed, that Pye should conduct field measurements in the Australian bush. We even considered equipment for mobile laboratory vehicles. The task was huge; it required considerable staffing, and graduate staff were scarce in the UK, so Pye had decided to locate the entire project in Australia. Dr Weighton himself was leaving to head up the enterprise and offered to take me with him. He said Jancsi too could come along; there would be plenty of opportunities for circuit designers. However, we had other commitments and concerns, so my association with Dr Weighton and with TV networks never continued. I often wonder how our family might have evolved in sunny Oz.

202 Chesterton Road, Cambridge. The author's husband Kaposi János, Mr Easton, the author (wearing the dressing gown donated by Donáth Judit in Paris), Mrs Easton.
Kaposi family collection

Where did we live?

Our first home was a room in Fulbrooke Road, in the house of a distinguished Cambridge don. His family included a toddler called Alistair and a newborn whose name I forgot. In the first five minutes it became clear that we were not welcome; we were all victims of a misunderstanding. Our hosts had contacted our employers, offering a room to a young refugee couple in exchange for the wife providing services as an au-pair. They never considered a working wife; such things were unusual in this country at that time. I did what I could after work each day. There were a few painfully funny incidents, like our landlady explaining to me that the iron needed no hot coals, it was heated by something mysterious called 'electricity' which came out of the wall. They never asked, and I never told them, about my Red Degree in electrical/electronic engineering.

We urgently looked for, and soon found, two cosy rooms in a little house at the end of Chesterton Road. Our rent was £2 per week. Our back room overlooked the 14th Century Church of St Andrews. Bells chimed on Sunday mornings. Our host Mr Easton was a veteran of World War I. Mrs Easton baked cakes and pies twice a week, and a plateful was always waiting for us on our return from work. We stayed with the Eastons until leaving Cambridge in November 1957, and we remained friends until they died.

We were practically rich. Jancsi's salary was £750 a year, mine £500. We soon managed to repay our debt of £56 to our Paris benefactor Monsieur Roder, bought ourselves a change of underwear, and got me a coat. Next, we sent a few parcels of tea, coffee, chocolate, dried fruit and other delicacies to our families from the famous grocery Matthews in Trinity Street, where every customer was treated like a celebrity. Who would have imagined that shopping could be a pleasurable experience?[148]

We made acquaintances. Local people asked no questions but showed us kindness. A celebrated Marxist historian (I forgot his name) did ask questions, but only to confirm his idea of idyllic life in a Communist regime, so he did not believe our answers. We met other distinguished academics from various branches of learning and were invited to tea by the legendary mathematician Paul Dirac, whose name we knew from our textbooks.

We were also received with warmth and generosity by my shambolic brilliant senior colleague Dr Lax and his vivacious Italian wife Violet. Dr Lax was my father's age, a Slovak Jew. He had arrived in Britain in the late 1930s. Almost all his family had been murdered in the Holocaust. He taught me a lesson for life. One day a new Hungarian refugee appeared on the scene, a Dr Kalapács, one of my erstwhile university lecturers, a feared Communist with an Arrow Cross past. Dr Lax treated him with his characteristic

---

148   Judy Wilson, OBE (née Matthew), *A Cambridge Grocer: Matthew's of Trinity Street*, Sawston Village History Society, 2012 Meeting Report

kindness and open-handedness. I tried to warn him off, recounting Dr Kalapács's past. Dr Lax' response to me was: 'My dear, he is a man.' So was Dr Lax, one of the best. He and his family remained our friends for life.[149]

Then work became a problem. With the Chief Scientist leaving for Australia, my opportunities at Pye were limited. We needed *two* other jobs. This was the first and not the last occasion of having to make compromises, coordinating the career development of us both.

Our move to Ericsson Telephones, Nottingham, was fortunate in every way. The company was imaginative and enterprising; our tasks – designing two of the main building blocks of Britain's first transistorised telephone exchange – were substantial and prepared us for work in the fast-developing computer industry. John Pollard, our boss and Head of Ericsson's Research and Development, was a formidable multitalented man with boundless energy, great charisma and a photographic memory. He is one of the heroes of this story. We had nothing in common, and yet he must have made it his project to help us settle into British society. An Englishman from the Midlands, he came from a working-class background, and it was sheer talent that lifted him to his distinguished position: his gold-lettered name adorned the wall of our professional institution, the IEE. We were scruffy, confused and bewildered, but he saw our potential, and gave us the chance to make major contributions to an innovative project of international importance, and to publish our work in prominent international journals. This is how our feet became firmly planted on the professional ladder. He insisted that we buy a house on a 90% mortgage when we were penniless, and bullied our employers into guaranteeing the remaining 10% of the purchase price. He even chose the house for us in Nottingham's newly built smart district Bramcote Hills. He marched us to the office of his own bank manager and arranged to open a bank account for us when we had not a penny and had no clue what a bank was, or what a bank account could be *for*. It was by his sponsorship that we became members of the IEE. Later, he and his family became our dearest English friends.[150]

Time proved that separation from our loved ones was not complete and not permanent. With the post-revolution exodus, Hungary lost a good proportion of its most enterprising and best educated young citizens, but the Communist regime discovered how to profit from the loss.

- By immediately re-allocating the homes of the departed, the housing shortage was eased somewhat. Also, the assets of emigrants were seized, and their salaries saved.

---

149   This name translates to 'Hammer'. It would have suited him, but it was not his real name.
150   The Institution of Electrical Engineers is now the Institution of Engineering and Technology.

- Within the year, elderly dependants of emigrants were allowed, perhaps even encouraged, to leave the country. This way the State gained access to more homes and resources, and saved pensions.

- After a couple of years, emigrants like ourselves who had left the country illegally were pardoned. By visiting relatives who stayed behind, emigrants brought in Western currency, and were the first wave of tourists.

My parents were allowed to leave Hungary late in 1957 and joined us in Nottingham. Neither of them spoke a word of English, and arrived with almost nothing, having renounced their pensions, and having forfeited their home and assets. They also parted from their family and friends.

My father left Hungary without a backward glance. He was joining his daughter and her husband, and was to live in the country whose liberal democracy had always been his ideal. He was 56 years old, suffering from Parkinson's disease, and was too ill to find employment. My mother, Jancsi and I were at work all day, and he was at home alone. One day the Anglican parish priest of Bramcote knocked on the door, wishing to welcome a new parishioner. My father tried to warn him off; he had just enough English to say that he was a godless Jew. The priest was not deterred – he was a tenacious scholarly man. At first the two of them conversed in Latin, then they became friends, and in course of regular weekly visits the priest taught my father English. What a country! My father lived to enjoy the first years of his first grandchild, and I will always regret that he died before the arrival of his second.

My mother's case was different. To come to live with us in our new country, she had to part from those dearest to her: her mother and sisters. She was 45 years old, resourceful, intelligent, tireless. Before the birth of my daughter Esther, she worked as a seamstress in one of John Lewis's workshops. Whatever her shortcomings as a mother, she more than made up for them when her grandchildren came along. She was devoted to my daughters and took charge of our household. Without her, I would never have been able to build my career. She was 50 when my father died, and for 40 years thereafter she remained physically active and mentally alert. She was keenly interested in the politics of her new country, travelled to three continents on her own, and was a discerning reader of English literature. She explored London, was intrigued by its social and architectural variety, and took advantage of its cultural opportunities: museums, galleries and art exhibitions. Most of all, she loved and understood good music. My friends and family admired her, and my daughter, sons-in-law and grandchildren will always remember her with great affection.

In a new country, things are strange, upside down, back to front. Vehicles drive on the other side of the road. Houses and buses have two floors. Open fires don't heat the room, they just burn you on one side, leaving your other side cold. To turn the light *on*, you flick the switch *down*. In different shops the same goods are sold at different prices, and in any case, who could make sense of pounds, shillings and pence, not to mention Guineas – and how about inches, feet and yards, gallons and pints, pounds and ounces? But there were huge bonuses. Telephones worked, the climate was moderate, neighbours were helpful, and in due course I learnt not to be afraid of people in uniform.

We showed our gratitude to this wonderfully generous country by being loyal citizens. We worked hard, built our careers. My husband progressed from designing electronic circuits and computer machinery to being managing director of a manufacturing company. As an engineer useless with gadgets, I resorted to research, higher education and consultancy. My PhD proved to be a turning point in my professional life. It came about some ten years after my graduation, almost by accident. The next paragraph tells the story for those interested in IT matters.

All engineers of our generation had been raised on analogue circuits, whereas the new computer circuits were digital. Testing them was a challenge, and to learn about it, I attended a conference at Sheffield University. I knew nobody, I was the only woman among 500 delegates, and to emphasise the point, the Chairman addressed the gathering: "*Lady* and Gentlemen". This did not make me feel more welcome or more comfortable. The lecturers were distinguished professors from all over the world, and one presented a method of testing digital circuits by simulating their operation on the computer. I did not understand this: it seemed that simulation could highlight only a few of the virtually countless ways in which a digital circuit might function; it was like shooting at a flea in a haystack. Why didn't we test the *design* of the product, rather than its *operation?* I sketched out a possible method on my way home on the train and showed it to my husband. He said this would make for a great PhD. Plessey, a major electronics and telecommunications company, were focusing on the problem at the time; they thought my idea promising, and decided to sponsor my research.[151]

Working on a PhD would have demanded full attention, but I was a mother and a wife, and was holding down a full-time job. This was the start of decades of 14-hour working days and seven-day working weeks.

My research caught the attention of employers and even governmental administrators. Uniquely for a woman, I was appointed Head of an Engineering Department. Our courses were innovative in content and style. In addition to full-time courses for students just leaving school, we provided part-time education for people at work, and conversion Masters programmes for unemployed science graduates. My department grew to be one of the largest undergraduate and postgraduate schools in the country. This was an inner-city Polytechnic, offering educational opportunities to people from all layers of society. My socialist father should have lived to see it.[152]

---

151   Agnes Kaposi, *Logic Design Testing.* London: CNAA, 1971. Plessey, a British company, was taken over in 1989 by a consortium of GEC and Siemens.

152   Anne Buckley, Women in Electrical Engineering Education. *The International Journal of Electrical Engineering and Education,* Vol. 21. (1984) 197-212.

My subject – software and systems engineering – was, and is, of wide interest. As a researcher and consultant, I found myself travelling to three continents, advising universities, research councils, banks and organisations such as BT, the Admiralty, Philips and Siemens. In the last decade of our working life my husband became full-time manager of our enterprise, drawing together teams of academic experts to suit each project. It was his illness that stopped us in our tracks. He died eight years ago, and as he neared the end of his life, I became his full-time carer, first giving up gainful employment, and later even resigning from honorary posts. These days I am a writer and educator, trying to contribute to the cause of liberalism and tolerance, but I will always think and reason like an engineer.

I am often asked whether I had experienced any antisemitism in the UK, or any prejudice as a foreigner. I assert with confidence that I have found no trace of either, neither in industry nor in academia. However, I could write a whole book about systematic discrimination against me as a woman. Here is an example. I was headhunted by a prestigious university for the post of Head of their Electrical Engineering Department. The appointment committee included some of my professional friends who told me afterwards that I was the committee's favoured candidate, but the rector vetoed my appointment, saying that "over his dead body" would one of their engineering departments be headed up by a woman. It happened decades ago. Nowadays he might not say such a thing aloud, but his attitude might not have changed.

And how about our family?

Esther, our first child, was born in 1959, and Anna, our second, in 1963. My bright strong mother, only 20 years my senior, looked after us all. Esther was the first Briton of the family: when she was born, the rest of us were still waiting to qualify for naturalisation. This brings me to my last story about the extraordinary country that became our home.

To apply for naturalisation, one had to fill in a lengthy questionnaire. In due course a letter arrived from the Home Office, stating the date on which an officer would interview us in our home. The time was well selected: early evening, after we had returned from work, when our toddler was in bed. At that time, we lived in a small rented Corporation house in Stevenage New Town. We expected a forbidding person in bowler hat or uniform. Instead, a casually dressed, smiley civilian appeared, not much older than us. By then I had learnt that a cup of tea was to be offered to any British visitor, but this young man asked for a dry sherry, inviting us to join him in celebrating his promotion, showing us the letter he had received that very day, announcing his new status. Encouraged by his informality, I asked if he minded if I got on with my ironing. He said of course I should. All three of us chatted pleasantly for some half an hour about the weather (of course), music (it turned out we had similar tastes), and beautiful Cambridge, where we had worked and he had studied; he had even been member of the University's rowing team. This was pleasant, but Jancsi and I were becoming anxious: when would the interview begin? Suddenly he stood up, assured us that our naturalisation documents would arrive through the post, shook our hands, and was about to leave. We were astonished. I said please may we have an explanation?

– we expected to be interviewed, questioned, our suitability for citizenship tested. Yes, he said, we *had* been challenged, and we had passed the test. How were we challenged? I queried – he had asked no questions at all. He said the questionnaire asked the questions. Our answers created the impression that we were honest people, and his visit confirmed that impression. When I persisted, he said: 'Here is just one example. The questionnaire asked whether either of you had been members of any Communist organisation. János said he had not; you (Agnes) said that at university you had been a member of the Communist youth organisation DISz. We knew that your husband was four years ahead of you, and it was during those years that DISz membership became compulsory. You might have tried ingratiating yourself to British authorities by denying DISz membership. Instead, you simply told the truth.'

What a country. A country after our own heart. A country of which Jancsi and I were proud to become citizens. A country in which we were happy to found a family.

The family tree is complete, but reality is fractured. My husband Jancsi and my beloved daughter Esther died years ago. There is a recent photograph of those of us still alive. My five beautiful grandchildren are now young adults. My hope is that telling this story will help their generation build a better world.

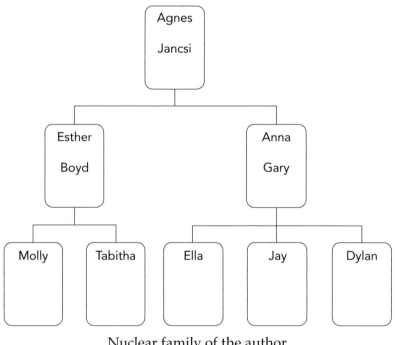

Nuclear family of the author

The author's family in London, 2017.
Back row: granddaughter Ella Kaposi, son-in-law Gary Bullock, granddaughter Tabitha Steemson, granddaughter Molly Steemson, daughter Anna Kaposi.
In front: grandson Jay Kaposi, grandson Dylan Kaposi, the author, son-in-law Boyd Steemson.

Kaposi family collection

WHO'S WHO IN THE AUTHOR'S FAMILY

Anna	younger daughter; husband Gary Bullock
Ági	first cousin, daughter of Terka; husband Gál Péter
Andras	first cousin Sir Andras Schiff, son of Pici; wife Yuuko Shiokawa
Bandi	Deutsch Endre, twin brother of Pici's first husband Pista
Bandi	Kaposi (Klein) András, brother of author's husband Jancsi
Dezső	maternal grandfather Csengeri Dezső
Dylan	grandson, Anna and Gary's son Dylan Kaposi
Ella	granddaughter, Anna and Gary's daughter Ella Kaposi
Ernő	father-in-law Kaposi (Klein) Ernő
Esther	elder daughter; husband Boyd Steemson
Éva	first cousin, daughter of Terka; husband Fonyódi János
Feri	Dr Sebes (Stern) Ferenc, husband of Terka
Gabi	son of mother's cousin Rosinger Sándor
Gabika	son of mother's cousin Dr Futó (Friedmann) Imre and Rácz Ilus
Giza mama	half-sister of grandfather Csengeri Dezső
Gyurika	son of Klári
Imre	father, Kristóf (Klein) Imre
Irén	mother-in-law, née Frankl
Jancsi	husband Kaposi (Klein) János
Jani	Stern János, brother of Feri; wife Székely Manci
Jay	grandson, Anna and Gary's son Jay Kaposi

Klári	first cousin, daughter of Imre's brother; husband Frankel Miklós (Can't Swim)
Laci	father's half-brother Klein László
Lipót	Klein Lipót (no relation); wife mother's cousin Schwartz Margit
Magda	mother, née Csengeri; husband Imre
Máli néni	Stern Mártonné, Terka's mother-in-law
Margit	sister of author's father, née Klein; husband Salamon Milchior
Miklós	Frenkel Miklós, Klári's husband (Can't Swim)
Molly	granddaughter, Esther and Boyd's daughter Molly Steemson
Nanóka	maternal grandmother, née Rosinger; husband Csengeri Dezső
Ödi	Dr Schiff Ödön, Pici's second husband
Pici	mother's sister, née Csengeri Klára
Pista	Deutsch István, Pici's first husband
Rózsi	Giza mama's daughter, née Winkler; husband Frank Ernő
Sámuel	paternal grandfather
Sándor	father's stepbrother, Szeréna's son
Szeréna	step-grandmother, second wife of Klein Sámuel
Tabitha	granddaughter, Esther and Boyd's daughter Tabitha Steemson
Terka	mother's sister, née Csengeri Teréz
Vera	second cousin, daughter of Lipót

INDEX